HUMANITARIANISM UNDER FIRE

The US and UN
Intervention in Somalia

HUMANITARIANISM UNDER FIRE

The US and UN
Intervention in Somalia

Kenneth R. Rutherford

Kumarian Press
An Imprint of Stylus Publishing

Humanitarianism Under Fire
The US and UN Intervention in Somalia

Published 2008 in the United States of America by Kumarian Press
22883 Quicksilver Drive, Sterling, VA 20166 USA

Design, production, and editorial services were provided by Publication Services, Inc., Champaign, Illinois. The text of this book is set in Adobe Sabon 10/12.5.

Printed in the United States on acid-free paper by Thompson-Shore, Inc. Text printed with vegetable oil-based ink.

∞ The paper used in this publication meets the minimum requirements of the American National Standard for Information Sciences—Permanence of Paper for printed Library Materials, ANSI Z39.48-1984

Library of Congress Cataloging-in-Publication Data

Rutherford, Ken, 1962-
  Humanitarianism under fire : the US and UN intervention in Somalia / by Kenneth R. Rutherford.
      p. cm.
  Includes bibliographical references and index.
  ISBN 978-1-56549-260-8 (pbk. : alk. paper)
  1. Somalia–History–1991-   2. Operation Restore Hope, 1992-1993.
3. Humanitarian intervention–Somalia–History–20th century.   4. United Nations. Unified Task Force Somalia.   5. United States–Relations–Somalia.
6. Somalia–Relations–United States. I. Title.
  DT407.42.R88 2008
  967.7305'3–dc22
                                                    2008010160

CONTENTS

Dedicated to Kim

Acknowledgments

This book could not have been written without the support of the many people, including archivists and librarians around the world, including those at the Pearson Peacekeeping Centre in Clementsport, Nova Scotia, the Dag Hammarskjöld Library at the United Nations in New York, and the United Nations High Commissioner for Refugees headquarters in Geneva, Switzerland.

It also would have been difficult to finish without the funding from Dean Frank Einhellig at Missouri State University in the form of a Graduate College faculty research grant. Also important to the project's realization were the editing assistance of Jeff Sjerven and the research help of Steve Henry.

I would also like to express my gratitude to two special librarians at Missouri State University—Ann Fuhrman, Director of the UN Depository Library, and Byron Stewart, Director of the Government Documents—who always responded quickly and thoroughly to research requests.

At Kumarian Press, I would like to thank Jim Lance and Erica Flock, who are both incredibly supportive of this book.

I am especially indebted to Tamara Morgan, who helped give me a second chance by providing me with immediate lifesaving emergency medical care in Lugh, Somalia, and Don Henderson, whose skilled guidance and genuine friendship helped me successfully reintegrate back into society.

I would also like to convey my appreciation to all the people I interviewed for this project regarding their involvement with the Somalia mission; I thank them for trying to help Somalia recover from years of conflict and drought. Any errors in the book are mine alone and should not be associated with them.

Also, I would like to give my heartfelt gratitude to Austin for coming into my life and allowing me to be part of his.

Finally, I want to express thanks to my parents and siblings, to the pillar of my life, my wife Kim, and to our children—Hayden, Campbell, Duncan, and Lucie—for their love and patience.

Acronyms

United Nations

SRSG	Special Representative for the Secretary-General to Somalia
UNDHA	UN Department of Humanitarian Affairs
UNDP	UN Development Program
UNDPKO	UN Department of Peacekeeping Operations
UNDRO	UN Disaster Relief Office
UNHCR	UN High Commissioner for Refugees
UNICEF	UN Children's Fund
UNITAF	United Task Force (Somalia)
UNOSOM	UN Operation in Somalia
UNSC	UN Security Council
UNSG	UN Secretary-General
WFP	World Food Program

United States Government

CENTCOM	Central Command
CIA	Central Intelligence Agency
DART	Disaster Assistance Response Team
DOD	Department of Defense

DOS	Department of State
NSA	National Security Advisor
NSC	National Security Council
OFDA	Office of Foreign Disaster Assistance
PCC	Policy Coordinating Committee on Africa (State Department)
QRF	Quick Reaction Force
RDJTF	Rapid Deployment Joint Task Force
SOLIC	Special Operations and Low-Intensity Conflict
TFR	Task Force Ranger
USAID	US Agency for International Development
USLO	US Liaison Office
1MEF	First Marine Expeditionary Force

Somali Groups

SNA	Somali National Alliance
SNF	Somali National Front
SNM	Somali National Movement
SPM	Somali Patriotic Movement
SSDF	Somali Democratic Salvation Front
SNDU	Somali National Democratic Union
SSDF	Somali Salvation Democratic Front
USC	United Somali Congress

Other

HOC	Humanitarian Operations Center
ICRC	International Committee of the Red Cross
MSF	Médecins Sans Frontières

NGO	Nongovernmental Organization
OAU	Organization of African Unity
OAS	Offensive Air Support
PYOPS	Psychological Operations
ROE	Rules of Engagement
TNC	Transnational Council

PREFACE

Why Somalia?

In 1993 I had a terrific job helping thousands of Somalis recover from years of civil war and drought as a credit union training officer. Lack of credit was one major tribulation confronting the Somali people. The others were multiple warlords operating unencumbered, except by each other; depleted food stocks and an imploded agricultural sector; the absence of a functioning central government with which the international community could communicate; and intensive clan divisions resulting in zero-sum outcomes.

My background made me well suited for the work: I was a former Peace Corps volunteer with an MBA degree and experience directing a business consulting firm. Of course, most Somalis didn't know that, nor did they care. "Bush Management 101"—garnered solely by field experience—was what mattered. My enthusiasm for the project derived from my idealistic notion that economics was the best way to alleviate poverty. However, I learned fast in Somalia that insecurity can waylay the best of intentions. In Somalia, I came to feel as if I were on a moving train that I knew was going to crash, in spite of the project's quality organization and people.

I felt uneasy some days, and a few times I had guns pointed at me. Staring at a pistol gave me pause to wonder what we were doing and whether it was possible to achieve what we had promised. Sometimes when Somali children saw foreigners, they would walk toward them, stop, and make a hand motion slitting their own throats. It was scary. I told my Somali colleagues, some of whom were fathers to these children, and they would say, "They are only kids. Do not worry about it." But I wondered how kids learned to hate at such an early age.

Despite the stress I enjoyed the wide open, astonishingly barren Somali desert panoramas, especially during sunrise. On December 16, 1993, the morning broke with a gorgeous gold and yellow sun, made all the more beautiful because my life was sailing in fair winds and on course, and I could barely contain my high spirits. I was living large, and everything in my professional and personal life was clicking in rhythm. I enjoyed my work with the Somalis, and I had just become engaged to Kim, who is the love of my life.

As I climbed into my Land Cruiser parked outside my office in the southwestern Somali city of Lugh, I could not have imagined the dreadful calamity that I was about to experience or the wonderful chain of events that would put my life into constant motion toward living a dream, which itself was clarified by the tragedy. The Land Cruiser carried us toward a loan applicant's project site, which we would never reach. None of us had any idea that something was lying in wait to try to kill us.

As we flew along the rocky dirt road, we passed people and animal herds walking into Lugh. There was a donkey cart and its owner, Mohamed Salet, approaching, so my driver, Abdual Ramen, eased off the gas pedal, lightly applied the brakes, and angled the Land Cruiser to the left side of the road. The cruiser tilted and then the right front exploded, rising off the ground and to the left, almost perpendicular to the road and leaning into a small, rocky, shadeless gully. The cab filled with dust as we skirted the donkey cart at the edge of the road, and I struggled to see. The Land Cruiser skidded sideways—it must have turned in the air as the front wheels left the ground—off the dirt road and into the gulley. I knew my feet were hurt, but I could not feel them.

The Land Cruiser stopped among thorn bushes and rocks on the hard Somali desert plain. Smoke continued to flow as the dust inside the cab settled. After the dust in the cab cleared, I could see everything. My foot was on the floorboard, bloodied and disfigured. I crawled out into the bright sun, and every inch of my lower legs was visible.

I thought that the rocky ground was my deathbed, and, initially, I did not have time to be afraid or fear death. No one rescued us for what seemed forever—but time is relative, especially when one is near death. I worried that completely stopping the flow of blood to the lower leg would risk losing the limb, but the limb was already lost.

My unhurt Somali staff huddled around me as I lay on the ground, and I told them matter-of-factly that I had enjoyed working with them. I called on the radio that people were hurt and bleeding and that we needed assistance and evacuation. Meanwhile, they put tourniquets around my legs just below the knees.

Lying back against the dry, hard ground, I stared up at the sky and thought to myself, "This is the end of the line of my life." But it wasn't. After being rescued and treated in hospitals in Kenya and Switzerland,

I returned to the United States a changed man who was to become a father, husband, and teacher.

When I departed Somalia, I was lying on my back on a stretcher, nearly bleeding to death. Throughout my recovery, which resulted in the loss of both my legs, I had endless questions that culminated in one that I would pursue professionally: Why did President George H. W. Bush send more than 30,000 troops in late 1992 to Somalia when there was neither security nor international norms at stake? I pursued this question while earning my doctorate at Georgetown University and after becoming a professor at Missouri State University. Although it was an interesting research question, I also wanted to know why so many American lives were put at risk and, in my case, why I lost my legs.

In the years immediately following the Cold War, there was a tremendous surge in UN peacekeeping and enforcement activities. From 1988 to 1993, there were substantially more UN military operations—more than twenty new operations were launched—than during the entire first four decades of the world organization. Euphoria reigned in pro-internationalist circles in the United States.

By 1992 Somalia was a nonfunctioning state. Its government and related services, except for violent repression, had collapsed in early 1991. Hundreds of thousands of Somalis had died, and more were on the verge of starvation despite the attempts by the UN, regional organizations, and numerous humanitarian nongovernmental organizations (NGOs) to alleviate the suffering.[1] In April 1992 the UN estimated that most of Somalia's population was under grave threat: "The lives of 1.5 million Somali people are at most immediate risk, and 3.5 million more require urgent assistance."[2] The key factor in the lack of major international action was Somalia's nonfunctioning governing system, which raised the question of how the UN could resolve the chaos and whether it should intervene without consent. At the same time, UN humanitarian relief operations were in organizational disarray because of internal bureaucratic changes. The concept of sovereignty and burdensome UN operational coordination led to further delays in addressing the growing Somali humanitarian crisis.

While the UN and the rest of the world watched, immobilized, President George H. W. Bush took action in a meaningful and dramatic way. Facing his first post–Gulf War humanitarian crisis, Bush resolved to help secure aid and protection for delivery to and within Somalia, and he volunteered the United States to lead the effort. The UN Security Council determined in December 1992 that the internal conditions in Somalia were a threat to the region and passed an American-drafted resolution to facilitate Bush's offer to have American military forces lead a UN armed intervention to protect and deliver humanitarian assistance.

In early December nearly 30,000 US military personnel deployed to Somalia and were supplemented by about 10,000 soldiers from nearly twenty other countries to form the United Task Force (UNITAF); the mission was called Operation Restore Hope by the United States. The immediate goal was to quickly establish a peaceful environment in southern Somalia to allow humanitarian relief distribution to vulnerable groups and then immediately turn the mission over to a UN force. However, UN Secretary-General Boutros-Ghali's plan was different. He wanted the US forces to disarm all Somalis, deploy throughout Somalia, and then transition to UN responsibility.

Arriving in the White House several weeks after American troops landed in Somalia, President Bill Clinton, who had personally approved his predecessor's humanitarian mission, focused on domestic policy and more pressing international matters, such as the political instability in Haiti and Russia. A few months later, in March, his administration supported the "whatever force is necessary resolution," UNSC 814, which US ambassador to the UN Madeleine Albright called a new era of "aggressive multilateralism." It launched UNOSOM II, a new mission authorizing UN personnel, including US military forces, to use whatever force was necessary to disarm Somali warlords and to ensure access to suffering civilians.

The UNOSOM II operation was the first UN military operation conducted solely for the sake of human rights. Previously, in such places as Nicaragua, El Salvador, Namibia, and Cambodia, UN forces observed but didn't enforce human rights. The immediate result of Resolution 814 was that US and UN military personnel became more aggressive in coercing Somali warlords to cooperate, and if they didn't, enforcing UNSC resolutions. The resulting conflict led to the Battle of Mogadishu on October 3, 1993, the subsequent US and UN withdrawal, and the effective end of UN and coordinated international action to help Somalia.

On October 3, 1993, in the sandy streets of the Somali capital, Mogadishu, US military forces were ambushed, suffering one of their most grave defeats, a blood-spattered tragedy that left the United States hesitant about utilizing military ground forces in the region and in future peacekeeping missions. The fighting started with the downing of two US Black Hawk helicopters and ended with the killing and wounding of nearly 100 US troops by factions loyal to Somali warlord General Mohamed Farrah Aidid. After the battle, Clinton precipitously announced a US pullout.

So compelling were the questions surrounding the mission in the public mind that they inspired the book and movie *Black Hawk Down*, which effectively described the battle. Many Americans are familiar with the fight in Mogadishu between American and Somali forces as the US attempted to capture Aidid loyalists.

A plethora of books and articles have been written about the tragic fighting during the Battle of Mogadishu and how it affected future US policy toward humanitarian interventions. This book is a straightforward, detailed historical and political narrative primarily focused on UN and US policy formulation toward Somalia. I describe some of the challenges involved that hitherto have received scant attention in the literature addressing the international intervention in Somalia. A presidential transition and conflicting goals between the Departments of Defense and State were some of the challenges that made it difficult for the US government to develop and implement a consistent foreign policy and military operation. These tensions are illustrative of the broader difficulties that US government officials face in determining an effective response to global humanitarian emergencies. I also investigate UN behavior toward Somalia and highlight reasons for failure, such as delayed and ineffective responses.

This book takes an explanatory approach and depicts many of the key decisions and personalities in light of new information obtained through interviews and documents resulting from intensive research in five countries. Some of this new information is significant in better understanding one of the first cases of international action in response to state collapse in the post–Cold War era, which was an experiment in a new form of multilateral peace operations. Until Somalia the UN Secretariat had no previous experience in running a Chapter VII exercise with large numbers of troops operating under a fighting mandate.[3] Somalia was a test of whether the UN could carry out a peace operation involving the use of force against an adversary determined to sabotage that operation. The original humanitarian mission was broadened for good reasons but without sufficient preparation or resources. The differing goals of the United States and the UN were never resolved, and the UN's firepower was insufficient to overcome wily opponents acting on their home turf.

The international intervention in Somalia was remarkably complicated. Initial involvement was intended to create a stable environment for effectively providing humanitarian relief to vulnerable populations. But it evolved stealthily toward creating a workable governing system and rehabilitating the destroyed social and economic infrastructures, including creating an indigenous police force and judicial system, while at the same time trying to induce a secure environment. It was also one of the most challenging and difficult operations ever conducted by US military forces. A key administration official (under Bush and Clinton) involved in both the planning and implementation of the Somalia operation remarked that

"Somalia was the messiest military peacekeeping operation until post-Saddam Iraq in 2003. The complexity of Somalia makes Iraq look like a day at the beach."[4]

The US and UN humanitarian and military actions in Somalia teach valuable lessons because there are very limited instances of internationally approved interventions without consent. Problems encountered in Somalia during the interventions redefined UN procedures and future US interventions. Somalia was the first international action in an imploded state after the Cold War, and also the first time the UN negotiated with nonstate actors on humanitarian and security issues. Nonconsensual intervention by the United States and UN in Somalia, therefore, had little in the way of precedent to guide its operations.

Notes

1. According to a report produced by the Refugee Policy Group and Centers for Disease Control and Prevention researchers, the population of Somalia during the 1991–1993 period was 5.1 million, around 4 million of whom faced extreme food insecurity. Steven Hansch, Scott Lillibridge, Grace Egeland, Charles Teller, and Michael Toole, "Lives Lost, Lives Saved: Excess Mortality and the Impact of Health Interventions in the Somalia Emergency," report, Refugee Policy Group, November 1994, 16, 35.

2. "Consolidated Inter-Agency Plan of Action for Emergency Humanitarian Assistance to Somalia covering 20 April 1992–20 July 1992," April 5, 1992, 5.

3. Some experts in UN affairs would argue that the Congo peacekeeping effort in 1960 was comparable to the one in Somalia, except that Chapter VII authority was not given by the Security Council at that time.

4. State Department official involved in UNITAF and UNOSOM II planning and implementation, interview with author. Conducted in confidentiality and the name withheld by mutual agreement. Washington, DC, July 6, 2004.

SOMALIA

- ⊙ National capital
- ◉ Regional capital
- ○ Town, village
- ✈ Airport
- — — — International boundary
- — · — · — Regional boundary
- — — Indeterminate boundary
- —— Main road
- —— Track
- —+— Railroad

0   50   100   150   200 km
0   50   100 mi

The boundaries and names shown and the designations used on this map
do not imply official endorsement or acceptance by the United Nations.

Map No. 3690 Rev. 7   UNITED NATIONS
January 2007

Department of Peacekeeping Operations
Cartographic Section

CHAPTER ONE

THE LAST DAYS OF THE
MODERN SOMALI STATE

Somalia comprises many things: an arid environment, plentiful sunlight, herds of camels, wonderful poetry—and these days, death and violence. The Somalis most love their poems. They speak to the immeasurable quality of Somali culture, ranging from the nomadic traditions to the dry, harsh, yet magnificent, land. Somalis and their herds wander the Horn of Africa following the rains for pasture and water. Like most people of the desert, Somalis are an independent and prideful group who can survive harsh circumstances and quickly adapt to available resources. Despite having two large river valleys in an arid region and the second largest coastline in Africa, most Somalis look with disdain on the farming and fishing occupations.

Belying the simplicity of Somalia's arid landscape and time-honored poetry is a clan system based on an intricate communal arrangement of extensive blood ties. This social structure is distinguished by inter- and intra-clan rivalry over everything from governing affairs to foraging rights and water privileges. Clan units break apart or unite in reaction to circumstances.[1] The traditional Somalia governing system is an anarchic condition, dependent upon clan self-regulation for sanctioning violators.[2] Some of the major manifestations of this complicated clan system are bursts of violence, which are sometimes generated by grievances that occurred in previous generations. In traditional Somali society, clans and sub-clans co-exist and are governed by aspects of consensus and compensation for violations decided by a "dhirr," a group of elders and religious leaders. These leaders and the clan system facilitated peace by consensus decision-making among antagonists or balancing weaker clans against stronger clans to produce equilibrium.

Somalia has several national blessings not inherent in most African states. Its population is primarily Somali, speaking the same language and sharing the Sunni Muslim faith. Yet Somalia also has challenges common

1

to many African states—irrational borders carved among colonial powers, traditional societies leading to a twentieth-century state in only a few generations, and a flood of weapons from Cold War rivals. Somalia's major obstacle to national political development is unique within Africa—the clan system. In most other parts of Africa, traditional governing systems are characterized by some form of hierarchical authority.[3] In Somalia, clan identity flows downward through paternal lineage that also determines political schisms and governing. From childhood, Somalis learn about their clans, sub-clans, and lineage, and they memorize significant events and honor founders of the clan. In lieu of an official social safety net program, clan affiliation and loyalty provide everything from insurance to security.

Somali clans and sub-clans are most united when there is an external threat. They cobble together an alliance to take on the threat and then break apart after it passes. Perhaps the most unifying factor among all Somalis is their combined loathing of the distribution of Somali lands to Ethiopia, Kenya, and Djibouti by the colonel powers. In the late 1860s, Britain established a protectorate in northern Somalia to complement its Crown Colony in Aden and as a protection hedge for the future Suez Canal. Not to be outdone, France formed French Somaliland at the northern edge of the British protectorate, and in the 1890s Italy claimed a huge swath of the southern Somalia region, which was less strategic but economically carried more potential because of the river valleys of the region's two largest rivers—the Shabell and the Juba. Meanwhile, the Somali lands in the very south were included in the British colony of Kenya, and the western Somali region was annexed in 1897 by the Ethiopian Emperor Menelik, who assured the British that he would not harm British interests in the Sudan or Somalia, which was Aden's main source of meat.[4]

As a result, Somalis in the south of Somalia (as opposed to those living in Kenya) experienced Italian colonial authority, whereas Somalis in the north of Somalia (as opposed to those living in Djibouti and Ethiopia) experienced British rule. These differing colonial experiences layered another division on the Somali people that manifested into a north-south rift soon after independence in 1960. The Somali government was controlled by southern Somalis, who, for the most part, had been trained by the Italians. Fearing southern domination and alien forms of governmental organization and rule of law based on the Italian model, the northern Somalis considered ways to make a claim for national power, and some considered creating their own state whose territory would cover former British Somalia.

Although the division of Somali land was conducted by external actors, the internal divisions among the Somali clans sowed the seeds for continued international intervention. "Reunification of all Somalis is the very reason for our nation," said President Aden Abdille Osman in 1965. Modern Somali nationalism is focused on reuniting Somalis under one state.[5] This nationalism threatens neighboring states. For example, Ethiopia has at various times invaded Somalia or supported Somali insurgencies.

The colonial legacy also exacerbated the self-induced Somali clan schisms. Further complicating an already complex social system, clan and sub-clan divisions do not associate with visibly distinct geographical boundaries but are territorially fungible.[6] Northern Somalia is an exception as it is primarily Issaq inhabited, whereas the central and southern regions are more clan diversified. Northern dissatisfaction with the Somali government, based in Mogadishu in the south, revealed itself in many ways, including violence one year after Somalia's independence in 1960. In December 1961 a group of British-trained military officers attempted to control major towns in the north. The Somali military, which was dominated by southern Somali officers, swiftly ended the revolt, but it left bitterness among northern Somalis that manifested in violence years later.

In 1964 Somalia held its first post-independence elections, which led to a government that increasingly consolidated its power to a small group of leaders. The 1969 election led to a "mushrooming of political parties on the eve of elections and their immediate disappearance (even after winning seats)," which "became a peculiar characteristic of the Somali experiment with liberal democracy."[7] The reasoning was that Somalis intensely chased rewards at the expense of debating national and governing issues. Also, absent external threats, clans easily subdivided when it came "to negotiating representation and benefits."[8]

In 1969, Mohammed Siad Barre, a member of the small Marehan sub-clan, which was part of the larger Darod clan, seized power in a military coup. He renamed the country the Somalia Democratic Republic and embarked on a program of "scientific socialism" based on the Soviet model that he and many of the leading military officers learned while studying in the USSR. He also outlawed clans but reverted to his sub-clan power base when his popularity dived in subsequent years.

In December 1974 Somalia's regional rival, Ethiopia, experienced a coup d'etat that would provide an opening for the Somalis to help fulfill their irredentist dream of reunifying greater Somalia. Ethiopia's strong American ally Emperor Haile Selassie was overthrown in a bloody coup by junior military officers led by Colonel Mengistu Haile Mariam, who announced the adoption of a Soviet-style state-centered socialist model. Seeing a greater geo-strategic partner in Ethiopia, the Soviets cultivated

Mengistu's friendship leading to the start of Soviet military aid in December 1976.

Meanwhile, Somalia continued to suffer from years of economic decline. The economic stagnation further delegitimized Barre's rule and the Somalis' belief in a central government. Sensing a quick military and political victory, he decided to invade the Somali-populated Ogden area of Ethiopia in 1977 in an attempt to rally Somalis to the nationalist cause and to take advantage of the new Marxist regime in Ethiopia. After initial success, the Somali army was badly defeated and beaten back by a combination of Ethiopian, Cuban, and Soviet forces, who switched support from Barre's Somalia to Ethiopia during the war. The Ethiopian war defeat led to Somali national introspection about the high number of casualties and increased questions about the legitimacy of the Barre government.

After its military thrashing in Ethiopia, an influx of more than one million Ethiopians of Somali ethnicity flooded into Somalia fleeing starvation. The Barre government had difficulty directing and managing an effective relief effort even though it controlled the transportation networks.

> At one point eighteen ships waited to dock in Mogadishu—a port capable of handling only three vessels at a time. Lack of coordination among the 100 different agencies, combined with inadequate harbor space, kept food from reaching millions of ethnic Somalis stranded in refugee camps. While grain lay by the ton in ships' holds, people starved to death.[9]

Because of Cold War politics, the United States, which had been a longtime supporter of Ethiopia's now deposed ruler Haile Selassie, commenced supporting Barre's government to maintain a geo-strategic position in the Horn of Africa. This support was intensified after February 12, 1979, when Islamic radicals led by Ayatollah Ruholla Khomeini took control of Iran and declared their hostility to the United States, thus posing a new threat to US regional interests. At that time, Saudi Arabia and most other Arab Persian Gulf states would not allow US troops on their soil.

Nine months later, the December 1979 invasion of Afghanistan by the USSR moved Somalia upward on the Carter administration's foreign policy priority list. The United States remained steadfast in its "over the horizon" Persian Gulf security strategy, which entailed continuing to position troops and supplies in Somalia. Subsequently, Somalia joined Egypt as the only Organization of African Unity (OAU) members on the US list of strategic states in the Middle East region. The US political and security goals in Somalia were significant, such as maintaining military access to the fuel bunker storage facilities at the port of Berbera and the Mogadishu airfield.

During most of the late 1970s and 1980s, US policy toward Somalia was based not only on Cold War strategy, but also on a desire to maintain peace between Ethiopia and Somalia. James Bishop, then deputy assistant for Africa at the State Department (and later US ambassador to Somalia) considered the Somali invasion of Ogden "foolish" and did not want it to reoccur.[10] The US foreign policy challenge was to provide enough military assistance to Somalia to ensure continued access to Somalia's ports and airfields, but not enough to encourage another invasion of Ethiopia. This friction was played out between US Ambassador to Somalia Robert Oakley and Bishop. Oakley kept asking for weapons for Somalis, while Bishop "reluctantly supported giving some arms to the Somalis after."[11]

Besides military aid concerns, another source of tension in US and Somali relations was the Barre regime's increasingly bad human rights record. Many members of Congress felt that the United States should not be associated with the Barre regime because of its human rights violations and formed "pressure groups to save lives."[12]

In Somalia, many national leaders wanted Barre to take steps to curb increasingly parochial selections for high-level government and military posts filled by his own Marehan clan. One estimate is that by 1987, 50 percent of the Somali Army senior officer command were Marehan and the majority of officers in the artillery and tank brigades in Mogadishu were Marehan.[13] His clan-based policy reinforced inter-clan differences and rivalries and led to repressive policies to preserve his rule.

Although the idea of a Somali national state was tenuous since its inception, immediately after the Ogden war a violent spark signaled the beginning of the end of a Somali nation focused on irredentism and the beginning of one focused on domestic clan violence. Soon after the Ethiopian war ended, the government launched severe reprisals in northern Somalia in April 1978 against the Mijerteen clan in retaliation for a failed coup led by Mijerteen military officers. Many Mijerteen leaders fled to neighboring countries, especially Ethiopia, to join other opposition groups and helped form the Somali Salvation Democratic Front (SSDF), which quickly evolved into a Mijerteen-centered faction.

As the Barre government continued to hunt clan opposition groups, new groups, also primarily identified by clan, were forming. For example, in April 1981 the Somali National Movement (SNM) was formed in London by northern Issaq intellectuals and leaders in opposition to

Barre's targeted abuse.[14] The Issaqs held a range of grievances against Barre and many planned his overthrow. They bore a disproportionate share of the casualties from the Ethiopian war because a large part of the battle front was in Issaq territory. As the Ethiopian military received reinforcements of Cuban armored units backed by Soviet air support, Barre cut his losses and decided on an immediate withdrawal of Somali forces on March 8, 1978. Many Issaqs believed that Barre had pulled the rug out from under them. During the war, one of the Somali Government's main worries was a possible Ethiopian invasion to seize the important northern seaport of Berbera. As a result of this fear, Barre sent his best troops and equipment to the north; they were either never put into Ethiopia or were put in last.[15] That meant the Issaqs and their region did not get the support they expected.

In response to US pressure, and to relieve their respective forces and combat the challenges of growing insurgencies in their countries, Somalia and Ethiopia signed the Agreement on Normalization of Relations between the Somali Democratic Republic and the People's Democratic Republic of Ethiopia on April 3, 1988.[16] One of the key provisions in the agreement was a nonaggression pact that included language forbidding each side to shelter the other's opposition groups. Seeing their days in Ethiopia numbered, on May 27, SNM fighters, funded by remittances from Issaqs working in the oil-based economies in the Persian Gulf, launched a distressed assault from Ethiopia into Somalia, taking Burao and Hargeisa in the northern part of the country and defeating Barre's better equipped army.

The Issaq assault was the serious start of all-out civil war. In retaliation, Barre ordered his brother-in-law, General Hersi Morgan, who attended the US Army's Command and General Staff College at Fort Leavenworth, Kansas, and the Somali armed forces to destroy the SNM rebels. Under Morgan's leadership, the Somali military recaptured the cities, destroying Issaq property, killing many SNM fighters and noncombatants, mostly Issaqs, and terrorizing the Issaq population. In many cases, no quarter was given. Barre also ordered aerial bombardments of the cities, which generated thousands of noncombatant casualties and displaced civilians, many of whom were non-Issaq. As the heart of the Issaq insurgency, the city of Hargeisa was particularly targeted. During one month of bombing by artillery and air, more than 50,000 died and 350,000 fled to Ethiopia.[17] Reports of these atrocities and other human rights violations prompted the US Congress to suspend military assistance to Barre. It also encouraged the State Department via "notification" demands to reprogram Economic Support Funds from Somalia to other African countries.[18]

In order to combat the violence of the Barre-led, Marehan-dominated Somali military, other clans started to form and organize militias, including the Ogden clan, who formed a large component of the military. The Ogden soldiers felt betrayed by Barre because the Ethiopia-Somalia Normalization agreement renounced Somalia's claim to the Ogden area of Ethiopia. Paradoxically, as Somalia's army was being weakened from demoralized Ogden soldiers, it was being attacked by the newly formed Ogden-dominated Somali Patriotic Movement (SPM). The SPM helped the already existing clan-based insurgencies, the SNM and SSDF, in generating internal instability by combating the Somalia military. Barre's government found itself increasingly under siege not only by these armed factions but also by the US government for human rights abuses. In July 1988 the United States suspended all military aid to Somalia for 1989, and in June 1990 the $20 million assigned to Somalia for nonmilitary purposes was frozen.

Anti-Barre protests started to occur in Mogadishu, where on July 14, 1989, during Friday prayers, the Islamic Somali Ulema Council in Mogadishu encouraged people to take to the streets to protest the continued national economic decline and government human rights violations. After leaving the mosque, protesters jammed the streets protesting governmental policies and then clashing with police, resulting in many casualties. Two days later, on governmental orders, Issaqs tied to anti-government activities were executed on Jezira Beach south of Mogadishu.

Despite continued congressional pressure for curtailing US support of the Barre regime, two events delayed dramatic US policy changes. First, General H. Norman Schwarzkopf, commander in chief of the US Central Command, impressed upon Herman Cohen, undersecretary of state for Africa, the need "to maintain access to Berbera, and, thus, further develop constrictive ties to the Barre regime."[19] Second, on August 7, a plane carrying US Rep. Mickey Leland, D-Texas, crashed in Ethiopia, where he was on a mission to learn more about the Ethiopian famine. Leland and fourteen other people aboard the plane died. With approval from the Ethiopian government, the US Air Force led a search mission. The incident provided a catalyst for future US military exercises in the Horn of Africa area, including Somalia.

US-Somali relations changed dramatically a few months later, when on November 24 Marehan-dominated Somali military forces killed more than 120 people, mostly from the large Hawiye clan, in Galcayo and 100 in Belet Weyn in central Somalia. The massacres occurred after Hawiye troops mutinied. At the time, the Hawiye-led United Somali Congress (USC) was based in Rome, but after the massacres, it started supporting on-the-ground violent actions by Hawiye militias against the government.

After the Hawiye massacres, Barre's government quickly lost control and the economy rapidly deteriorated. These trends were compounded by President George H.W. Bush's decision to end major US financial support and a serious drought that began in 1989 and would last into 1991. These problems led to a sense among some Somali leaders that the Barre regime might be open to political compromise. In April 1990 a group of 114 Mogadishu-based Somali leaders, primarily Hawiye clan members, made public a manifesto that, among other things, identified political compromises, such as a more representative government and political rights protections.

Barre reacted immediately and harshly. Without discussing the manifesto or meeting with its authors, who were considered relatively moderate in their demands and political outlook, he ordered the arrests of many signatories. Most opposition groups realized well before then that the Barre government would not tolerate dissent and adopted the view that violence was the only path to political change. That, ironically, is exactly what the manifesto authors wanted to avoid.

As the manifesto leaders were being arrested, James Bishop was sworn in as US ambassador to Somalia on June 11, 1990, and his credentials were accepted by the Barre government. Among Bishop's many challenges was the escalating fighting between government forces and clan militias resulting in a complete breakdown of law and order. Within months after his swearing-in, all nonessential UN personal were evacuated in September on orders from UN headquarters, and on October 6 unidentified gunmen carried out a deadly ambush on International Committee of the Red Cross (ICRC) staff returning from an emergency assistance mission.[20]

In November Mike Harvey, Africa officer of the Office of US Foreign Disaster Assistance (OFDA) took a trip to Mogadishu, where he met with Bishop in the ambassador's embassy office. Meanwhile, there were daily incidents of hundreds of deaths, vehicle thefts, and expatriate shootings in and around Mogadishu. Harvey thought that "this place is going to blow" and that "there was no sense of urgency" among embassy officials.[21] Two weeks later clan militias entered Mogadishu battling government troops.

Also arriving at the US Embassy in November was US Agency for International Development (USAID)/Somalia contractor Jan Westcott, who was hired to promote NGO programming. Soon after her arrival she discovered that most of her time was devoted to tracking security incidents involving NGOs.[22]

Bishop found himself in an awkward position. Some of the weapons being used in Mogadishu's streets were American-supplied and approved by him when he was deputy assistant for Africa. He had attempted to assuage the demands of then-US Ambassador Oakley, who kept requesting more US military weapons for Somalia. When he heard those weapons, primarily the howitzers, firing in the streets, Bishop called it a "sad day."[23]

The resulting violence forced Bishop to recommend the voluntary departure of US government dependents and nonessential personnel on December 5, reducing the number of official Americans in Somalia from 150 to 37.[24] Westcott believes that the incident that triggered Bishop's evacuation decision was an early December brazen daylight attack on an American-based NGO office in Mogadishu. As bandits armed with hand grenades, knives, and AK-47 assault rifles robbed the NGO office, they forced the NGO director's wife and small children into a back bedroom.[25] Rather than departing Somalia, Westcott stayed to monitor the relief situation and assist in packing out American employee belongings from their houses. She managed to get many houses packed out, but the warehouses and everybody's personal effects were looted or destroyed when the militias moved into Mogadishu. Westcott left in early December on a Somali Airways plane, which was the last commercial flight out of Somalia for nearly ten years.[26]

As the magnitude of the violence increased, Bishop on December 30 ordered all US Embassy personnel to move to a secure location on the grounds, where he and embassy staff strengthened security procedures under the direction of a former SAS and Scottish mercenary Bob Nobel, whom Bishop hired out of Nairobi to assist with security.

On January 2, 1991, Bishop cabled Washington, DC, requesting military helicopters and airborne troops from US military bases in Saudi Arabia to help protect the embassy's grounds until evacuation ships arrived. At first there was some resistance from the Department of Defense (DOD) and National Security Council (NSC). One DOD official told Bishop that helicopters could not be used because Somalia is too dusty for them, and Bob Gates at NSC (later CIA director and defense secretary) replied that parachutists were not available to assist with the rescue.[27]

As a result of Bishop's request, on January 3 Washington started planning the evacuation mission, which was called Operation Eastern Exit. The following day was the worst day at the US Embassy because looters started climbing over its walls, trashing the outlying buildings and facilities, including the golf club. On the morning of January 5, Marine and SEAL teams arrived by helicopter and evacuated most of the US Embassy in Mogadishu and other expatriate personnel to US ships waiting offshore. These teams had been prepared for Operation Desert Storm in Iraq and were transported on two helicopter boats to the rescue.[28] There was an initial mix-up as the first Marine helicopters passed over the embassy because they were looking for a golf course, "maybe a Westchester type golf course" according to Bishop.[29] But the embassy golf course was only nine holes and was covered with debris and trash—and herds of grazing goats.

Two CH53s flew evacuation flights during the day on January 5, and then five stacks of CH47s came late at night and into the early morning of January 6. Bishop, Noble, and Marines and SEALs left on the last helicopter. Thirty-seven of the 116 or so evacuees were Americans, whereas the other evacuees included the Soviet Embassy staff. On the morning of January 5, Bishop received a call for help from the Soviet ambassador with the greeting "Yankee, Yankee, this is Ivan." Bishop relayed the request to Washington, where Secretary of State James Baker sent a message to the Marines: "Don't leave Soviets."[30]

During the evacuation, some shots were fired, but fortunately there were no casualties, although the Kenyan ambassador was beaten and a Sudanese embassy staffer was stabbed. The US Embassy staff from Mogadishu were overjoyed, and US State Department personnel in Washington, especially those in the African Affairs Division, were also thrilled with the embassy evacuation's success and the fact that Barre was defeated and exiled.[31]

Americans and other international diplomatic personal were not the only people to flee as anti-Barre forces continued to infiltrate Mogadishu. The day after the US-led evacuation, UN agencies and NGOs began evacuating their personal, including CARE, who lost all their vehicles, which had been parked in the US Embassy with Bishop's permission.

On January 20 a UN Inter-Agency Mission traveled to Mogadishu to collect information and confirmed earlier reports of the total looting and destruction of UN and its staff's property.[32] Another UN mission a month later resulted in a similar, bleak conclusion about the impossibility of returning for the short term and the level of destruction. Its report stated that "there is nothing left of either except a few desks. Both safes in hcr [UN High Commissioner for Refugees (UNHCR)] have been blown and even the windows and toilets have been taken. . . . I believe it would be fair to say that all of us were shaken by the damage that has been done in such a short span of time."[33]

The departure of the UNHCR significantly damaged the relief effort because it had the mandated responsibility for the international protection, material assistance, and promotion of durable solutions for the 600,000 Ethiopian refugees. The UN staff's apprehension and horror of possibly returning to Somalia are evidenced in a post-evacuation report from UN staff returning to Mogadishu on a one-day visit:

> The ferocity with which the diplomatic and UN offices and the
> homes of expatriates were looted and the killing of a number

of local and expatriate personnel of these organizations give rise to a very real concern for the safety of staff who would have to work in Somalia. A return of nonessential personnel and of any dependents must be ruled out for a long period. . . . Mogadishu and all other locations [in Somalia] are undoubtedly the most difficult duty stations in the world.[34]

As rebels increasingly won the running gun battles with government forces, the Mogadishu residents joined the fighting and pillaging, especially targeting foreigners. The price of AK-47s rose from $80 to $150 as the fighting increased. Somali militias soon turned on each other, targeting members of the Darod clan, especially sub-clan members of the Marehan, who had supported Barre, and the northern Issaqs, who, ironically, had had helped the anti-Barre forces.[35] Historical hostility toward the northerners violently manifested itself once the Barre threat unifying them disappeared as the country returned to time-honored clan groupings.[36]

On January 27 Barre was forced from his bunker by rebels and fled Mogadishu in one of his army's few remaining tanks escorted by his battered army. With the support of Kenyan President Daniel arap Moi, Barre attempted to set up a government in the southern Somali city of Kismayu. Tens of thousands of Somalis also evacuated Mogadishu on foot, on animals, and in animal-pulled carts. Many of the initial Somali groups leaving Mogadishu were connected to Barre's clan or government.

Bishop and others from the Mogadishu embassy were sent back to Washington, and Somalia was lowered on the US foreign policy priority list. Some of the Mogadishu embassy staffers were angry at the Somalis after literally having their suitcases ripped from their hands as they were evacuating Mogadishu. The assault on the embassy compound by looters and the resulting destruction of US government property ended US interest in Somalia. Although the United States no longer had an embassy in Somalia, it had basing rights in the Persian Gulf, something it did not have during the Cold War, and thus, Somalia no longer served America's strategic needs.

The international exodus from Somalia had detrimental effects on addressing the Somalia crisis efficiently and quickly. Typically, if there is not a USAID mission attached to an embassy, the ambassador is disabled in projecting a humanitarian crisis. If the embassy is evacuated, that further reduces US capability to detect a crisis and determine whether conditions for famine are forming. In this case there was no USAID mission or US Embassy in Mogadishu, and most of the media and NGOs were outside of Somalia. Those that remained were run mostly with local staff who did not have the benefit of a free press or international presence supporting their work.

Nearly one week after her evacuation, Westcott and other relief personnel representing NGOs involved with Somalia met at the USAID office in Nairobi to share information. It became the first of a series of regular NGO coordination meetings for the "Emergency Relief Assistant to Post Civil War Somalia." Future meetings determined the main priorities to be coordination of resources, establishment of communications with Somali authorities, sharing of knowledge of existing and planned programs, and promoting donor confidence through effective communication.[37]

US congressional representatives concerned about human rights violations under the Barre regime now began pressuring the State Department to get involved in humanitarian aid operations. On January 22, 1991, a Senate letter signed by Edward Kennedy of Massachusetts, Nancy Kassebaum of Kansas, Paul Simon of Illinois, and five others was sent to Secretary of State James Baker, encouraging US aid to the ICRC and other relief agencies involved in Somalia and highlighting their concern about the growing Somalia humanitarian crisis.[38]

Less than two weeks after the Senate letter, the House also started to act on Somalia. On February 5, 1991, Harvey provided testimony before the House Foreign Affairs Committee staff.[39] He said the US government had to pay attention to the Somali problem or the costs were going to speed out of control.

> We just watched for four years and finally had enough to initiate Operation Lifeline in Sudan, and five years before that we ignored Ethiopian famine that the size got so big, we had to do something. During the Ethiopia drought in 1987 there was no attention because there was no famine because we managed it. What I was saying is that these are not unmanageable problems. If you manage the problems, they don't become big problems because front pages don't carry it. In Somalia, I don't know if we couldn't prevent something from happening; we just didn't try.[40]

On February 21 OFDA and USAID officials briefed Senate Foreign Relations Committee staff on the status of emergency relief activities in the Horn of Africa and pooled funds to create and support a newly created position for a Somalia emergency relief coordinator, Jan Westcott. Because of her East Africa experience with emergency food aid, it was decided that she should be based in Nairobi to help direct US government humanitarian relief supplies with the ICRC, UN agencies, and other NGOs and be pre-positioned to go into Somalia as soon as it was safe to assess emergency food and nonfood needs.[41]

Also based in Nairobi was political officer John Fox, who was the only American representative tasked solely with following the events in Somalia. Fox and Westcott sent Somalia updates to Washington, DC, where they ended up on the desk of Mike Harvey, the 25-year-old OFDA/USAID action officer for Sudan, Ethiopia, and Somalia, who wrote the Somali OFDA reports, which were the primary source materials for Somalia read by US government and UN officials. He told everyone who would listen, "If you don't allow us to do something in Somalia, then it will be god-awful."[42] Much of his information came from Westcott, who was rallying the NGOs in Nairobi and continually soliciting feedback from those few NGOs with contacts in Somalia. Fox and Westcott also starting working on a plan to get Westcott clearance from the State Department to visit Somalia to conduct an assessment and gather information to be sent on to Washington.

Meanwhile, Mogadishu was now the center of a violent struggle for control of the country. The city was attacked by the recently deposed former president, Barre. He and his supporters, primarily the Marehan-dominated Somali National Front (SNF), made a push to retake Mogadishu. Outside Mogadishu's outskirts he was met by a USC counterattack directed by warlord Mohamed Farrah Aidid. Meanwhile, Westcott became the first US government official to visit Mogadishu since Barre's fall. This trip was supported by Harvey, who wanted to "drop the veil" to get the US government more involved in Somalia and establish a presence in Mogadishu by getting Westcott in safely.[43] Since the State Department was risk-averse about sending in a staffer, Harvey suggested sending in non–US government staff contracted by OFDA; if someone died, he or she wouldn't be a US government official.[44] When Westcott complained to Fox about the tight travel restrictions—only twenty-four-hour visits, always travel with armed guards, stay in the Conoco compound—he replied, "All you have to do is not get shot and then we can go for increasingly longer visits."[45]

It helped Harvey's case that Westcott wanted to go to Mogadishu. Even though she knew the situation was a disaster from the reports she was receiving from Somalia, she wanted to go back in to start a US government response. Once that visit was completed and she came back and sent out a report on the situation, it became easier for her to travel to Somalia for longer periods."[46] In Westcott's view, she "was just trying to get back and help as much as we can and send the message that the US government had not deserted the people of Somalia, especially our employees."[47] For the next two years, Westcott was the sole US government representative traveling in and out of Somalia on a regular basis to track US food aid shipments and visit ICRC and NGO relief programs.[48]

US policy toward Somalia began to change with Westcott's trip and Harvey's raising the volume on Somalia. On March 25, 1991, Assistant Secretary of State for African Affairs Herman Cohen declared that Somalia was in the midst of civil strife. His official pronouncement prompted the OFDA to respond. Harvey and others within OFDA argued that "interventions are needed to keep it from spiraling out of control," but the response was that "it is too dangerous."[49] After Westcott's reports were sent to Washington through Harvey at OFDA, the US government started to provide money to ICRC and encourage American NGOs to get into Somalia to support relief efforts. For example, Harvey met with Roy Williams, head of the International Rescue Committee (IRC), who was working with Harvey on its southern Sudan programs, to convince him to go into Somalia."[50]

As the humanitarian situation in Somalia continued to deteriorate throughout April, Congress and the UN started to take a greater interest. By late April Kassebaum spearheaded calls for greater US action. On April 15, 1991, she introduced Senate Resolution 115, which asked President Bush to "lead a worldwide humanitarian effort in Somalia to relieve the suffering and for the United Nations to make the humanitarian crisis in Somalia an item of high priority."[51] According to Ted Dagne, who was on loan from the Congressional Research Service to the House Committee on Africa, it was not until after Kassebaum's appeal to Bush that the US government became more assertive toward the growing Somalia humanitarian crisis.[52]

At the same time, Mogadishu quickly descended into violent chaos. From May until December 1991, the Ali Mahdi Mohamed and Aidid factions representing different Hawiye sub-clans fought nearly daily battles throughout its streets and neighborhoods, resulting in an estimated 5,000 killed and 15,000 wounded, mostly by indiscriminate firing and shelling at civilian neighborhoods. Hundreds of thousands fled Mogadishu.

On May 18, 1991, the formerly British-controlled area of Somalia declared its independence at a SNM Special Congress meeting held in Burao. The meeting declared independence for a new state to be called "Somaliland" and named Hargeisa as its capital. Although Somaliland's independence was not recognized internationally, within days the UN, through the UN Children's Fund (UNICEF), re-established its permanent presence in Somalia, in the northwestern area away from the major humanitarian suffering and in the region now known as Somaliland.[53] UNICEF became the first UN agency to re-enter Somalia permanently, albeit only in Somaliland. This decision was made despite the fact that "the apparent creation of a new independent entity in northwestern Somalia [is] still under review by UNHCR."[54]

The deployment of UN staff to support Somaliland laid seeds of distrust among the southern Somalia population that were harvested by warlords, especially Aidid, in the next several years. Even though UN reports refused to use the term Somaliland, so as not to give anyone the impression that it was accepting the country's independence, Somalis living in southern Somalia felt betrayed that the UN was helping the breakaway region and not helping the regions of the greatest suffering. Perceptions about equal distribution along regional lines were important in the UN's action plan, which stated that equal geographical operations should be emplaced "to evidence commitment of UN system to respond to needs of all affected Somali people."[55] Yet the UN was not following its own plan. It was establishing a presence in a region that was not recognized internationally—even by itself—yet remained absent from the recognizable entity, which retained its UN seat.

On June 5 the first Somali reconciliation conference took place in Djibouti under the auspices of its president, Hassan Gouled Aptidon. The conference was supported by Egypt, Italy, and other regional states to implement a cease-fire among the contesting anti-Barre forces. The conference produced arrangements for political reconciliation in order to form a transitional government, which made US government officials, including Cohen, initially optimistic.[56] However, the conference agreements failed because many Somalis believed that the conference was manipulated by Italy because of its support of the moderate manifesto group and its desire to fill the space vacated by its former ally, Barre.[57] Rather than establishing peace, the conference propelled and intensified the fighting between Mahdi and Aidid forces.

As the UN treaded lightly and slowly back into Somalia, its effort was impeded by internal bureaucratic fighting and security instability in Mogadishu.[58] In light of the increased violence and UN ineffectiveness, President Gouled sponsored a second reconciliation conference, or Djibouti II, July 15 to 21 with support from Kenyan President Moi.[59] The conference came at a moment of high tension among and within the Somali factions. Warlords, clan elders, and former government officials jockeyed to preserve or increase their authority after the flight of Barre, by far the most solidifying and influential Somali figure. This was another reason why it was so hard to get a read on Somali leaders and what they wanted—they still had not figured out what type of government they wanted themselves and, more importantly, who would be its leaders.

At Djibouti II the Somali participants agreed to a cease-fire beginning the following week on July 26 and a two-year transitional government headed by Mahdi, who accepted the conference resolutions, was sworn in as president the following month, in mid-August, and later appointed a government cabinet in mid-October.

The US government accepted the conference's resolutions as a mandate for a Somali national government. Assistant Secretary of State for Africa Herman Cohen "thought Mahdi was a perfectly civilized guy" and that "he was chosen in a fair way."[60] Shortly after the conference ended, Cohen visited the region and in a press conference "endorsed the decisions, including Mahdi's designation as interim president" and "pledged US support for the restoration of a Somali governmental structure and reiterated our refusal to recognize Somaliland."[61]

After Ali Mahdi's inauguration as interim president on August 8, the UN quickly lent its support to his claim, including organizing the delivery of more than 12,000 mega tons of US donated food aid to coincide with the inauguration ceremony and generate publicity for the new government. UN agencies and personnel were pleased because their challenge in Somalia was not having a government to work with; UN agencies typically work through governmental agencies. Later in November UN officials cheered as Ali Mahdi's forces temporarily took over some of Aidid's territory in Mogadishu.[62]

Aidid rejected the conference resolutions and especially disapproved of Mahdi's election. The way Aidid saw it, the Somalis owed him the presidency and not a position as a member of a UN-organized governing coalition, marginalized by a political process that he did not control. After all, he was the general who stood up to Barre and was imprisoned for doing so, and later he came back to lead a coalition of rebel forces against the Barre government, forcing its collapse and flight.

Following the conference, violence between the Mahdi and Aidid Hawiye subclan militias continued to increase. In the meantime, Barre and his loyalists gathered and rearmed in southwestern Somalia's Gedo region and northwestern Kenya bases, where he and his followers watched the increasing breakdown of peace and relations among the clan militias, which had been held together by their common hatred and fear of Barre. The continued threat by Barre's forces delayed the dispute between Mahdi and Aidid forces, yet Mahdi's claim to the presidency finally led to a breakdown in intra-Hawiye relations. Mahdi consolidated his forces with the support of the manifesto group and those supporting the Djibouti I and II resolutions. With Barre seemingly out of the way, the clans and sub-clans, especially the Hawiye sub-clans, started to turn on each other.

Taking advantage of the Hawiye conflict, Barre forces launched new attacks from their Kenyan and southwestern Somalia bases against Hawiye forces. After successfully capturing Baidoa, Barre marched to Mogadishu, coming within 150 kilometers of the city before his assault ground to a halt and he and his forces retreated back to the Kenyan border. Much of the Barre-Aidid fighting took place between the Shabelle and Juba rivers, Somalia's only two permanent rivers, feeding most of Somalia's 15-percent arable land. The inter-clan fighting propelled food insecurity by destroying harvests, confiscating farming assets required for planting, closing transport routes for agricultural goods, and instilling fear in farmers of producing surplus crops for markets because warehouses were common militia targets.[63] The fighting devastated the farming communities and domestic food production already shattered by drought. Elsewhere, fighting also damaged local economies, but not as severely as the river valley farming areas, because other areas tended to focus on livestock herds. Past government neglect had made the Somali herders relatively self-sufficient, and they survived better than most other Somalis.[64]

As the Barre threat passed for the final time, the Hawiye-dominated USC, which controlled Mogadishu, separated along sub-clan lines. Aidid formed the Somali National Alliance (SNA) centered on members of his Habar-Gidir sub-clan, which had its roots in a nomadic lifestyle and whose members were pejoratively labeled the "camel people."[65] Ali Mahdi continued his control of the USC based on support from his sub-clan, Abgal, which had a more sedentary lifestyle. The intra-Hawiye fighting in early September caused thousands of casualties in Mogadishu. The worst fighting occurred on November 17, when Aidid's SNA forces unleashed a successful attack on Mahdi's Mogadishu positions. Within one month of Aidid's attack, NGOs estimated there were more than 13,000 casualties, including 4,000 killed.[66] The November attack commenced hostilities for another four months and began a humanitarian disaster leading to hundreds of thousands of deaths. The Mogadishu seaport shut down for several weeks as a result of the chaos, and on October 30 Aidid closed the Mogadishu airport to prevent an official Italian government delegation from arriving for a meeting with Mahdi.[67]

By mid-November US embassies in Nairobi and Djibouti, as well as NGOs and UN personnel working in Somalia, were "reporting the situation as out of control."[68] Compounding the Somalia humanitarian crisis was the UN's extended absence from Mogadishu and southern Somalia.[69] The few international NGOs remaining in the region continued to experience violent attacks, such as the following:

- On September 17 an ICRC plane was hit by a missile while flying from Mogadishu.[70]

- In October forty-five ICRC vehicles were looted and ICRC workers were repeatedly robbed.[71]

- On October 14 gunmen entered the Médecins Sans Frontières (MSF) Mogadishu compound, opened fire on MSF security guards, and attempted to steal a vehicle.[72]

- On December 5 a CARE expat was shot execution-style while distributing food.[73]

- On December 9 armed bandits attacked the Italian Cooperation compound in Berbera, stealing one generator and killing three people.[74]

- On December 11 an ICRC Belgian employee died on board an aircraft evacuating him to Antwerp after he was shot by a gunman in front of the Somali Red Crescent HQ.[75]

- On December 11 six gunmen robbed two UNICEF foreign nationals when they broke into the UNICEF compound in Berbera.[76]

Seeing that Somalia was degenerating into further violence, congressional action picked up. The US Congress continued providing the strongest source of support for international action in Somalia. In late December 1991 and early January 1992 Senators Kassebaum and Simon organized petitions to the Bush administration and sponsored congressional resolutions demanding urgent action, including use of troops if necessary to alleviate the Somalia crisis.

In addition, several congressional delegations visited Somalia, and the House Hunger Committee sponsored a weeklong fact-finding tour of northern Somalia, Eritrea, Ethiopia, Sudan, and Djibouti. Kassebaum became the first member of Congress to visit food-scarce and war-torn southern Somalia. According to the chair of the House Subcommittee on Africa and a researcher for the Congressional Research Service, "By the end of the second session (December 1992), a total of seven hearings had been held on Somalia—two in the Select Committee on Hunger, three in the House Subcommittee on Africa, and two in the Senate Subcommittee on Africa. Over a dozen letters were sent out by members to key players," including Secretary of State Baker, President Bush, UN Secretary-General Boutros Boutros-Ghali, Somali faction leaders, and several international organizations "urging stronger efforts to provide a secure environment for humanitarian assistance and peace talks to bring an end to the civil war."[77]

The UN's slow response to Somalia is explained by three factors. First, some UN agencies said that the security situation was too dangerous for staff to be sent into Somalia.[78] Until a cease-fire could be achieved, the delivery of humanitarian aid would be exposed to diversion before reaching vulnerable populations and risk the lives of UN and NGO staff. Other international organizations that had international staff in Somalia disputed the UN's reasoning. The ICRC's delegate-general for Africa, Pierre Glassman, asked, "How come UNICEF Somalia has thirteen people in Nairobi and no one inside Somalia?"[79] Westcott said that one UN staff member remarked that "the UN did not work in war zones," but NGO and government representatives pointed out that UNICEF had a successful program in southern Sudan.[80] Westcott recounted how UN personnel tried to claim credit for work they were not doing following a 1991 Somali coordination meeting in Nairobi:

> A camera crew from a major network asked to interview individuals carrying out relief programs in Somalia. The UNICEF representative rushed before the other NGOs and demanded to be interviewed (UNICEF was not operational in Somalia at the time). His inflated claims of what UNICEF was doing in Somalia elicited so many hoots of laughter from us, however, that the cameraman had to stop filming several times until we settled down.[81]

A characteristic of the 1991 and early 1992 UN missions to Somalia were that they usually lasted only one day. Among NGO relief officials these trips became known as "doing a UN woofie [a term denoting quick in and out visit with no substance]."[82] The head of the UN Operation in Somalia (UNOSOM) (and soon to be UNSG special representative to Somalia), Mohamed Sahnoun, also criticized the lack of UN presence in Somalia:

> Most Somalis still could not comprehend why the world community had deserted them. . . . Above all, they could not understand why the UN and all its agencies kept a distant and suspicious stance toward Somalia when their needs were so obvious. They could not but compare the behavior of the UN with that of the charitable institutions and NGOs that had provided essential relief and come to the rescue of the starving and the sick.[83]

The second reason why meaningful UN action in Somalia was slow is that the organization is a bureaucratic leviathan, where decision making is slow and turf battles easily erupt. The result was a lack of coordination among several of the key UN specialized agencies, a disconnect between the secretary-general and UN members, and a failure to work with the key Somali leaders and parties to establish relief plans.

The lead UN disaster relief agency, the UN Disaster Relief Office (UNDRO), which President Bush helped create in 1972 when he was US ambassador to the UN, was being replaced by the UN Department of Humanitarian Affairs (UNDHA), ironically because of pressure from the Bush administration. UNDRO's main purpose was to help coordinate UN actions toward natural disasters, but it failed to live up to expectations. The Nordic countries wanted it replaced by UNDHA, and the US and UK governments concurred. UNDRO could not adequately address the emerging Somali crisis because it was being phased out, and UNDHA was bureaucratically unprepared when it was launched in January 1992. Besides Nordic pressure for its elimination, UNDRO's elimination was also directly due to Bush's pressuring of Boutros-Ghali to reduce the secretariat's bureaucratic staff, which he did by eliminating or downgrading twelve of the seventeen undersecretaries-general.

The UNDRO dissolution and UNDHA transition could not have come at a worse time for Somalia. Despite being the lead UN agency charged with coordinating field assessments and launching international appeals for humanitarian emergencies, UNDHA failed to move in Somalia. It entered into immediate competition for funds and attention in a bruising bureaucratic environment without the bureaucratic experience to assert itself. It was also leaderless for months because its first undersecretary-general, Jan Eliasson, did not assume office until April 1992, more than four months after UNDHA's creation. Finally, UNDHA's effectiveness in Somalia was undermined because it was also trying to manage a major drought in southern Africa and large-scale relief efforts in Yugoslavia, Afghanistan, and Cambodia.

After Boutros-Ghali became UN secretary-general on January 1, 1992, the organization became more assertive and engaged in Somalia.[84] Boutros-Ghali not only had a personal interest in the Horn of Africa, especially in Somalia, but he was also more active in terms of engaging the UN in humanitarian emergencies and nation-building than his predecessor.[85]

On the morning of January 2, his first full day in his UN headquarters office in New York, Boutros-Ghali must have read the *New York Times*, which printed an opinion piece titled "Save Somalia From Itself" written by Senators Kassebaum and Simon. The senators called for the UN to work toward a cease-fire, start political negotiations, appoint a special envoy for Somalia, and impose an arms embargo. In Washington, DC, the senators also spearheaded a joint House and Senate letter to Secretary of State Baker calling on the UN to appoint a special envoy, implement an immediate cease-fire, and possibly create "neutral zones" for emergency relief distribution.[86]

One of the first reports that Boutros-Ghali received was from Undersecretary-General James Jonah, who led the first UN political mediation mission to Somalia, where he met with a range of Somali leaders, including warlords Aidid and Mahdi. Jonah reported that Mahdi said UN security personnel were welcome and needed in Somalia "to put an end to the fighting and maintain law and order," whereas Aidid thought that "the presence of a UN force were not necessary to restore peace as "the fighting in [Mogadishu was] a strictly internal USC matter which he can solve without outside assistance."[87] Jonah concluded that the disagreements between Aidid and Mahdi made a cease-fire unlikely.

After the ICRC reported in mid-January that its food stores were looted and that thousands of Somalis continued to starve, Boutros-Ghali called on the UN Security Council (UNSC) to adopt the Cape Verde-sponsored Resolution 733, which was designed to put an immediate stop to the violence and humanitarian suffering in Somalia. Incredibly, while members of Congress were pressing for UN action, the US mission at the UN was instructed to weaken the resolution. Two days later, the council unanimously adopted Resolution 733, which declared a total arms embargo and called for an increase in humanitarian aid and imposition of a cease-fire, including the deployment of fifty unarmed Pakistani troops to serve as cease-fire monitors.

When Secretary of State Baker found out that the resolution passed with the peacekeeping component, he was annoyed. The UN peacekeeping budget was in arrears and he was worried about spiraling costs for the twelve ongoing peacekeeping operations. Moreover, since the United States was running a considerable arrear in UN dues itself, the US mission at the UN insisted that UN involvement in Somalia be limited to humanitarian operations, which are financed within the regular UN budget, which assessed the United States at a 25% rate, rather than the peacekeeping budget, which assessed the United States at a 30 percent rate. American concern was understandable because costs for humanitarian operations had dramatically increased by the late 1980s. From 1978 to 1985, there was an average of five ongoing complex emergencies each year; by 1989 there were fourteen; and by 1992, seventeen.[88] The United States had supported all peacekeeping at the UN until the $2 billion for the total Cambodia peacekeeping costs. At that point, the United States decided that it couldn't afford many more such operations.[89] During the first half of 1992, the continuing demands of ongoing peacekeeping operations and the proposal of new peacekeeping operations led to diplomatic and financial exhaustion, which, in turn, directly contributed to the slow response to Somalia. According to Cohen, "Peacekeeping fatigue was settling in. . . . Cambodia was the straw that broke the camel's back."[90]

Cohen continued to hold meetings to highlight the Somalia emergency and consider possible options, most of which would fall on deaf ears as "the question of peacekeeping and Somalia was mainly question of dollars."[91] In effect, the growing financial burden was influencing US actions toward Somalia. Although the US still classified the situation in Somalia as a food crisis, there were financial worries concerning the exploding UN peace-keeping operations. Cohen started increasing the frequency of Somalia meetings, "to get people agitated about the situation."[92] Others within the State Department also began calling for military intervention in order to alleviate the disaster. The former US ambassador to Somalia, James Bishop, who was now deputy assistant secretary for human rights, became the first person within the State Department calling for US armed forces to go to Somalia.[93]

Boutros-Ghali was very receptive to Cohen's push for greater UN action in Somalia. They had known each other when Cohen was US ambassador to Senegal and then assistant secretary for Africa and Boutros-Ghali was Egyptian foreign affairs minister. Cohen traveled to Egypt to discuss African issues, including the Sudan problem. As an African diplomat and expert on the Horn of Africa, Boutros-Ghali decided to champion the Somalia cause.[94]

At the State Department, Cohen and Bishop were not alone in calling for more robust American action. Assistant Administrator for the Bureau for Food and Humanitarian Assistance Andrew Natsios, Undersecretary for International Security Affairs Frank Wisner, and Assistant Secretary for Political-Military Affairs Robert Gallucci were also supportive of a greater response. They each had prominent Pentagon contacts, and Wisner had become good friends with Boutros-Ghali when he served as ambassador to Egypt for five years.

Boutros-Ghali viewed the growing humanitarian crisis in Somalia as a threat to the multilateral system and began talks with Wisner on how best to achieve a solution.[95] He suggested to Wisner that the UN should launch a major Chapter VII peacekeeping operation with the UNSC's permission to use force to protect humanitarian relief operations. Although he wanted US military personnel to be part of the airlift and logistical com-ponents, Boutros-Ghali wanted to exclude Americans from the proposed ground force because he believed that Americans tended to be nervous about endangering US troops, and that could prevent the operation from getting off the ground. Also, the Somali peacekeeping mission would be a showcase for augmenting UN leadership, something that the presence of US military forces would water down.[96]

On January 23, the day after the Security Council passed Resolution 733, Boutros-Ghali sent the resolution text to Mahdi, Aidid, and other Somali leaders to seek their commitment to the cessation of hostilities as outlined in the resolution. He also invited them to participate in consultations in New York "to explore the best ways of reaching a cease-fire agreement and to draw up a framework for a sustained peacemaking effort in Somalia."[97]

On January 26 Mahdi confirmed his acceptance of the resolution. On January 31 Aidid replied that he had questions regarding the resolution and called upon the Security Council to reconsider the matter, but he did not state whether he accepted Resolution 733.[98] On the day he received Mahdi's message, Boutros-Ghali hosted his first meeting of the Security Council at the level of heads of state or government and had a chance to meet President Bush.[99]

Meanwhile, the US Congress remained engaged with the Somalia issue. On January 30 the House Hunger Committee heard Andrew Natsios, who had recently been appointed administrator for USAID, call Somalia "the greatest humanitarian emergency in the world." The following day, thirty members of Congress (twenty-four representatives and six senators) wrote letters to Mahdi and Aidid requesting their assistance with Resolution 733, especially in ensuring the delivery of food aid.

The month of February saw a rapid increase in Somalia activity among the UN, the United States, and international NGOs. Some of this attention was due to Mahdi's declaration that he was interim president, which provided a government entity for the international community to work with. Especially noteworthy is that the international media was still disengaged from the conflict and rarely mentioned Somalia despite the horrible humanitarian devastation. In order to attract media and public attention to garner international support, on February 1 the UN launched an Inter-Agency Consolidated Appeal for the Horn of Africa, and the following week Senator Kassebaum introduced Senate Resolution 259, which urged the UN to increase efforts to end the conflict.

On February 12 the Mahdi and Aidid groups met with a range of officials at UN headquarters in New York but never together. Boutros-Ghali met separately with the two factions and attempted to highlight a common approach for reconciliation by stressing the importance of humanitarian assistance by the UN and regional organizations.[100] The Aidid and Mahdi delegations gave their assurances that they would work toward a cease-fire by signing an ambiguous cease-fire agreement.

There were two important and troubling incidents during the New York meetings that put Boutros-Ghali, Jonah, and other UN officials on notice that the agreement would not work. First, Aidid delegation members refused to go along with UN efforts to meet with Mahdi representatives because they did not recognize Mahdi as Somalia's interim president or his delegation as true representatives of Somalia, instead viewing them as temporary imposters deserving nothing.

Second, the Mahdi delegation informed UN officials that any cease-fire without an international presence and support would not work.[101] In contrast, Aidid's delegation was silent except for Aidid's original concern about the UNSC resolution, specifically the insertion of UN forces in Somalia. At this time, Boutros-Ghali, Jonah, and other leading UN officials should have realized that UN troops in Somalia would be perceived by Aidid and his forces as an alien force bent on securing Mahdi the presidency and, therefore, an enemy.

After their meetings with Boutros-Ghali and Jonah, the Aidid and Mahdi delegations traveled to Washington, DC, for discussions with Cohen at the State Department. The Mahdi representatives again lobbied for international intervention to provide a cease-fire monitoring force that they said was indispensable to success.[102] Again, it is noticeable that the Aidid representatives did not comment on the possibility of international intervention.

Based on the cease-fire agreement signed at UN headquarters in New York, Boutros-Ghali sent another mission to Somalia to settle the interclan fighting. After arriving in Mogadishu on February 29, the delegation participated in four days of concentrated talks among the Somali parties. At the end of the four-day trip, the Aidid and Mahdi factions signed another cease-fire agreement on March 3 that included provisions for a UN technical team to visit Mogadishu to help implement a monitoring mechanism for cease-fire implementation.[103]

Aidid and Mahdi swiftly re-established the cease-fire, resulting in relative peace and little fighting in Mogadishu for several weeks. As the agreements were implemented, additional countries started to transport more humanitarian aid. Intuitively one would think that the increased amount of humanitarian aid to Somalia would enhance and support the peace agreements. However, the increased levels of food aid ignited a new round of fighting among the smaller Mogadishu armed gangs as Aidid and Mahdi declared their forces were standing down. The other clan militias and smaller, breakaway armed gangs that were not under the authority of the two Mogadishu-based leaders were determined to get their share of the food aid. They also felt slighted by the UN, which did not consult or invite rival clans and militias into the reconciliation discussions.[104]

As the international community brought in more aid, armed gangs started to skirmish with each other, eventually waging outright warfare throughout the Mogadishu area and drawing in Aidid and Mahdi forces interested in protecting their territories. Several weeks after the March agreement, fighting levels were above pre-agreement levels as the Aidid and Mahdi forces joined the fray and resumed fighting each other and the armed gangs.

On the first and last days of the delegation's four-day visit, two UN flagged ships unsuccessfully attempted to enter Mogadishu's harbor to unload relief supplies. The first vessel, loaded with 340 tons of food, hit a reef, where it got stuck and was thus unable to unload the critically needed food. Four days later on March 4, another relief ship was shelled from on-shore artillery positions when it reached Mogadishu's harbor. Although there were no casualties or damage, the ship had to return to Mombassa and the UN suspended further food deliveries because the shelling was in violation of the cease-fire agreement, which included language committing parties not to obstruct food delivery efforts.

The failures of the relief ships were emblematic of the UN's challenges in coordinating humanitarian relief—namely, a lack of competence among some UN relief officials and the lack of a secure environment in which relief delivery could be protected. The difference between the pre- and post-agreement violence was that international humanitarian aid was now the center of gravity for the fighting. The militias hijacked relief vehicles, charged astronomical fees for protection to relief convoys and warehouses, and killed those who opposed their looting of goods. The relief supplies provided the militia leaders with currency to buy guns and khat for their soldiers. According to a British reporter covering Somalia, "Aidid had realized that increased deaths among the Somalis, whether by fighting or starvation, led to increased international humanitarian aid, which, in turn, led to increased riches for himself."[105]

Besides halting relief shipments, the March ship incidents also forced the UN and relief officials to look to the United States to take the lead in directing and organizing the humanitarian operation. Other March events also conspired to bring a more intense US involvement in Somalia. Boutros-Ghali's personal interest in Somalia led to a continual flow of negative reports about Somalia to the US and other Security Council members. He kept pressing the delegation for more US involvement.[106] The delegation was also receiving pressure from Congress, the administration, and the media, including CNN, which in March "discovered Somalia and filled the tube almost daily with pictures of starving mothers with dying children."[107] The CNN coverage, coupled with increased Boutros-Ghali pressure and the continuation of congressional demands, persuaded the US delegation at the UN to "adopt a more flexible policy beginning in March 1992."[108] That same month, the US government signed an "agreement with the ICRC to provide 24,270 metric tons of food aid to Somalia."[109]

As a result of the United States softening its posture on Somalia, on March 17 the UNSC passed Resolution 746, which urged Somali factions to abide by the cease-fire agreement and supported dispatching a UN technical survey team to Somalia. Pushed by Senator Kassebaum, who had earlier criticized the Bush administration for watering down the language of UNSC Resolution 733 calling for the deployment of UN peacekeeping troops to Somalia, the State Department announced on March 20 that it would be taking a more activist position toward Somalia, including working with the UN on considering proposals to flood combat zones with food.

Later in the day, Boutros-Ghali announced the appointment of a fifteen-member technical team to visit Somalia headed by Canadian Robert Gallagher, who was selected in part because of Canada's support for greater UNSC engagement in Somalia. The team's purpose was to examine the possibility of sending military observers. The team arrived in Nairobi, where on March 21 it met with Mahdi, who informed the team that without a stronger UN military presence, the cease-fire would not hold and effective distribution of food and other supplies would not be possible.[110]

During the Somali visit, the technical team met with local authorities and clan leaders, including Aidid, who repeatedly told the team that he opposed the presence of foreign forces, including those associated with the UN, in Mogadishu. Aidid feared that a foreign or UN military presence would solidify Mahdi's interim presidency, a post he thought was his. He also did not want a foreign military threat to his growing zone of control in the more profitable and strategic southern Mogadishu. Aidid controlled all the activities in southern Mogadishu through his bodyguards and an elaborate administrative structure. His location gave him a significant advantage over his rivals, including Mahdi, and could be used as leverage with the international community. Since he controlled areas near Mogadishu's port and international airport, which could handle any size of aircraft, he could have power over humanitarian relief deliveries.

In contrast, Mahdi controlled the smaller northern Mogadishu airport, which had a runway that could handle only smaller aircraft. Aidid, therefore, thought he was in a better negotiating position than Mahdi to control the food aid coming into the country. It was in his interest to get food through his territory because he could skim profits, hire out his men to international aid agencies, and increase his international profile. While continually opposing the introduction of UN peacekeepers, Aidid consistently called for the international community to provide humanitarian assistance, especially food, which could be distributed by his forces.[111] Further strengthening Aidid's position was the fact that his forces had produced significant casualties to Mahdi's militia, including key military officers, during the recent fighting, and that Mahdi had lost control over most of Mogadishu and remained confined to the Karaan area.[112]

Regardless, after many days of intense and complex negotiations, the team was able to cobble together an agreement from Aidid and Mahdi.

They agreed to fifty UN military cease-fire monitors to be deployed on both sides of the Mogadishu green line dividing the two factions. In addition, a 500-man force would be deployed to provide protection for humanitarian relief convoys and provide security for UN personnel and, if necessary, international and NGO personnel. In his final report to Boutros-Ghali, Gallagher wrote, "From the beginning, Ali Mahdi's team insisted a large armed and well-equipped UN military force was necessary immediately to resolve his problems while General Aidid's team insisted that beyond a few civilian UN observers, no military presence was acceptable."[113] Instead, the agreement called for UN peacekeepers, which upset Aidid, whereas Mahdi was disappointed at the small size of the UN force and its limited mandate.

On April 7 the Congressional Black Caucus officially got involved for the first time in lobbying for US action in Somalia. The caucus sent an April letter to Secretary of State Baker asking that the United States take "the initiative in the United Nations in forcefully advocating a high-level UN presence in Somalia."[114]

In reporting to the UNSC, Boutros-Ghali continued to highlight the depressing and ominous humanitarian crisis and called for increased UN military forces. These reports were forwarded by the US mission in New York to State Department officials, including Cohen, who commented that "Boutros-Ghali was a great proponent of intervention. He kept sending reports that always said the only solution is to use force."[115]

By mid-April, people with the State Department and the Senate become distressed and desperate by the lack of success in alleviating the swelling Somalia crisis. For example, Andrew Natsios, assistant administrator for USAID, proposed to address the security problem in Somalia by deploying 5,000 Nepalese Gurkhas. Many were about to be demobilized by the British Colonial Service. Although Natsios met twice with the British security firm representing the Gurkhas, the State Department "got very upset" and quickly killed the idea.[116]

April also saw the UNDHA finally receive its first undersecretary, Jan Eliasson, more than four months after its creation. Although Somalia was emerging as a priority at UNDHA, it still had to compete for attention with other international humanitarian challenges, such as "the major drought in southern Africa, and handling large-scale relief efforts in Yugoslavia, Afghanistan and Cambodia." Compounding UNDHA's problems—and indirectly those of the Somali relief operation—was that Eliasson had little authority and even fewer resources. He did not visit Somalia until September, more than five months after he assumed office.

On April 21 Boutros-Ghali approved and released the consolidated interagency 90-day Plan of Action for Emergency Humanitarian Assistance to Somalia, which was based on Gallagher's report of the UN technical team's visit to Somalia the previous month. In the plan Boutros-Ghali proposed relief distribution and safe passage for aid personnel and supplies through designated "corridors" and "zones of peace."[117] The challenge would be getting the relief supplies out of southern Mogadishu, where the port and airport were under the control of Aidid and thus military targets for Mahdi.[118]

Several days after receiving the plan from Boutros-Ghali, the UNSC passed on April 24 Resolution 751, which established UN Operations in Somalia I (UNOSOM I), a military force that would help implement a cease-fire in Mogadishu and protect UN humanitarian relief personnel and their activities.

Not surprisingly, Aidid did not endorse many parts of the resolution, especially those paragraphs concerning the deployment of UN military observers and an open-ended call for the possible deployment of a larger force. At best, Aidid probably read UNSC Resolution 751 as an intrusion into Somali politics and at worst as another attempt to take away the presidency. He did not like the UN plan for fifty unarmed cease-fire observers and 500 armed guards to protect food relief in Mogadishu. Aidid argued that the soon-to-arrive military observers should dress as civilians but wear UN blue berets and armbands, whereas Mahdi accepted the agreements, including allowing the military observers to wear their uniforms.[119]

At UN headquarters in New York, there was celebration at the passage of UNSC 751. It was assertive, aggressive, and unprecedented by the UN to deploy troops into a country with no functioning government and no peace treaty. It also was the UN's first time negotiating with nonstate actors. Aidid most likely assumed UNSC 751 to be an aggressive move by Boutros-Ghali, who was closely tied to the former colonial power Italy and a supporter of Barre and Aidid's main rival, Mahdi. Meanwhile, happenings in Somalia emboldened Aidid not to reconcile or heed UNSC resolutions, UN peacekeepers, or Boutros-Ghali's initiatives. On April 26 his forces captured Baidoa and Garba Harre, which was Barre's hometown in the heart of Marehan territory in southwestern Somalia. Two days later, on April 28, Barre fled Somalia for the final time to northern Kenya, never to return to Somalia.

Emboldened by Resolution 751's passage, Boutros-Ghali urged the UNSC to continue the momentum in Somalia by passing another resolution, 767, on April 27 authorizing an airlift of relief supplies and sending another technical team to Somalia. The following day, Boutros-Ghali appointed Mohamed Sahnoun to be his special representative to Somalia and to begin implementing the 90-day action plan.

As the UN secretary-general's special representative, Sahnoun received Boutros-Ghali's strong support, but the position had many drawbacks. Its major weakness was that Boutros-Ghali did not have the support of the

UN's implementing agencies, and its New York headquarters lacked administrative capability to handle Somalia's large-scale emergency relief situation. Compounding the confusion was that there was no UN lead agency to coordinate the Somalia operation. Typically, the main UN model for coordinating humanitarian relief operations is the secretary-general assigning a specific crisis to one agency. For example, UNHCR was the lead UN agency in Bosnia, whereas in southern Africa it was the World Food Program (WFP), and in Sudan and Kurdistan it was UNICEF. According to Natsios, this model was "unmanageable" and "neither the secretary-general nor his staff was capable—temperamentally, intellectually, or organizationally—of centrally supporting extended field operations in Somalia."[120]

By early May, the first significant amounts of food aid poured into Mogadishu accompanied by Sahnoun, who arrived on May 4 to open UNOSOM I headquarters. Without delay, he met with selected Somali representatives to discuss how better to distribute humanitarian aid, supervise the cease-fire, and plan for a national reconciliation conference. By this time the UN had already hired 10,000 gunmen from both the Aidid and Mahdi militias to guard food supplies in Mogadishu's port.[121] The ICRC was also accused of "hiring of Red Cross mercenaries" or "the hiring of gunmen" to protect humanitarian distributions.[122]

The straws that kept Somalia burning in Washington were the distressing reports of hunger and food insecurity sent by Westcott and Fox in Nairobi. Westcott's reports were rich with primary information, as she had developed an extensive network of Somalia-related personalities and NGOs in Kenya. She also had a strong desire to help the Somali people and return there herself, so she organized the interested NGOs in Somalia and Nairobi to generate information channels to encourage and lobby their governments and the broader international community for aid to Somalia. One of the first readers of Westcott's reports to OFDA Washington was Jan Coffey, who was the OFDA information specialist for the Sudan, Ethiopia, and Somalia Desk. She remembers receiving Westcott's reports, on which she would base her OFDA reports to Congress, that "screamed there was a crisis, but no one was listening."[123]

On May 13 Westcott returned to Mogadishu and was shocked. She cabled to Washington a horrifying report that graphically described how many Somalis were dying or going to die.

Although I have previously worked in drought and famine areas elsewhere in Africa, I never expected to see the catastrophic situation that prevailed in Mogadishu in May; the number of adults suffering from malnutrition was shocking.

One watched adults and children dying of starvation in camps for the displaced. At the ICRC beach landing sites, Somalis were seen picking through the sand for grains of rice or drinking vegetable oil directly from tins. Security problems linked to the delivery of food aid were also on the rise, especially at the port of Mogadishu.[124]

Several days after her report, four Senate staffers were sent to New York to meet with Sahnoun and other UN officials.[125] The next day, on May 19, 1992, the Senate passed Resolution 258 supporting more Somalia relief operations, and on May 22 Senator Simon met with OFDA, NGOs, and a group of Somali principals to explore ways to facilitate more relief more quickly.

In the meantime former Somali President Barre accepted an asylum invitation from Nigeria, where he arrived on May 17 and lived his remaining few years in exile. The immediate ramification for Somalia was that Barre became an impotent force in Somali politics, which further weakened Somalia militia unity. Rebel forces, faction leaders, and many clan elders lost the one thing that helped bond them, although tenuously, the fear that Barre and his forces would again attempt to retake Mogadishu and Somalia. When Barre was nearly successful, the disputing factions laid down their differences long enough to turn him and his forces back to southwestern Somalia and eventually Kenya. The factions now had very little in common to unite them to form a national government.

Increasing divisions among the Somali factions and Boutros-Ghali's assertive vision of the UN peacekeeping led to a collision that would entangle the US and make it hesitant to use its military for purely humanitarian operations ever again. Despite increased humanitarian relief shipments, the UN estimated that 4.5 million of the 6.5 million Somalis were facing starvation and that 100 to 200 people were dying every day in and around Mogadishu.[126] In the following months, intense US planning to help the UN and then exasperation at its incompetence would finally lead to a dramatic US attempt to save hundreds of thousands of Somalis from starvation and civil war by sending in US Marines.

Notes

1. Peter D. Little, *Somalia: Economy Without State* (Bloomington: Indiana University Press, 2003), 48.

2. I. M. Lewis, *A Modern History of the Somali,* 4th edition (Athens: Ohio University Press, 2002), 11.

3. Peter J. Schraeder, *African Politics and Society: A Mosaic in Transformation* (Boston: Bedford/St. Martins, 2000), 63–82.

4. John Drysdale, *Whatever Happened to Somalia?* (London: HAAN Associates, 1994), 131; Lewis, *Modern History*, 40–41.

5. The Somali national flag has a white five-pointed star representing the five Somali areas colonized by outsiders. The flag's background color is the light blue color of the United Nations, highlighting the country's appreciation for the organization's support of its independence.

6. Little, *Somalia*, 48.

7. Terrence Lyons and Ahmed I. Samatar, *Somalia: State Collapse, Multilateral Intervention, and Strategies for Political Reconstruction* (Washington, DC: The Brookings Institution, 1995), 13.

8. Little, *Somalia*, 47.

9. Philip Johnston, *Somalia Diary: The President of CARE Tells One Country's Story of Hope* (Atlanta: Longstreet Press, 1994), 13–14.

10. Ambassador Jim Bishop (deputy assistant for Africa, 1981–1987; US ambassador to Somalia 1987–1990), interview with the author, Washington, DC, May 28, 2003.

11. Bishop, interview.

12. Ted Dagne (specialist in international relations, Congressional Research Service; professional staff member, Subcommittee for Africa 1993–1994), interview with the author, Washington, DC, May 12, 2004.

13. Lewis, *A Modern History*, 356.

14. Drysdale, *Whatever Happened to Somalia?* 136; Lyons and Samatar, *Somalia*, 17–18; and Ken Menkahus, "Somalia: Political Order in a Stateless Society," *Current History* (May 1998): 226.

15. US government intelligence officer for Africa (service in Somalia, including UNOSOM II, 1993), discussion with author, November 11, 2004. Discussion conducted in confidentiality, and the name withheld by mutual agreement.

16. Mengistu's regime was under military pressure from liberation movements in Eritrea, Ogden, and Oromo.

17. Menkahus, "Somalia," 226.

18. Peter J. Schraeder, "The Horn of Africa: US Foreign Policy in an Altered Cold War Environment," *Middle East Journal*, vol. 46, no. 4 (Autumn 1992): 576.

19. Herman J. Cohen, *Intervening in Africa: Superpower Peacemaking in a Troubled Continent* (New York: Macmillan Press Ltd, 2000), 202.

20. "Four ICRC Staff Ambushed in Somalia," ICRC Press Release No. 1645, October 6, 1990.

21. Michael T. Harvey (USAID grants officer for Sudan, Ethiopia and Somalia, 1989-1992), interview with author, Amman, Jordan, April 18, 2005.

22. Jan Westcott, "The Somalia Saga: A Personal Account 1990–1992," Refugee Policy Group, November 1994, 2.

23. Bishop, interview.

24. John G. Sommer, *Hope Restored? Humanitarian Aid in Somalia: 1990–1994* (Washington, DC: Refugee Policy Group, 1994), 9.

25. Westcott, "The Somalia Saga," 2.

26. Jan Wessel (Westcott) (special relief coordinator for Somalia, Office of US Foreign Disaster Assistance), e-mail correspondence with author, May 4, 2005.

27. Bishop, interview.

28. The August 2, 1990, Iraqi invasion and occupation of Kuwait further pushed Somalia to the margins of the world's attention. In response, the United States requested and was granted basing rights in Saudi Arabia and in the Persian Gulf region, where by January 1991 over half a million allied troops were deployed. Thus the "over the horizon" bases, such as those in Somalia, were no longer necessary because Saudi Arabia and other Persian Gulf countries welcomed US forces on their soil for the first time. After President Bush ordered a cease-fire on February 27 and Iraq accepted the cease-fire terms on March 3, the US had significant military assets in the region, where they remained, and no longer required Somali basing rights. The Cold War was over and the Islamic fundamentalist threat from Iran could now be countered from locations closer to the Persian Gulf.

29. Bishop, interview.

30. Ibid.

31. Cohen, *Intervening in Africa*, 203.

32. "Framework for Possible Resumption of UNHCR's Activities in Somalia," Report prepared by the Branch Office Somalia Unit in Nairobi, February 27, 1991, 2.

33. Cable from UNHCR Nairobi to UNHCR Geneva "for bwakira from perkins," February 22, 1991.

34. "Framework for Possible Resumption of UNHCR's Activities in Somalia," 11.

35. For example on February 21 more than 200 unarmed civilians were killed in Belet Weyne in the Darood region. *Amnesty International Report 1992*, 232.

36. The Mogadishu violence against the Issaqs already fueled their dislike of the southerners and propelled them toward breaking away from southern Somalia and creating a self-declared state of "Somaliland" on May 18, 1991.

37. Westcott, "The Somalia Saga," 6.

38. Sommer, *Hope Restored?* B-2.

39. Ibid.

40. Harvey, interview.

41. Wessel (Wescot), correspondence.

42. Author interview, Michael T. Harvey, USAID grants officer for Sudan, Ethiopia, and Somalia (1989–1992), Amman, Jordan April 18, 2005.

43. Harvey, interview.

44. Ibid.

45. As quoted in Westcott, "The Somalia Saga," 14.

46. Wessel (Wescot), correspondence.

47. Ibid.

48. Ibid.

49. Harvey, interview.

50. Ibid.

51. Harry Johnston and Ted Dagne, "Congress and the Somalia Crisis" in *Learning From Somalia: The Lessons of Amred Humanitarian Intervention*, ed. Walter Clarke and Jeffrey Herbst (Boulder, CO: Westview Press, 1997), 192. "S.R. 115 referred to Senate Committee on Foreign Relations (SCFR), April 25, 1991; reported to Senate by SCFR June 27, 1991; agreed to in Senate without amendment and with a preamble by voice vote June 18, 1991." Johnston and Dagne, footnote 3, 203.

52. Dagne, interview.

53. UN Secretary-General Report, Consolidated Inter-Agency 90-day Plan of Action for Emergency Humanitarian Assistance to Somalia. April 21, 1992. S/23829.

54. Regional Bureau for Africa: UNHCR's Plan of Action for Somalia, June 14, 1991.

55. Ibid., Annex A.

56. Ambassador Herman J. Cohen (assistant secretary of state for Africa, 1989–1993), interview with author, Washington, DC, May 12, 2004.

57. Drysdale, 33; Samuel M. Makinda *Seeking Peace From Chaos: Humanitarian Intervention in Somalia* (Boulder, CO: Lynne Rienner Publishers, 1993), 31–33.

58. The UN special coordinator for Somalia, Osman Hashim, faxed Undersecretary-General Jonah stating that there were "divergent views and approaches" among WFP, UNHCR, and CARE, and that he was trying, albeit unsuccessfully, to get food aid approved and released from WFP but that "this somehow was not possible." Moreover, he reported "serious incidents in Mogadishu demonstrating the growing threat created by food shortages." UN Special Coordinator for Somalia Osman Hashim fax to Undersecretary-General Jonah, July 19, 1991.

59. In July, Italy and Egypt attempted, but failed, to convene a peace conference in Cairo. Boutros-Ghali and Secretary of State Baker also meet in Cairo to discuss international issues, including Somalia.

60. Cohen, interview.

61. Cohen, *Intervening in Africa*, 205.

62. Westcott, "The Somalia Saga," 20.

63. Steven Hansch, Scott Lillibridge, Grace Egeland, Charles Teller, and Michael Toole, "Lives Lost, Lives Saved: Excess Mortality and the Impact of Health Interventions in the Somalia Emergency," report, Refugee Policy Group, November 1994, 3.

64. Little, *Somalia*, 66.

65. Helen Fogarassy, *Mission Improbable: The World Community on a UN Compound in Somalia* (Lanham, MD: Lexington Books, 1999), 53.

66. Westcott, "The Somalia Saga," 18.

67. Ibid., 18.

68. Cohen, *Intervening in Africa*, 205.

69. A few weeks later, the first humanitarian supplies since the January evacuation arrived when UNICEF established a Mogadishu presence, though its staff kept a low profile in the relief efforts and stayed confined to a bunkered office. It was the first UN presence in Mogadishu in 11 months. 4/21/92 UNSG Consolidated Inter-Agency 90-day Plan of Action for Emergency Humanitarian Assistance to Somalia. Report of the SG . . . S/23829/Add. P. 6. [and] Report of the SG in pursuance of para 13 UNSC Res. 954 (1994), S/1995/231 March 28, 1995, 7.

70. UNHCR Situation Report, Somalia Unit-Djibouti, September 20, 1991.

71. Sommer, *Hope Restored?* 14.

72. UNHCR Situation Report for Northwest Somalia, Somalia Unit-Djibouti, October 31, 1991.

73. UNHCR Situation Report for Northwest Somalia for period December 5–12, Somalia Unit-Djibouti, December 12, 1991.

74. Ibid.

75. ICRC Press Release 1698, "Somalia: ICRC Worker Dies," December 15, 1991.

76. UNHCR Situation Report, December 12, 1991.

77. Johnston and Dagne, "Congress and the Somalia Crisis," 193.

78. Mohamed Sahnoun, *Somalia: The Missed Opportunities* (Washington, DC: US Institute for Peace, 1994), 18.

79. Jane Perlez, "Somali Fighting Keeps Aid From a Suffering City," *New York Times*, December 11, 1991.

80. Westcott, "The Somalia Saga," 18.

81. Ibid., 18.

82. Ibid., 11.

83. Sahnoun, *Somalia*, 16.

84. At the time of his appointment by the General Assembly on December 3, 1991, Boutros-Ghali had been deputy prime minister for foreign affairs of Egypt since May 1991 and had served as minister of state for foreign affairs from October 1977 until 1991. During this period he and the former Somali President Barre became friends, which was to be a source of much hostility among much of the Somali population, especially Aidid.

85. In his 1992 book, *An Agenda for Peace*, Boutros-Ghali provides his vision and roadmap for how the UN should operate going forward. In the book, he calls for a more aggressive and assertive UN that would be empowered to help states rebuild and that would become more independent from state sovereignty requirements for non-intervention. For example, Boutros-Ghali wrote to the UNSC that "the interdependence between peace and security in Somalia and the provision of increased humanitarian assistance to the country" are intertwined and require the deployment of "United Nations security personnel to ensure the unimpeded delivery of humanitarian assistance to Somalia." Secretary-General Boutros-Ghali, letter to His Excellency Mr. Paul Noterdaeme, President of the Security Council, June 5, 1992.

86. Sommer, *Hope Restored?* B-2.

87. Report of the Under Secretary General James O.C. Jonah on his Exploratory Mission to Somalia, January 3–6, 1992, 5.

88. As quoted in Natsios, 1.

89. Cohen, interview.

90. Ibid.

91. Ibid.

92. Ibid.

93. Ibid.

94. Ibid.

95. Cohen, *Intervening in Africa*, 205.

96. Ibid., 210–211.

97. UN Secretary-General Report, "The Situation in Somalia," March 11, 1992. S/23693. 5.

98. Ibid., 3.

99. According to Boutros-Ghali, Bush seemed pleased to be back at the UN and made two demands: As long as Saddam Hussein remained in power, there would not be normalization, and Libya must accept responsibility for the Pam Am Flight 103 and UTA Flight 772 terrorist

bombings. Boutros Boutros-Ghali, *Unvanquished A U.S.–U.N. Saga* (New York: Random House, 1999), 23–24.

100. UN Secretary-General Report, "The Situation in Somalia." March 11, 1992. S/23693. 6.

101. Ibid., 7.

102. Herman J. Cohen, "Intervention in Somalia," in *The Diplomatic Record: 1992–1993*, ed., Allan Goodman (Boulder, CO: Westview Press, 1995), 55.

103. The agreement also included the following provisions: 1) Both sides were to disengage forces and efforts to seize land. 2) Troops were to remain in their respective positions. 3) Both sides were to facilitate distribution of relief. 4) Both sides were to support withdrawal of forces from airports and seaports, with UN observers invited to monitor records.

104. Jeffrey Clark, "Debacle in Somalia," *Foreign Affairs* (1993): 115.

105. Aidan Hartley, *The Zanzibar Chest* (Atlantic Monthly Press: New York, 2003), 180.

106. Cohen, interview.

107. Cohen, *Intervening in Africa*, 207.

108. Ibid., 207.

109. James L. Woods, "US Government Decisionmaking Processes During Humanitarian Operations in Somalia" in *Learning From Somalia: The Lessons of Amred Humanitarian Intervention*, ed. Walter Clarke and Jeffrey Herbst (Boulder, CO: Westview Press, 1997), 153.

110. UN Secretary General Report March 21, 1992. S/23829. 5.

111. "The Situation in Somalia: Report of the Secretary-General," April 21, 1992. S/23829.

112. "Somalia: Time to take Stock," *Africa Confidential*, vol. 33, no. 8 (April 17, 1992): 4.

113. Robert Gallagher, "Support for the Mission," UN Technical Team Report on Somalia to the UN Secretary-General [not dated].

114. Johnston and Dagne, "Congress and the Somalia Crisis," 195.

115. Cohen, interview.

116. Susan Rosegrant, "A 'Seamless' Transition: United States and United Nations Operations in Somalia–1992–1993," Kennedy School of Government Case Program (Cambridge, MA: President and Fellows of Harvard College, 1996), 6, footnote 12.

117. UN Secretary-General Report, "Addendum to the Consolidated Inter-Agency 90-day Plan of Action for Emergency Humanitarian Assistance to Somalia," April 21, 1992. S/23829/Add. 1.

118. Ibid., 14.

119. UN Secretary-General Report, "The Situation in Somalia." March 11, 1992. S/23693. 10.

120. Andrew S. Natsios, "The International Humanitarian Response System," *Parameters* (Spring 1995): 76.

121. "Armed relief," *The Economist*, May 9, 1992, 48.

122. "Somalia: Security Set-Up Food Aid in Mogadishu," ICRC Press Release, No. 1714. May 8, 1992.

123. Jan Coffey (US Office of Foreign Disaster and Assistance, Information Specialist, Sudan, Ethiopia, and Somalia Desk, April 1991 to May 1992), interview with author, Egypt, May 27, 2005.

124. Westcott, "The Somalia Saga," 32.

125. Sommer, *Hope Restored?* B-3.

126. OFDA Somalia Situation Report #10, "Somalia—Civil Strife," June 23, 1992, 2.

CHAPTER TWO

INEFFECTIVE EFFORTS TO STOP
THE CHAOS AND DEATH

By June 1992 Somalia was experiencing one of the most severe famines of the twentieth century, based on death rates as a percentage of the affected population. There was a wide-ranging deterioration of security in Mogadishu and an increase in organized piracy and looting by large, well-armed factions who raided relief food facilities, including convoys, distribution centers, and warehouses. By mid-March 300,000 Somalis had died, 3,000 were dying daily, 500,000 had fled to refugee camps in neighboring countries, and more than 70 percent of the livestock had died.[1] Not only were many Somalis not receiving food but also food prices were soaring—in some areas by 1,200 percent over a few short months.[2] The combination of drought in southern Somalia, which is the country's most fertile region, and inter-clan violence affected commercial transportation networks and put weaker clans at the mercy of stronger clans.[3]

On June 5 Boutros-Ghali wrote to the UN Security Council (UNSC) President Paul Noterdaeme, highlighting the linkage between peace and security and saying they were an "indispensable prerequisite" for delivering humanitarian aid. As an example of why the UNSC needed to support the insertion of UN military personnel to protect humanitarian relief distribution, he noted the May 31 looting of one metric ton of medicine from an International Committee of the Red Cross (ICRC) Cessna aircraft and six metric tons of high-protein food mix from a WFP Antonov aircraft by armed elements in Mogadishu. As a result, on June 1 he suspended all UN flights to Mogadishu. UNICEF launched a feeding center, which in turn attracted international humanitarian NGOs, followed by armed bandits stealing vehicles and supplies.

As a result of UN Special Representative Mohamed Sahnoun's patience and persistence with Aidid, he was granted a face-to-face meeting June 21 in Baidoa, where Aidid gave his formal permission for UN troops to accompany humanitarian aid convoys, provided they were unarmed and deployed on both sides of the Mogadishu demarcation line. He also accepted the immediate deployment of fifty cease-fire monitors after giving up his demand that they wear civilian clothes but still argued against further international military intervention.

A June 23 US Office of Foreign Disaster Assistance (OFDA) report titled "Somalia—Civil Strife" indicated that more than 4.5 million people out of the 6.5 million total Somali population were facing starvation. It went on to note that hundreds of people were dying each day in Mogadishu and that people were dying daily in the nearly 175 makeshift camps in and around the city. Further propelling the Somalia crisis, according to the OFDA, was a rise in violence as food shipments arrived "as armed gangs fight civilians and each other for the food."[4] Meanwhile, the UN reported that the food aid "aggravated tensions" and served as a "catalyst for flare-ups of fierce fighting as heavily armed bandit groups attempted to attack [Mogadishu's] port."[5] Further adding to the Mogadishu port violence was the UN's June decision to cease all flights to the city's main airport because of looting of relief flights.

By the end of June, the Bush administration was facing pressure to do more to improve security in Somalia. The month ended with a House letter to Bush, signed by eighty-eight members of Congress, in part a response to the June 23 OFDA report, urging his administration "to devote the highest priority to this unprecedented humanitarian disaster." The letter noted the likelihood of armed intervention in the Balkans but urged Bush not to forget the "catastrophe" facing Somalia. It went on to highlight Sahnoun's statistics of "as many as 5,000 children under the age of five are dying on a daily basis," "over half the population is at risk of starvation," and "over 30,000 people have been killed or wounded." The House letter also mentioned that "tens of thousands of refugees are now risking their lives in a desperate attempt to escape Somalia."[6]

In the Senate, Senator Paul Simon declared Somalia the worst humanitarian tragedy in the world and then organized a letter to the administration urging delivery of additional aid to Somalia. In his push for greater US action toward Somalia and support of the UN, he also quoted Sahnoun's estimates that nearly 5,000 Somali children were dying each day. Twelve Senators sent a letter to Ronald Roskens, US Agency for International Development (USAID) Administrator, urging him to mobilize OFDA and other agencies to speed relief deliveries.

July proved seminal for US policy in Somalia. In Washington, DC, outrage about the humanitarian crisis broke the bureaucratic logjam. President Bush pressed the State Department to come up with possible policy solutions. Spearheading the Somalia policy discussions at the State

Department was Ambassador Herman Cohen, Assistant Secretary of State for African Affairs. He convened meetings of the Policy Coordinating Committee on Africa (PCC) at the State Department to discuss the distressing intelligence reports coming in from Somalia.

At the PCC meetings, Cohen used direct questioning of otherwise "passive agencies" to push the Somali action agenda. He eventually persuaded the Bureau of Human Rights to join in support of a security operation, but the Bureau for International Organizations and representatives from the National Security Council (NSC) and Department of Defense (DOD) were not convinced. For example, Cohen asked the Joint Chiefs of Staff representative whether the US military could offer airlift support to deliver food to Somalia's interior. The representative said, "We plan for operations like Desert Storm. We do not plan for humanitarian airlifts that can be done more cheaply through civilian charter."[7] Cohen then asked the Bureau of International Organization representative whether the United States could introduce a UNSC resolution sanctioning "all necessary means" to counter Somali armed factions halting food distribution. The representative's response: "We have already been burned by a similar resolution concerning Bosnia. Nobody in the Security Council would support such a resolution covering Somalia."[8]

As the July PCC meetings concerning Somalia became more intense, momentum toward greater UN and US action in Somalia increased. During an early July meeting, Cohen invited USAID Assistant Administrator Natsios to present on his recent Somalia trip. Natsios described the horrible situation and made a personal plea that helped lead the US administration to take the "forward-leaning" position toward Somalia. Somalia finally hit the headlines of such important publications as *The New York Times* and *The Economist*. For example, on July 19 *The New York Times* ran a front-page story about the Baidoa famine with a heart-wrenching photo.[9] *The Economist* also carried a Somalia story in July titled "Death by Looting" that reported that food-aid theft by warlord-run militias was resulting in Somalis "dying of hunger, possibly at the ghastly rate of several thousand per day."[10]

On July 5 Pakistani Brigadier General Imtiaz Shaheen, appointed as the chief military observer by Boutros-Ghali, and three staff arrived in Mogadishu to prepare for the arrival of the UN Operation in Somalia (UNOSOM I) team. The complete fifty-member military cease-fire team would not arrive for two weeks because the UN was waiting for permission from Aidid, who continued to oppose deployment of UN forces to Somalia. A June 25 incident further alienated him from the UN and reinforced his belief that the UN was pro-Mahdi. A UNICEF-chartered Antonov aircraft with World Food Program (WFP) markings landed in

Mogadishu carrying money and arms for Mahdi's forces. Immediately, Aidid supporters alleged that the UN was providing the plane to Mahdi and that it was carrying Somali currency and military equipment for delivery to the Mahdi faction. A subsequent UN investigation into the Antonov aircraft incident concluded that it was an illegal flight.

As Mogadishu continued to spiral into violence and food insecurity mounted, the UN remained immobilized over how to establish security and deliver aid. Yet, it remained satisfied in its effort. Jan Eliasson, undersecretary-general for the UNDHA said that "given the political and security environment" in Somalia, the UN humanitarian assistance to Somalia "represents a praise-worthy effort."[11]

In a confidential cable from Secretary of State James Baker to the US Mission at the UN, speaking points were given to Edward Perkins, the US ambassador to the UN, for his expected July 7 meeting with Sahnoun to discuss the latter's draft report. Baker endorsed Sahnoun's call for urgent humanitarian distribution and dividing Somalia into zones to increase a nationwide relief effort. However, Baker did not support Sahnoun's suggestion for a meeting of Somali experts in Nairobi and Sweden because the State Department was "aware that Somalis are capable of talking as long as they are housed and fed." Baker did support Sahnoun's idea for regional conferences and for introducing UN military personnel into Somalia as long as they were not involved in police functions or activities other than protecting "UN humanitarian supplies and those UN and NGO personnel involved in distribution."[12]

During the meeting with Sahnoun, the US delegation told him that the United States supported the concept of securing reconciliation within the regions prior to moving to a national reconciliation conference. The OFDA director then informed Sahnoun that the United States would help with funding of the conference, provided that the conference also tackle the issue of humanitarian relief. Finally, Baker notified the US Mission at the UN that the State Department would "be willing to take under consideration any other specific requests for US assistance to UN relief and reconciliation operations in Somalia."[13]

In early July the US ambassador to Kenya, Smith Hempstone, visited Somali refugee camps near the Somali border in northern Kenya. After his trip, Hempstone cabled a July 10 message titled "A Day in Hell" to the State Department in Washington, where it later made the rounds of officials, including Walter Kansteiner, the NSC director for African affairs, who forwarded part of the letter to National Security Advisor (NSA) Brent Scowcroft and President Bush. Besides describing the horrible humanitarian situation, the letter included attention-grabbing quotes, such as "if you love Beirut, you'll love Mogadishu," "Somalis are born warriors," "no good deed goes unpunished," and there will be "blowback because of tar baby angle." According to Kansteiner, Bush returned it a few days with "a number of questions and comments scribbled in the margins."[14] "This is a terribly moving situation. Let's do everything we can to help," Bush wrote in the margin.[15]

On July 12 Sahnoun returned to Mogadishu to begin preparations for the UNOSOM arrival and sought Aidid's and Mahdi's permission for its continued deployment in meetings on July 15–16. Aidid agreed to allow the UNOSOM four-member advance party, including Brigadier General Shaheen, to remain in Mogadishu and to allow the arrival of the forty-seven military observers currently waiting in Nairobi contingent upon Sahnoun getting Mahdi's agreement to refrain from circulating newly printed currency that had been brought in on the illegal Antonov flight. Mahdi finally agreed not to circulate the currency and informed Sahnoun on July 16. In return, Aidid consented to allowing the full complement of observers and said he would support their deployment at the end of the week.

More than three months after the UN and Somali parties agreed to the UNOSOM military cease-fire team of fifty observers, the forty-seven Pakistani observers arrived in Mogadishu on July 20. Two days later, Senator Kassebaum described her two-day visit to Somalia at the House Select Committee on Hunger. She relayed the horror of her Somali experience, saying that "as many as 30,000 people have been killed just in Mogadishu alone since November. Estimates are that there could be as many as 5,000 to 7,000 dying a week from the famine and conflict that exists throughout Somalia." Kassebaum called for UN armed troops to ensure safe relief distribution: "The mandate would be simple: to provide protection for relief workers and guard relief supplies en route to those most in need."

Her idea was immediately backed by InterAction, the growing association of private voluntary agencies engaged in international humanitarian efforts. InterAction's credibility on Somalia was high within Washington, DC, because five of its members were operational on the ground in Somalia in July 1992. Its president and CEO, Peter Davies, said, "I enthusiastically support the senator's proposal to authorize sending 500 United Nations peacekeeping troops to Somalia to help ensure the distribution of relief commodities."[16]

Meanwhile, Representative Bill Emerson also testified that "Somalia is, without reservation, the world's greatest disaster." His opinion was reinforced by Andrew Natsios, USAID assistant administrator for food and humanitarian assistance, who wrote to the House Select Committee on Hunger that there was a huge disparity between the US and UN level of support for Bosnia and Somalia: "The number of people who perish in

Yugoslavia each month equals the number of people who die in Somalia each day. Yet there is little international concern, and no outrage."[17] As a result of bipartisan concern for Somalia, Senators Kassebaum and Simon introduced a resolution that called for greater protection for food aid delivery, which quickly passed both houses unanimously at the end of the week on July 31.[18]

Although the State Department's Africa Bureau was sympathetic to deploying a force to protect aid to Somalia, its International Organization Affairs Bureau, headed by Assistant Secretary John Bolton was opposed. He said that the administration was continuing to encourage the UN to take increased action in Somalia toward relief and reconciliation attempts and to establish a cease-fire.

In addition, the Africa Bureau maintained that Somalia was a security crisis, whereas Bolton and his bureau said that Somalia was a food problem. According to Cohen, the International Organization Affairs Bureau's position was that "if people were starving in Somalia, the UN's main job was to coordinate the shipment of food assistance, nothing more."[19] Bolton's deputy was John Wolfe, who also opposed any military intervention and said that there "had to be a red line which US would not get involved, and Somalia was below the red line."[20]

The Africa Bureau's main ally in the interagency community was Natsios, who leveraged his USAID position "as the lone Africa Bureau voice supporting its contention that Somalia was a security problem."[21] According to Bishop, who at the time was acting assistant secretary for human rights and humanitarian affairs, "Natsios was a real hero. He and Cohen argued for military intervention in Somalia in opposition to Bolton."[22] Cohen remembers that Bishop was the first person to say that US troops should be sent in. "He kept saying that we had to send in US troops over and over," Cohen said. "I was not thinking of that; rather I was thinking that we need UN forces and we'll pay for it."[23]

On July 22 the same day as Kassebaum's Somalia testimony on Capitol Hill, Boutros-Ghali angrily told the UNSC that it was "fighting a rich man's war in Yugoslavia while not lifting a finger to save Somalia from disintegration."[24] The next day *The New York Times* ran an editorial titled "The Hell Called Somalia," and *The Washington Post* ran a Somalia story with the headline "Bush, UN Face Pressure to Aid War-Torn Somalia." The day after the newspaper stories ran, President Bush instructed Deputy Secretary of State Lawrence Eagleburger to be "forward-leaning" on Somalia. In response, Eagleburger established a Somalia task force. "I will be blunt," Eagleburger said. "There was lots of pressure to get involved and to get in Yugoslavia and some, but not as much, to get into Somalia. In Somalia, it was humanitarian aid, and in Bosnia, there was a really a call for military intervention."[25] In the meantime, Secretary of State Baker notified the US Mission at the United Nations that the United States was "gearing up to be responsive" to Somalia events.[26]

Cohen, who led many of the Somali PCC meetings, thought White House pressure came from Walter Kansteiner, the young Republican who regularly attended the meetings in his position as NSC director for African affairs.[27] Although he was relatively quiet during the meetings, Kansteiner provided briefings to National Security Adviser Scowcroft. The president's directives on Somalia addressed the same issues that were addressed at the PCC meetings, which is why Cohen believed Kansteiner was responsible for bringing the meetings to the notice of the president.

Deeply disturbed by the Somalia crisis, the United States lent its support to UNSC passage of Resolution 767 on July 27 calling for an urgent airlift operation to relieve the growing starvation. The UNSC also implicitly warned that the United Nations would take unilateral action: "In the absence of such cooperation, the Security Council does not exclude other measures to deliver humanitarian assistance to Somalia." Although UNSC Resolution 767 did not call for security forces other than those already authorized by UNSC Resolution 751, it "does not exclude other measures to deliver humanitarian assistance to Somalia."

Resolution 767 marked the first pro-security signal from the Bush administration. A few weeks earlier at the July 7 meeting, Baker and Ambassador Perkins told Boutros-Ghali that they did not believe UN security guards should be involved in any other activities, including disarmament and demobilization, because it would detract from their protective mission.[28] Moreover, Baker said that "UN security guards should not be involved in police training."[29]

Four days after Resolution 767's passage, the Senate passed a Senator Kassebaum and Simon Resolution calling for US pressure on the UN to fulfill the resolution's food delivery goals: "The UNSC [should] deploy these security guards immediately, with or without the consent of the Somali factions in order to assure that humanitarian relief gets to those most in need, particularly the women, children and elderly of Somalia."[30]

By the end of July, the administration decided to take greater action in Somalia as it felt protected by a pro-intervention Congress led by the bilateral and respected leadership of Senators Kassebaum and Simon and Representatives Hall and Emerson. Moreover, the media was compassionate toward the Somalia disaster, and many American religious and relief organizations began writing pro-intervention letters to Bush administration officials and submitting op-eds to newspapers. For example, InterAction President Peter Davies called for the international community to take more aggressive action in Somalia by committing peacekeepers and suggested race was a factor by drawing comparisons between the high level of international security and relief effort in Bosnia and not in Somalia:

> For civilians in former Yugoslavia, the international community has decided that starvation is unacceptable and must be prevented. . . . Why have civilians in Sarajevo commanded a united international response—including humanitarian military intervention—while we ignore Somali children who are dying? . . . If Somalis were white, more strategically located in the geopolitical sense, or had ethnic cousins in the US, would the capacity of the international community to care increase?[31]

On July 31 *The New York Times* ran a story headlined "US Says Airlifts Fail Somali Needy; Relief Team Warns Fighting Prevents Delivery of Food to Tens of Thousands" that detailed official American exasperation with the UN relief effort. The same day, David Beckmann, president of the Washington, DC–based Christian citizens' movement Bread for the World, which claims more than 45,000 members, sent a letter to Eagleburger asking for a drastically increased effort by the United States to avert considerable starvation in Somalia by quickly deploying military personnel to protect food relief operations. He also noted that 25 percent of Somalia's children under five had died "in the last twelve months and the majority of them in the last three to four months" and that "further delay could conceivably mean death and destruction for a generation of people." Beckmann told Eagleburger that Bolton's view that a security deployment should wait until there was a cease-fire is "unconscionable for the United States."[32]

OFDA Director James Kunder, who visited Mogadishu for five hours with international relief expert Fred Cuny, returned to Washington, DC, to brief US government officials and the media in an August 3 press conference. He also briefed Eagleburger's newly created Somalia task force. As the highest-ranking American official to visit Somalia since the civil war broke out eighteen months earlier, Kunder carried great weight in Washington. Kunder reported that the effort to save the Somalis must be increased because the situation in Somalia was grave, with more than 1.5 million Somalis—one-quarter of the country's population—at risk of starvation. His briefs further propelled interagency debate about how to alleviate the humanitarian disaster, including the use of the US military.

After receiving Kunder's starvation reports in early August, President Bush "reacted with a burst of energy."[33] The NSC Office of International Programs, which covered UN affairs and Africa, looked at different ways of getting food to Somalia, including possible US military airdrops.[34] Asked at an NSC meeting, the military representatives thought that moving food by air was inefficient. According to Richard Clarke, the NSC director of international programs, "They were right because weight loads were limited."[35] One military official also expressed concern that "US airplanes would be dropping palates of food from the air by parachute and that the people could chase the palates and get squashed underneath them." Clarke responded, "They're going to die anyway, and it will be acceptable if one person is squashed in order to feed many others who are starving."[36] On August 12 President Bush made up his mind to begin airlift relief flights to Somalia even though the Joint Chiefs of Staff considered taking part in any operation in Somalia to be a "bottomless pit."[37]

The following day White House press secretary Marlin Fitzwater announced that the president had ordered the DOD to make available its aircraft to transport the 500-member UN guard force and its associated equipment authorized under UNSC 751 to Somalia.[38] The next day, on August 14, Fitzwater made another, more dramatic announcement: "The United States will take a leading role with other nations and international organizations to overcome the obstacles and ensure that food reaches those who so desperately need it."[39]

The major contributors to Bush's airlift decision, according to Kunder, were his assessment of his July trip to Somalia coinciding with Bush's reading of US Ambassador to Kenya Smith Hempstone's cable concerning the Kenya-Somalia border situation. After reading the cable, the president was "deeply disturbed by what he read in the ambassador's report."[40] He was also influenced by Senator Kassebaum's Somalia report based on her July trip.[41] Less influential in Bush's calculation to intervene was the media, who paid little attention to Somalia until his decision.[42] For example, the three major television networks—ABC, CBS, and NBC—broadcasted only fifteen Somali stories, almost half as part of the evening's forty-second wrap-up, in the seven and a half months of 1992 before Bush's August 14 announcement.[43]

After his appointment as the president's special coordinator for Somali relief and President Bush's airlift announcement, Natsios and Kunder were regularly invited to testify on Capitol Hill and had the authority to conduct press conferences as they wished.[44] Initially, the press conferences on Somalia generated little media attention, but coverage significantly increased after Bush's airlift announcement.

Bush's airlift pronouncement prompted others within the State Department to promote the president's new Somalia policy. Eagleburger immediately sent a confidential cable with the president's announcement to US embassies around the world. He then followed up with another confidential cable asking US ambassadors to approach host governments to share with them the White House announcement on Somali relief and "ask them for a status report on their relief plans, determine where they can increase their relief efforts in concert with our and UN efforts now under way, and solicit their views on and support for UN donors conference."[45]

Eagleburger notified the US embassies through confidential cables of more details concerning the president's Somali relief plan. The emergency airlift was designed for two operations. The first was to move relief supplies from the Kenyan seaport of Mombassa to Wajir, near the border of Somalia, for Somali refugees and at-risk Kenyans. The second operation was to airlift humanitarian relief from Mombassa to four cities in Somalia—Baidoa, Bardera, Belet Weyne, and Oddur. These airlift operations "in and of themselves," according to Eagleburger, "can address only a small part of relief needs and are intended to expand on, not substitute for, ongoing relief efforts."[46] Operation Provide Relief was a measurable and attainable mission as insisted by the US Central Command (CENTCOM).[47]

As a sign of continued Senate interest, from August 13 to 22 Tim Rieser visited Somalia as a staff member of the Senate Appropriations Subcommittee on State and Foreign Operations "to check out airlift operations and port facilities in Mogadishu." During his trip, Rieser remembers "seeing technicals and refugees all over the place" in Mogadishu.[48] He also visited Baidoa, where he went into a goat barn, which did not have windows, and saw a Somali having a leg amputated—"I remember that the guy assisting was a dental student from Penn."[49]

On the weekend of Bush's announcement, US Ambassador to Kenya Smith Hempstone was on a weekend safari in southern Kenya, where he was notified via radio to return to Nairobi concerning a "subject too sensitive to discuss over an open channel."[50] After returning to Nairobi, he heard that President Bush had ordered an air relief operation into Somalia. "When?" Hempstone asked. "The advance party, under a Marine brigadier, is in the air and will wheels-down in Mombassa at 9 a.m. tomorrow," responded a US Embassy official. Hempstone retorted, "Good Christ," before booking a seat on the last flight to Mombassa. Although he was not surprised that the US was launching the food-relief operation, he was taken aback that it had not notified the Kenyan government. President Daniel arap Moi "did not like surprises" and, given the Kenyan "sensitivities," notice would have been prudent.[51] When he was notified that the relief mission would be called "Provide Relief," Hempstone moaned, "I hope they got the permission of the Rolaids people."[52]

The day after the White House announcement (August 15), General Frank Libutti was ordered from CENTCOM in Tampa to Mombassa,

Kenya, to organize an airlift under the name Operation Provide Relief.[53] A Disaster Assistance Response Team (DART), which is a unit within the OFDA, was also assigned to the operation to help coordinate NGOs, prepare and locate food aid delivery sites, and track humanitarian relief donations. Upon arriving in Kenya, one of Libbuti's first questions concerned local security at the airport. Hempstone replied, "A bad sunburn is always a danger. And, even as we speak, every hooker in East Africa is on her way to Mombassa, intent on making her fortune and giving you all AIDS."[54]

Libutti also arrived without US notification of the airlift mission to the Kenyan government. Libutti and Hempstone had to do some fast talking with Kenya's President Moi after Kenyan newspaper headlines decried the "US invasion."[55] A few hours after Libutti's landing, Hempstone was notified that Moi had canceled the operation because of the US "disregard for Kenya's sovereignty" and because it had not sought "prior clearance to land at Moi International Airport [Mombassa] or overfly Kenyan air space."[56] Several days later, on August 21, Hempstone telephoned Moi: "Mr. President, I'm sure I've been misinformed: I'm told you intend to cancel Operation Provide Relief." Moi responded, "You have not been misinformed, Ambassador." Hempstone replied, "I cannot believe, Mr. President, that a man of your compassion would deny the hungry people of northeastern Kenya free food, particularly in your election year, let alone the people of Somalia. As you must know, the international press is here in great numbers, and such a move would be very bad for your image in the world."[57]

Within an hour, Hempstone, Libutti, and other American officials met Moi and his advisers in the State House, where they agreed with Moi's litany of complaints about lack of adequate notice and operation details. Hempstone emphasized that he, too, was upset because he had been informed only on Sunday afternoon, "when Libutti's aircraft was already airborne from Tampa."[58] After Libutti informed Moi that his orders also included sending "one plane of food to Wajir [a northern Kenyan city with food insecurity issues] for every four that go into Somalia," Moi seemed placated.[59]

At the largest press conference held in Kenya since its independence more than thirty years earlier, the Kenyan government announced that Operation Provide Relief would proceed and "claimed full credit for Kenya."[60] Since the operation was a UN-authorized mission, it helped alleviate fears of Kenya and neighboring states concerning US military involvement.

The airlift was quickly established, consisting both of DOD assets and OFDA civil charter and coordinated by a US Air Force team on site in

Kenya. Because of the deteriorated conditions of the short Somali runways, the pilots were only US Air Force pilots.[61] Humanitarian aid was delivered by 570 American troops under the direction of General Libutti and a DOD joint task force command.[62]

The initial task for the operation was to partner with organizations that had relief infrastructures in Somalia. The leading candidate was the ICRC, which had the largest footprint in Somalia with more than 500 feeding stations. Under an agreement hammered out by the United States and ICRC officials, US aircraft would fly from Kenya into Somalia for the food aid drops, but would do so unarmed and with ICRC markings on the outside of the planes. In response to President Bush's offer to deliver food via American military transport planes, Jeff Loane, the ICRC relief coordinator in Somalia, informed Hempstone and Libutti that the ICRC had two nonnegotiable requests: The aircraft "must be marked with a Red Cross, and there must be no armed men on board."[63]

Hempstone and Libutti agreed, so long as the Red Cross markings did not cover the US insignias. Regarding the carrying of weapons on the plane, they had dissimilar views. Libutti's responsibilities were American personnel and equipment, and he was not open to leaving them without protection. However, he realized that he needed the ICRC Somali network to distribute the food. In contrast, Hempstone understood the ICRC restrictions about carrying armed personal. As a former Marine, he also understood Libutti's concerns. To alleviate Libutti's concerns, appease the ICRC and get the operation moving, Hempstone diplomatically accomplished all three goals. He informed Libutti that he was going to agree to Loane's conditions, and "if you do anything other than that, I don't want to hear about it."[64] As added security insurance, US Special Forces were placed in an orbiting aircraft above the Somali airfields and would land if NGO or aircrew personnel were attacked.[65]

While President Bush seized the leading role in providing relief to Somalia, Boutros-Ghali waited for a Somalia trip report from a UN technical team created by UNSC Resolution 767. Nearly one month after UNSC 767 authorized the team, he received the team's report and resulting recommendations on August 24.[66] The report recommended that UN security forces be deployed in the northeast, southwest, and south and that they should cover a wide range of responsibilities, including monitoring cease-fire agreements, escorting and protecting humanitarian aid activities, and securing the sea ports. The report also stated that around 4.5 million Somalis were threatened by lack of food, and that many were dying due to famine. The report said that although the UN had the capacity to deliver food, it had been prevented from doing so by gunmen controlling delivery routes and raiding supply points, including ports and airports. Therefore, the team concluded that UN security personnel were needed to facilitate relief.

By the end of August, international NGOs were disagreeing publicly on a range of Somalia relief issues. Whereas some NGOs feared introducing military personnel to protect food aid would "escalate the conflict," many other NGOs advocated for relief-worker protection. Perhaps the biggest inter-NGO disagreement occurred between InterAction and Africa Watch and its parent organization Human Rights Watch. In an August 31 letter to Holly Burkhalter, the Washington, DC, director for Human Rights Watch, InterAction's Tony Gambino expressed his view that Africa Rights Watch Associate Director Alex de Waal's calls for "the donating public to stop giving money to UNICEF or UN Development Program" were "highly irresponsible." De Waal also said the UN officials "who are responsible for hundreds of thousands of deaths must face the prospect of persecution, not promotion."[67] Gambino also expressed his opposition to Africa Watch Director Rakiya Omaar's suggestion that large ships should be anchored off the coast to deliver food to Somalia and that aid agencies should "abandon qualms about feeding armed men."

One of the items that NGOs were also discussing was the difficulty of estimating Somali deaths. It was almost impossible to find accurate statistics to verify NGO, UN, and US government claims. In *The Road to Hell*, Michael Maren, who worked for USAID in Somalia, writes that the fall 1992 Somalia statistics of the dead and dying were not accurate and were inflated to promote NGO fundraising efforts.[68] It was also difficult for NGOs and the media to get accurate statistics from Somalia regarding the humanitarian crisis. As an example, in response to a Reuters news agency question about how many children had died in Somalia (because NGOs were quoting 25 percent of all children under the age of 5 had died in Somalia) InterAction made a calculation from 1990 figures. It found in the 1992 UNICEF State of the Children report that in 1990 there were 1.4 million children under 5 in Somalia. So it divided 1.4 million by 4 and subsequently reported the 350,000 figure to Reuters and the Associated Press and recommended to its staff to use those figures "until we come up with a better one."[69]

Two days later, on August 23, Lawrence Eagleburger was appointed acting secretary of state, replacing Jim Baker, who had been chosen to manage President Bush's re-election campaign. Also, the recently appointed president's special coordinator for Somalia relief, Natsios, visited ICRC, UN High Commissioner for Refugees (UNHCR), and UN Department of Humanitarian Affairs (UNDHA) officials in Geneva on his way to Kenya and Somalia. During his August 26 meetings, Natsios informed them of the Kenya and Somalia airlift operations moving

250–275 tons per day to Wajir in northern Kenya. All three organizations indicated support of the US airlift and also "were very critical of UN coordination of assistance to Somalia."[70] The ICRC deputy delegate-general for Africa, Harold Schmid De Gruneck, and relief division chief Andreas Lendorff were especially "critical of the continued disarray and lack of coordination within the UN on assistance to Somalia."[71] The UNHCR Africa Bureau director, Nicolas Bwakira, also expressed disappointment with the lack of UN coordination on Somalia.[72] Natsios' last Geneva meeting was with the UNDHA Geneva office staff and its director, Charles Lamuniere, who concurred that the UN coordination in Somalia was lacking.[73]

On August 28 the Bush administration officially responded to Boutros-Ghali's August 25 Somalia report by proposing draft "all necessary measures" language for a UNSC resolution to authorize an additional 3,500 men to bolster 500 already approved for deployment to protect food aid convoys and oversee distribution. In gathering support for the proposed resolution and before leaving his position, Secretary of State Baker sent a confidential memo to the US Mission at the United Nations asking it to present the draft to the United Kingdom and French missions for consultations. The proposed resolution stated that if the Somalis needed greater assistance, they would "require measures beyond the level that could be addressed by the proposed security force, the UN may need to call upon its members to take additional necessary measures to permit distribution of relief supplies."[74]

It is with this last point in mind that the United States sought British and French support for the "all necessary measures" resolution. The resolution was passed on August 28 as No. 775. According to Boutros-Ghali, Resolution 775 signaled that the UNSC "finally decided to take firmer action." It also carried historical significance because it called for "secure humanitarian assistance, and it was something new for UN peacekeepers, a form of 'peace enforcement.' No Somali government approval for the mission was obtained, because there was no Somali government."[75]

Ironically, the passage of Resolution 775 alienated both UN officials and Somali leaders in Somalia, especially Aidid and Sahnoun, two key figures whose support was critical for the cease-fire, food aid security, and alleviating the crisis in general. Neither individual was consulted on the resolution, which in turn caused a hostile response from Aidid, who felt that he had been tricked into agreeing with Sahnoun for deployment of the 500-man Pakistani contingent. Sahnoun also had not been informed of the proposal and blamed the UN leadership for failure to communicate and undercutting his cease-fire efforts.[76] As a result of Resolution 775, Aidid boxed in the fifty-member UN security forces, composed of Pakistanis, at the airport. Further complicating the already complex situation for the UN in Mogadishu was Aidid's decision in August to break away from the United Somali Congress (USC) to form his own militia, the Somalia National Alliance (SNA) composed primarily of Hawiye sub-clan Habar Gidir members.

As the flow of international humanitarian relief to Somalia increased in midsummer, violence also increased as armed bandits and factions fought among themselves to control the ever-increasing amounts of aid. Most seriously, there was chaos at Mogadishu's seaport, which had the potential of being the greatest channel and the least costly way to get relief into Somalia. According to the August 14 OFDA report concerning the civil strife in Somalia: "CARE and ICRC are currently paying a 900-man security force to guard the port. Recently, these guards have begun demanding higher wages to protect the port. The port remains closed to commercial traffic, and given the tenuous security situation, is still not a reliable relief route."[77] An international reporter covering Somalia described the chaotic port scene:

> When a ship was unloading the seaport fizzed with gunfire day and night, so inevitably we tended to spend our time there—along with most of the population of Mogadishu. It was a place surrounded by mobs of heaving rags, rolling eyes, and angry mouths. Rival clan gangs competed to control the fortified port perimeter. Inside the docks it was like a circus with various freelance gangs killing one another: militias, the private armies of grain and sugar merchants, stevedores, and unemployed members of the defunct police forces in tattered uniforms. Worst of all were the cripples. My guards were hardened killers, but they went pale with fear when they saw a squadron of these deformed creatures barreling across the tarmac toward us. They charged in wheelchairs, on crutches, or on trolleys like skateboards—paraplegics, victims of polio and landmines. One had the swollen legs and the gourd-sized testicles of elephantiasis. They bristled with guns and grenades and we would have to speed off before they could skid to a halt or drop their crutches to take aim at us.[78]

Other areas of Somalia were also experiencing a rapid decline in security and, more specifically, attacks on international organizations and the relief distribution system. For example, armed bandits stole 800 tons of ICRC food from a Belet Weyne warehouse, and Mogadishu-based UN Development Program (UNDP) personnel and property were attacked by Somali workers demanding more money.

Although the airlift was well under way by September, most of the food delivered was not getting to the targeted populations. At the time, OFDA estimated that only 40 percent of the airlifted food was reaching those it was intended to feed. For example, Baidoa was ruled by armed gangs that charged relief NGOs $20,000 per week to allow the relief flights to land. If they didn't receive payments, they would shoot the planes.[79] William Garvelink, OFDA assistant director for relief and head of the DART team, highlighted the difficulty of delivering food: "If you flew into Baidoa in a C-130, which holds about twelve tons of food, you'd load up two or three trucks and one of them would always disappear. Plus they charged landing fees. Plus they charged a fee for each truck to get out the airport gate."[80] The only vehicle not requiring security protection was a truck that every morning collected around 300 dead bodies from "the orphanage, the hospital, and abandoned houses were those who had died the during the night were brought to be washed and wrapped for burial."[81] A *National Geographic* reporter was present in the CARE Baidoa office in September when the Somalis extorted $1,500 to allow the American relief planes to land.[82]

Throughout September the US government was peppered with demands for airlift support. On September 1 in a confidential message, Belgian Deputy Premier Van Daele informed the US Mission at the United Nations that it would accept US airlift assistance in transporting a Belgian battalion and all needed supplies from Brussels to Somalia.[83] On September 14 forty armed Pakistani troops were carried to Mogadishu by a US flight.[84] Less than two weeks later, on September 29, 500 Pakistani troops arrived in Mogadishu on US aircraft. Yet, as the US military continued to fly food and UN troops into Somalia, the situation on the ground got worse. On September 18 the US was forced to suspend all relief flights because one of them was hit by a bullet when departing the desert air strip Beledweyne.[85] Three days later, a major relief warehouse in Mogadishu was looted.[86]

At an October 1 hearing held by the Senate Committee on Foreign Relations Subcommittee on African Affairs, Kunder called Somalia "the worst humanitarian disaster in the world today." He also testified to the same mind-numbing figures he used in August before the president's airlift announcement. He said that an estimated one-third of Somali's population was at starvation risk, that 25 percent of the children had died, that 1,000 to 2,000 were dying daily, and that there were more than 800,000 Somali refugees in neighboring countries.[87] Kunder told the Senators that more UN troops to secure Mogadishu's port and open up ground operations were necessary because the airlift could not adequately solve Somalia's food insecurity situation.[88]

Airdrops would not be enough to alleviate the food famine. Moreover, the airlift operation was very expensive to maintain. UN or US armed forces had to regain control of the ports, but the US presidential election was going on and Bush was on the campaign trail. According to NSC's Clarke, who as the director of international programs participated in the Somalia meetings, "There was no way Bush was going to make a decision for US forces to intervene during the campaign."[89]

Notwithstanding US government efforts to alleviate the crisis, the enormity of the disaster remained.[90] The assistant secretary of state for international organization affairs, John Bolton, also testified at the October 1 hearing but argued against introducing further military personnel into Somalia. He said that "the UN system was not ready to meet fully its new responsibilities."[91]

By mid-October, Cohen and other State Department officials expressed surprise that Somalis would destroy their cities and kill their own citizens in order to control food, which was the only viable economic activity left in the country. This was something that they had never experienced in previous African famines.[92] Cohen believed that Somalia was the only case where there was "an inability to get aid through because food was used as currency."[93]

Natsios was also shocked that Somali leaders would not cooperate on allowing food aid to be delivered to starving people. Like Cohen, his previous experience with Horn of Africa famine and relief operations showed that negotiations between the United States and warring parties resulted in free flow of aid. Typically, when governments or militaries hindered relief delivery, the US government was successful in negotiating with them to clear the way without the use of force. Natsios noted that the United States had a successful record of dealing with obstinate and uncooperative governments and militias. Negotiations were previously successful with the governments of Sudan (1988–1989) and Ethiopia and Eritrea (1989), laying the foundation for successful relief operations.[94]

On October 2, the day after the Senate hearing, a member of the Congressional Black Caucus, Rep. John Lewis of Georgia, introduced Resolution 370 that asked the president to support the deployment of armed personnel to Somalia. The resolution sailed through the House and Senate, passing the former on October 2 and the latter on October 8.

As the crisis escalated throughout October, US CARE President Philip Johnston called for a UN trusteeship of Somalia. As the largest American NGO operating in Somalia, including functioning in Mogadishu's volatile port area and feeding more than one million Somalis per day, CARE carried tremendous political weight on the Somali issue. On October 5 Johnston said a UN trusteeship was the "only logical option" because Somalia's void could only be filled by the presence of the UN serving "as the country's surrogate government."[95] Johnston made his view known on the national news show *MacNeil/Lehrer News Hour,* where he said that the "UN as the only capable entity in our world, has to put a unit in there and take over the administration of that country until they help the Somali population develop the capacity, again, to govern themselves. . . . Put a military unit in there and take over the city of Mogadishu."[96]

The increased UN pressure for more forces in Somalia and discussion of a UN trusteeship over Somalia further reinforced Aidid's reservations about the UN role in Somalia. Aidid especially feared Boutros-Ghali's role because when he was Egypt's foreign minister, Boutros-Ghali and Somalia's then-President Barre were good friends—this during a time when Aidid was serving a prison sentence imposed by Barre. One of Aidid's fears was that the UN was simply an extension of Egyptian foreign policy in Somalia. Natsios noted that Egypt's "centuries of unwelcome involvement in Somali affairs" made the Somalis think that "the Egyptian pharaohs had been reincarnated in Boutros-Ghali."[97]

On October 12 the UN's 100-Day Action Plan was approved at a UNDHA major donor conference in Geneva. The plan's purpose was to generate momentum for the aid effort and, according to Jan Eliasson, it was "a race for the survival of the Somali people. That's why we felt the name '100-Day Action Plan for Accelerated Assistance to Somalia' was needed. We chose this 100-Day theme because we wanted to set a sprint pace. We have to turn this thing around quickly."[98] The 100-Day Plan was comparable to the previous 90-Day Plan, which had been stagnated by UN bureaucratic disorganization and infighting and insecurity on the ground in Somalia. The plan was designed to overcome past challenges by including a key ingredient—security—that was missing from previous UN plans.

International supporters contributed significant amounts of money to UN agencies and NGOs, but that good news was overshadowed by Sahnoun's criticisms of UN agencies for moving too slowly to return to Somalia. He assessed the UN's efforts to date: "We know that it [Somalia] is a crisis of frightening proportions and that we are paying the price for past neglect. A whole year slipped by whilst the UN and the international community, save for the ICRC and a few NGOs, watched Somalia descend into this hell."[99] After hearing Sahnoun's negative remarks, Boutros-Ghali reprimanded him.[100]

During his October 1st speech to the UNGA, President Bush had supported a proposal by Boutros-Ghali for the creation of a UN standing army. He said that the US was prepared to use its military knowledge and to make its military bases available to bolster UN peacekeeping operations.

Unfortunately, the situation in Somalia was getting worse, not better. The famine was intensifying and expanding, and death rates were rising. The port of Kismayu had to be closed because of militias fighting over control of the food aid being unloaded. That further deepened food scarcity throughout southern Somalia. In addition, diseases such as hepatitis, measles, and tuberculosis were killing more Somalis than the famine. Natsios feared that a medical emergency would soon be more dangerous than the food emergency.[101]

The UN stalemate with the Somalia reconciliation process further highlighted the lack of security to deliver food aid. According to Cohen,

> By mid-October, it was clear that the warlords were giving Sahnoun the runaround. They were not only refusing to acquiesce in the deployment of additional guards but they were also not allowing the five hundred Pakis to accomplish their mission in MOG. . . . The prime villain in this affair was Aidid, who from the beginning had been against any foreign intervention.[102]

International CARE President Malcolm Fraser, formerly prime minister of Australia, and US CARE's Johnston met with Boutros-Ghali at the latter's office in New York. Fraser had just returned from Somalia and wanted to brief Boutros-Ghali, who was eager for ideas on how to resolve the crisis. Fraser presented his expanded-force concept to Boutros-Ghali, who was positive yet remained reserved. According to Johnston, Boutros-Ghali said he would gladly send 15,000 troops but did not know where the United Nations would find the manpower and the money to pay for them. The secretary-general told Fraser that if he, Fraser, could energize the donor community to seek the money and advance troops movements, he would support the plan. Fraser left undaunted, taking his plan to acting Secretary of State Eagleburger.[103]

On October 21 Eagleburger met with Fraser, who called for expanding the UN military presence from 3,000 to 15,000. He also suggested that "a force could be drawn from a collection of Asian, African, and 'public spirited' European countries." They also started pressuring Bush administration officials to take the lead in Somalia by accepting robust action with American troops. The CARE officials and Boutros-Ghali most likely realized that a greater military presence was needed but that only the United States could provide the manpower and organizational skills to do the job. After all, the Americans were providing the airlift capacity for food aid, troop movement, and supplies already.

Near the end of the month, CARE's pressure on the Bush administration started to get attention. Peter Bell, chairman of CARE's board of directors, called Alexander Watson, deputy chief of the US Mission to the UN, campaigning for the United States to "show leadership, including the willingness to send troops in order to protect the international relief effort in Somalia, all within the framework of the UN." According to Johnston,

"By the second conversation Watson was seeing the security issue through Peter's eyes. Encouraged, Peter then went to work on the staff at the National Security Council and White House."[104]

CARE's lobbying effort resulted in Johnston being appointed by Boutros-Ghali as operational manager of the UN's 100-Day Action Program for Accelerated Humanitarian Assistance for Somalia. Johnston was to work within the framework of UNOSOM under the overall leadership of Sahnoun and in support of the coordinator for humanitarian assistance in Somalia, David Bassiouni.

Unfortunately, Johnston's arrival coincided with increasing UN disorganization in Somalia and insecurity in Mogadishu. Johnston departed for Somalia via Nairobi as manager of the UN 100-Day Plan. Soon after meeting Sahnoun and Bassiouni, who were the main UN contacts and the people that he would count on in his capacity as manager of the UN's 100-Day Plan, both men would leave their posts and Somalia.[105]

Johnston's first observations were that relief personnel feared for their safety and were concerned that they could not serve the starving and needy populations. NGOs were finger-pointing at the UN and blamed it for failing to provide security for the relief effort. He also saw that the UN humanitarian operation was disorganized, incompetent, and worse, more focused on political reconciliation efforts rather than the pressing humanitarian relief operation.[106] He observed,

> From the first senior staff meeting I attended, it was obvious that UNOSOM was not well-organized. The program was hugely understaffed. Sahnoun placed a great deal of importance on political reconciliation as a means to stabilize Somalia. I didn't get the impression that he was engaged in the humanitarian and military elements to the same degree . . . [my office] had no telephone, no file cabinets, and no office supplies.[107]

The teetering UN operations in Somalia sustained two severely damaging blows in a matter of weeks. First, on October 29 Sahnoun resigned after refusing Boutros-Ghali's request to "refrain from any criticism of the UN agencies."[108] Sahnoun had openly criticized UN policies, primarily through the media, including an appearance on *60 Minutes,* which angered UN headquarters staff and Boutros-Ghali. Sahnoun unceasingly complained about lack of UN headquarters support, especially mistakes that undercut his reconciliation efforts among the Somali warlords and leaders. Sahnoun believed he could not shake past mistakes, such as the UN-marked plane delivering arms and currency to Mahdi. He thought this hurt the UN's major asset—impartiality.

Sahnoun's main point of contention with UN leadership was the UN
headquarters announcement of the UNSC Resolution 775 to deploy a further 3,000 troops without notifying Sahnoun. The announcement's timing
could not have come at a worse moment for Sahnoun. He was in the midst
of difficult and sensitive give-and-take discussions with Aidid, who mis-
trusted Boutros-Ghali at best. At worst, Aidid thought the UN was targeting him unfairly as he controlled Mogadishu's airport and harbor,
locations where the UN troops would be deployed. The UNSC resolution
for dramatically augmenting the UN military presence by sixfold threatened Aidid's power base.

Sahnoun could not garner the confidence of the Somali warlords, especially Aidid, after the plane incident and UNSC 775 troop-increase resolution. Although they may have looked fondly upon his consensus negotiating
style, they perceived him as a UN instrument with little power. Conversely,
NGOs thought Sahnoun wasted precious energy, time, and resources to pla-
cate the warlords at the expense of the relief effort. For example, Johnston
thought that Sahnoun showed a lack of interest in the immediate humanitarian crisis because he seemed to focus more on political reconciliation
as the best way to stabilize Somalia.[109] Boutros-Ghali believed that
Sahnoun's focus on valuing the militia's leaders cooperation "perpetuated
the criminal establishment that had taken over the country."[110] Moreover,
the UN-Somali partnerships that Sahnoun established were, in Boutros-
Ghali's estimation, nothing more than a "Somali protection racket" resulting
in continuous armed threats if demands were not met.[111]

Boutros-Ghali immediately appointed Pakistani UNOSOM Commander Shaheen as acting special representative of the secretary-general until
the permanent replacement, Iraqi-Kurd and former president of the UN
General Assembly, Ismat Kittani, arrived. The following day on October
28, Aidid ordered Shaheen to clear the Pakistani troops from Mogadishu's
streets and evacuate the troops in Kismayu and Berbera. Aidid also alerted
the UN that further military deployment under UNOSOM auspices would
be countered violently by his forces and that UNOSOM coordinator for
humanitarian assistance, Bassiouni, should leave Somalia "within forty-
eight hours on the grounds that his activities went counter to the interests
of Somalis."[112] According to Johnston, "Aidid falsely accused Bassiouni of
participating in a meeting of clan elders arranged by Ambassador
Sahnoun." At Shaheen's request, Aidid extended Bassiouni's expulsion
order by seven days.[113] While Bassiouni sought shelter in Mogadishu,
Shaheen unsuccessfully tried to get Aidid to retract the expulsion order.
None was forthcoming, so Bassiouni went to Nairobi.

After arriving in Somalia on November 8, Kittani reported back to
Boutros-Ghali that Sahnoun's "practice of paying protection money" had

led Aidid to seek "further payoffs."[114] Kittani's arrival helped the UN slowly get the relief effort rolling, but persistent violence in Somalia killed much of the 100-Day Plan before some of its key tenants could get on track. The 100-day plan was also hindered from the start by mismanagement; although the plan was designed by the UN, "implementing the plan was more in the hands of the NGOs than the UN agencies."[115] Moreover, "at the time the UN agencies in Somalia were thinly staffed" and there was a "lack of cooperation and trust that currently existed between UNOSOM and the NGOs."[116]

In addition, the onset of November also saw the Somali security situation deteriorating further, and the UN and its members continued to search for ways to resolve the crisis. In the meantime, thousands of Somalis were dying daily, and the international media started to focus more intensely on the famine. Despite statements from the Organization of African Unity, Organization of Islamic Conference, Arab League, and European Union for greater relief support to Somalia, it was too little too late, and enthusiasm was low. The United States continued to be the main humanitarian relief provider and proponent for greater UN military presence on the ground. Soon after the US presidential elections in early November, the lame-duck Bush administration elevated the Somalia issue on its priority and political agenda. By the end of the month, President Bush made a decision that would save thousands of Somalis. But it also resulted in the bloodiest UN military operation on record and forced the United States and the UN to curtail military activities in other countries, even in the face of genocide.

Notes

1. Mohamed Sahnoun, *Somalia: The Missed Opportunities* (Washington, DC: US Institute for Peace, 1994), 15–16. Church World Service/Lutheran World Relief writes that reports suggest that as many as 5,000 children were dying daily. Norman E. Barth (executive director, Lutheran World Service) and Lani J. Havens (executive director, Church World Service), letter to Secretary of State James Baker, July 24, 1992; The ICRC estimated that "every day, hundreds of children die of starvation." ICRC Somalia Report, July 9, 1992, 3.

2. Andrew S. Natsios, *US Foreign Policy and the Four Horsemen of the Apocalypse: Humanitarian Relief in Complex Emergencies* (Westport, CT: Praeger Publishers, 1997), 12.

3. "Two hundred Rahanweyne died every day in mid-1992" in the Bardera area after being displaced from the Bay region in central Somalia. John Prendergast, "The Gun Talks Louder Than the Voice: Somalia's

Continuing Cycles of Violence," Discussion Paper, Center of Concern, July 1994, 19.

4. Office of US Foreign Disaster Assistance (OFDA), Situation Report No. 10, "Somalia-Civil Strife," June 23, 1992, 3.

5. The UNICEF Somalia Situation Report of June 1992.

6. On June 25 a Yemeni ship carrying Somali refugees was denied entry by the Yemeni government. Before the ship could turn around the panicked refugees dived overboard in an attempt to reach Yemeni land. More than 150 drowned trying to swim to shore. Walter S. Clarke, "Somalia: Background Information for Operation Restore Hope 1992–1993," Strategic Studies Institute Special Report, Department of National Security and Strategy, US Army War College, Carlisle Barracks, Pennsylvania, 1992, 26.

7. Herman J. Cohen, *Intervening in Africa: Superpower Peacemaking in a Troubled Continent* (New York: St. Martin's Press, 2000), 208.

8. Ibid., 208.

9. The *New York Times* writer Jane Perlez was a guest of the ICRC during her trip to Somalia. Her coverage was to play an important role in generating support for more robust humanitarian action.

10. "Somalia: Death by Looting," *The Economist* (July 18, 1992): 41.

11. Jan Elliasson, undersecretary-general, UN Department of Humanitarian Assistance, inter-office memorandum to the secretary-general, July 8, 1992.

12. Secretary of state confidential memo, "United Nations Operation in Somalia Approved," to the US Mission at the United Nations, July 1992.

13. Secretary of state confidential memo, "US Follow-Up Actions on Secretary-General's Report on Somalia and UNSC Resolution 767," to the US Mission at the United Nations, July 1992.

14. Walter H. Kanstiner, "US Policy in Africa in the 1990s," in *US and Russian Policymaking With Respect to the Use of Force,* ed. Jeremy R. Azrael and Emil A. Payin (Santa Monica, CA: RAND, 1996), 107.

15. Quoted from Don Oberdorfer, "US Took Slow Approach to Somali Crisis: Delay in Action Attributed to Civil War." *The Washington Post,* August 24, 1992.

16. InterAction Press Release, July 20, 1992.

17. Andrew S. Natsios, assistant administrator for food and humanitarian assistance, Agency for International Development, testimony at "Somalia: The Case for Action," Select Committee on Hunger, House of Representatives, July 22, 1992.

18. US Senate Concurrent Resolution 132, July 31, 1992.

19. Cohen, *Intervening in Africa*, 207.

20. Ambassador Jim Bishop (deputy assistant for Africa, 1981–1987; US ambassador to Somalia 1987–1990), Washington, DC, May 28, 2003.

21. Cohen, *Intervening in Africa*, 207.

22. Bishop, interview.

23. Ambassador Herman J. Cohen (assistant secretary of state for Africa, 1989–1993), interview with author, Washington, DC, May 12, 2004.

24. John G. Sommer, *Hope Restored? Humanitarian Aid in Somalia: 1990–1994* (Washington, DC: Refugee Policy Group, 1994), 22.

25. The Honorable Lawrence Eagleburger (secretary of state, December 8, 1992–January 20, 1993; acting secretary of state, August 23, 1992–December 7, 1992; deputy secretary of state, 1989–August 22, 1992), telephone interview with author, July 29, 2004.

26. Secretary of state confidential memo, "US Follow-Up Actions on Secretary-General's Report on Somalia and UNSC Res. 767" to the US Mission at the United Nations, July 1992.

27. Cohen, interview.

28. Secretary of state confidential memo, "Somalia: Reaction to Sahnoun Report," to the US Mission at the United Nations, July 1992.

29. Ibid.

30. Harry Johnston and Ted Dagne, "Congress and the Somalia Crisis" in *Learning From Somalia: The Lessons of Armed Humanitarian Intervention,* ed. Walter Clarke and Jeffrey Herbst (Boulder, CO: Westview Press, 1997), 194.

31. Peter Davis, CEO and president, InterAction, Op-Ed on Somalia submitted to *The Los Angeles Times*, July 28, 1992.

32. David Beckmann, president, Bread for the World, letter to acting Secretary of State Lawrence Eagleburger, July 31, 1992.

33. Cohen, *Intervening in Africa*, 207.

34. Richard A. Clarke (National Security Council, director, Office of International Programs, 1992; Department of State, assistant secretary of state for politico-military affairs, 1989–1992 and deputy assistant secretary of state for intelligence, 1985–1988), telephone interview with author, July 16, 2004.

35. Ibid.

36. Ibid.

37. Dan Oberdorfer, "The Path to Intervention," *Washington Post,* December 6, 1992. A1.

38. Statement by White House Press Secretary Fitzwater on the military airlift for humanitarian aid to Somalia, August 13, 1992.

39. Statement by White House Press Secretary Fitzwater on the military airlift for humanitarian aid to Somalia, August 14, 1992.

Besides ordering the Department of Defense to begin airlifts as soon as possible, the White House, through Fitzwater, made the following announcements: 1) The US would work with the government of Kenya to launch airlift operations from its airfields to deliver food into Somalia and to Somali refugees and drought-stricken Kenyans in Kenya; 2) The US ambassador to the UN, Edward Perkins, would begin immediate UNSC consultations for a resolution authorizing the use of further measures to guarantee that humanitarian relief will be delivered; 3) The US proposed that the U.N. call a donors' conference for Somalia and also invite leaders from the various Somali factions; 4) The US would donate an additional 145,000 tons of food for relief operations in Somalia; and 5) Andrew Natsios, assistant administrator of AID, was appointed special coordinator for Somali relief.

40. Andrew Natsios, testimony before the US Senate Committee on Foreign Relations Subcommittee on African Affairs, September 16, 1992.

41. James Kunder, testimony before the US Senate Committee on Foreign Relations Subcommittee on African Affairs, October 1, 1992.

42. Warren P. Strobel, *Late-Breaking Foreign Policy: The News Media's Influence on Peace Operations* (Washington, DC: United States Institute of Peace Press, 1997), 132–133.

43. Ibid., 132–133. In contrast, after the president's announcement the major television networks broadcast 30 evening news stories during the last two weeks in August, or more than five times the number aired in the first two weeks of August before the announcement. Strobel, *Late-Breaking Foreign Policy*, 136.

44. Andrew Natsios was appointed special coordinator for Somali relief on August 14, 1992, while at the same time retaining his position as assistant administrator of AID. James Kunder replaced Natsios as OFDA Director.

45. Confidential cable, "Demarche on Somali Relief," from Eagleburger to more than twenty American embassies and missions. August 1992.

46. Ibid.

47. As its name implies, USCENTCOM covers the "central" area of the globe located between the European and Pacific Commands. When the hostage crisis in Iran and the Soviet invasion of Afghanistan under-lined the need to strengthen US interests in the region, President Jimmy Carter established the Rapid Deployment Joint Task Force (RDJTF) in March 1980. To provide a stronger, more lasting solution in the region, President Ronald Reagan took steps to transform the RDJTF into a permanent unified command over a two-year period. The first step was

to make the RDJTF independent of US Readiness Command, followed
by the activation of CENTCOM in January 1983. LTC Christopher
L. Baggott, "A Leap into the Dark: Crisis Action Planning for Operation
Restore Hope," Monograph, Army Command and General Staff
College, School of Advanced Military Studies, Fort Leavenworth,
Kansas, December 20, 1996, 14.

48. Tim Rieser (Senate Foreign Affairs Committee), interview with
author, Washington, DC, July 7, 2004. Technicals are customized pickup trucks with mounted weapons, such as machine guns or anti-aircraft
guns. The term "technical" was derived by humanitarian NGO staff
placing armed protection fees or bribes in the "technical assistance"
expense account.

49. Ibid.

50. Smith Hempstone, *Rogue Ambassador: An African Memoir*
(Sewanee, TN: University of the South Press, 1997), 214.

51. Ibid., 215.

52. Ibid., 215.

53. CENTCOM has jurisdiction over US military operations in Horn
of Africa.

54. Hempstone, *Rogue Ambassador*, 218.

55. Sommer, *Hope Restored?* 33.

56. Hempstone, *Rogue Ambassador*, 217–218.

57. Ibid., 218.

58. Ibid., 219.

59. Ibid., 219.

60. Ibid., 220–221.

61. Major Eric F. Buer, USMC, "United Task Force Somalia
(UNITAF) and United Nations Operations Somalia (UNOSOM II): "A
Comparative Analysis of Offensive Air Support," master thesis, United
States Marine Corps, Command and Staff College, AY 2000–2001, 8.

62. Lieutenant Commander James C. Dixon, "UNOSOM II: UN
Unity of Effort and US Unity of Command," master's thesis, Army
Command and General Staff College, Fort Leavenworth Kansas, June 7,
1996, 2.

63. Hempstone, *Rogue Ambassador*, 222.

64. Ibid., 223.

65. Buer, "United Task Force Somalia," 8.

66. UN Secretary-General report on situation in Somalia. August 24,
1992. S/24480. On August 22, Operation Provide Relief's first flight
took off for Baidoa.

67. Tony Gambino, InterAction, letter to Holly Burkhalter,
Washington director, Human Rights Watch, August 31, 1992.

68. Michael Maren, *The Road to Hell: The Ravaging Effects of Foreign Aid and International Charity* (The Free Press: New York, 1997).

69. Tony Gambino InterAction inter-office memorandum regarding Somalia, August 18, 1992.

70. Confidential US Mission in Geneva cable to the secretary of state, August 1992.

71. Ibid.

72. Ibid. At the meeting, Bwakira asked Natsios if the United States could donate $6–9 million dollars for UNHCR Kenya-Somali cross-border operations. The cross-border program proposal was designed to limit refugee outflows and in the medium and long term promote repatriation of Somali refugees. Natsios also made it a point to tell Bwakira that his "recent remarks to the press about the West not doing enough to help Africa" were misplaced as USAID spent most of its resources in Africa. In response, Bwakira stated that he didn't mean any criticism of the United States and acknowledged US contributions.

73. Confidential cable from the US Mission in Geneva to the Secretary of State, August 1992.

74. Confidential cable, "'All Necessary Measures' Resolution on Somalia and Talking Points," from the Secretary of State to the US Mission at the UN and US embassies in London, Nairobi, Paris, Moscow, and Beijing, August 1992.

75. Boutros Boutros-Ghali, *Unvanquished A US-UN Saga* (New York: Random House, 1999), 55.

76. Sahnoun, *Somalia*, 39.

77. Office of US Foreign Disaster Assistance (OFDA), Situation Report No. 11, "Somalia: Civil Strife," August 14, 1992.

78. Aidan Hartley, *The Zanzibar Chest* (Atlantic Monthly Press: New York, 2003), 200.

79. Robert Caputo, "Tragedy Stalks the Horn of Africa," *National Geographic* (August 1993): 105.

80. Susan Rosegrant, "A 'Seamless' Transition: United States and United Nations Operations in Somalia—1992–1993," Kennedy School of Government Case Program (Cambridge, MA: President and Fellows of Harvard College, 1996), A, 9.

81. Caputo, "Tragedy Stalks," 105.

82. Ibid., 105.

83. Confidential cable from US Mission at UN to secretary of state titled "Belgian Mission Confirms US Offer of Airlift for Belgian Battalion to Somalia," September 1, 1992.

84. Clarke, "Somalia: Background Information for Operation Restore Hope 1992–1993," 37.

85. Ibid., 37.

86. Ibid., 37.

87. Kunder, testimony before the US Senate Committee on Foreign Relations Subcommittee on African Affairs, October 1, 1992.

88. Ibid.

89. Clarke, interview.

90. Kunder, testimony.

91. Bolton, testimony before the US Senate Committee on Foreign Relations Subcommittee on African Affairs, October 1, 1992.

92. Cohen, interview.

93. Ibid.

94. Natsios, *US Foreign Policy*, 39.

95. Philip Johnston, *Somalia Diary: The President of CARE Tells One Country's Story of Hope* (Atlanta: Longstreet Press, 1994), 28–29.

96. Ibid., 62.

97. Natsios, *US Foreign Policy*, 146.

98. Quote from Jan Eliasson Johnston in Sommer, *Hope Restored?* 30.

99. As quoted in Sahnoun, *Somalia*, 28.

100. Ibid., 40.

101. Keith B. Richburg, "Diseases Sweep Somalis, Kill More Than Famine," *Washington Post*, October 2, 1992. A1 and A46.

102. Herman J. Cohen, "Intervention in Somalia," in Allan Goodman, ed., *The Diplomatic Record: 1992–1993* (Boulder, Colorado: Westview Press, 1995), 62–63.

103. Johnston, *Somalia Diary*, 64.

104. Ibid., 60–61.

105. Ibid., 33–35.

106. Ibid., 36.

107. Ibid., 38, 41.

108. Sahnoun, *Somalia*, 40.

109. Johnston, *Somalia Diary*, 38.

110. Boutros-Ghali, *Vanquished*, 56.

111. Ibid., 57.

112. Johnston, *Somalia Diary*, 42.

113. Boutros Ghali letter to UNSC (S/24859) November 27, 1992.

114. Boutros-Ghali, *Vanquished*, 57.

115. Quote from Jan Eliasson Johnston in Johnston, *Somalia Diary*, 30.

116. Ibid., 31.

CHAPTER THREE

PRESIDENT BUSH
SETS OUT TO SAVE SOMALIA

As the fall of 1992 came and went, administration officials realized the UN-organized relief effort in Somalia, buttressed by Operation Provide Relief, was not working. Moving food by air was inefficient because of restrictions on weight. The key to transporting large amounts of food was to regain control of the ports from the Somali warlords, and that could occur only with robust military action.

The US presidential election campaign was going on, and there was no way that President Bush was going to intervene in Somalia during the campaign. His opponent, Bill Clinton, had accused Bush of focusing more attention and money on international concerns than on domestic issues, as evinced by the ongoing economic recession. While less than two years before Bush had enjoyed a record high approval rating of more than 90 percent, his re-election chance was rapidly fading. Although the 1990–1991 economic recession ended before the election, Clinton was able to depict Bush as disengaged from the lives of ordinary Americans, detached from domestic affairs, and absorbed with foreign affairs.

A month before the November election, administration officials started looking at different ways of getting food into Somalia. A series of interagency meetings illustrated the sad state of affairs in Somalia and the inability of the United Nations to prevent starvation there. However, intervening in Somalia would further embolden Clinton's attacks on Bush. Thus, according to one administration official, the United States never faced up to the Somalia famine until after the election.[1]

After his November 3 electoral defeat by Bill Clinton, Bush continued to request reports concerning Somalia and the available options. He instructed his senior advisers to prepare a set of policy options for dealing with the Somalia crisis, indicating that he wanted to put an end to the famine. Defense Secretary Dick Cheney's principal policy adviser, Paul Wolfowitz, was engaged in a number of serious foreign security issues, such as NATO enlargement, unrest in Bosnia, and the rogue states of Iraq, Iran, and North Korea. Therefore, when he was informed of the White House's interest in Somalia, Wolfowitz referred the matter to a lower bureaucratic level, which included the assistant secretary of defense for special operations and low-intensity conflict (SOLIC).[2] SOLIC received word that Bush was serious about an American military intervention and that the main question for them to decide was what form it should take. National Security Council (NSC) staffers repeatedly called SOLIC personnel for suggestions concerning Somalia.

As a result, on Thursdays and Fridays during the first two weeks in November 1992, SOLIC held staff meetings concerning the options in Somalia, and their opinions were sent to the NSC. On the following Mondays and Tuesdays, they received calls from NSC staffers asking, "Is there not anything else we can do?" and stating, "More options are needed, so show us more options."[3] Therefore, SOLIC members reconvened the following Thursday or Friday to discuss further options. One SOLIC staffer recalls "drilling the form" covering everything from high-end intervention, such as "making Somalia like Maryland, to low end, such as minimal involvement to do something and then get the hell out."[4]

But SOLIC did not see Somalia as a national security priority. The officials concurred that it was a terrible and sad situation, yet they concluded Somalia did not hold any true US security interest or strategic links to recommend a robust US military intervention. Therefore, SOLIC recommended that if the president wanted to use US military forces in Somalia, they should be used to support a UN mission, which would carry less political risk.[5]

NSC officials believed the US military could conduct the Somalia operation relatively easily because it was familiar with the Horn of Africa after recent military exercises there. The military could conduct humanitarian operations without much strain, because numerous post–Desert Storm military assets remained in the region. Officials also realized that several hundred thousand people were about to die and that only the US military could save them.[6] Within SOLIC there was a feeling of "we know how to do operations of this kind" because the US military had just finished Desert Storm and "could use our forces still out there to get relief supplies flowing.[7]

Compounding the president's pressure on the Pentagon to act in Somalia was the increasing interest in the Somali crisis by the media and by NGOs. The NGOs' common call for greater US involvement did not go unnoticed among administration and Pentagon officials. For example, former ambassador Morton Abramowitz, board member of several humanitarian NGOs, kept calling Richard Clarke at the NSC saying,

"You're a big military crisis manager. Why don't you use your military planning skills?"[8] The ongoing humanitarian devastation was the key pressure point for NGOs lobbying the administration for action in Somalia. Some NGO reports claimed that more than 80 percent of the humanitarian relief was being diverted or stolen, or being used to pay Somali security guards.[9]

NGOs coordinated media trips to the most tragic Somali sites to generate stronger action from the United States and the international community. Some NGOs also encouraged the media to write heart wrenching stories and take dramatic photos capturing the suffering in order to increase their fundraising efforts and gain large amounts of aid.[10] As one US official who helped coordinate the Somali effort stated, "The more dramatic and heart-wrenching the scenes of disaster in the developing world, the more income NGOs can expect from their solicitations."[11]

For example, on November 1 a group made up of British Broadcasting Corporation (BBC), Voice of America (VOA), and *New York Times* reporters accompanied CARE officials on a flight from Mogadishu to Bardera, where they visited a CARE project and toured the city's relief facilities. Based on CARE figures, the media subsequently reported that "because of fighting in the area, no food had arrived. As a result, 250 to 300 were dying each day."[12] That same day *New York Times* reporter Jane Perlez wrote that newspaper's first front-page story covering the Somali humanitarian crisis. Three days later, she wrote another cover story, headlined "Don't Forsake Somalia," that urged more US and international action in Somalia. The following day, November 5, a letter from CARE chairman Peter Bell was published in *The New York Times*, crying out for "leadership" by the Bush administration, noting that "if the United States waits until Bill Clinton's inauguration before galvanizing a more principled policy, 100,000 more Somalis will needlessly die."[13]

Watching the media coverage was Joint Chiefs Chairman Colin Powell and his staff, who "hovered over Somalia" as it "wrenched our hearts, night after night, with images of people starving to death before our eyes." Powell wrote that "the UN effort was practically at a standstill, while images of the fleshless limbs and bloated bellies of dying children continued to haunt us. I was not eager to get involved in a Somalian civil war, but we were apparently the only nation that could end the suffering."[14]

In early November, the UN announced that US CARE president Philip Johnston would be acting head of the UN Department of Humanitarian Affairs (UNDHA) based in Somalia until UN representative Ismat Kittani arrived. Johnston immediately made his mark by inviting his NGO counterparts to daily security meetings that were previously attended only by UN agency representatives.[15]

The UN ordered Pakistani soldiers to take control of Mogadishu airport on November 10, based on an agreement between the UN Operation in Somalia (UNOSOM) and local warlords. Despite the agreement, local militias continued to pressure UN staff and the Pakistanis for payments of NGO relief flight and airport fees. Warlord Mohamed Farrah Aidid was furious because he claimed he was not consulted on the UN takeover of the airport, and he was upset to see other militia groups benefiting from the agreement. The Mogadishu airport situation was symbolic of the chaos reigning in other parts of the city. The following day, Somali gunmen killed four CARE Somali employees while ambushing CARE humanitarian trucks carrying wheat from Mogadishu to the southern city of Baydhabo, which was hard hit by starvation. Of the thirty-four trucks in the convoy, only one reached Baydhabo.

Because of conflict at the airport and in light of the CARE ambush, UN officials visited Aidid in an attempt to prevent future ambushes and to keep the humanitarian relief flowing. Aidid denied involvement in the ambush and demanded the immediate withdrawal of the Pakistani troops from the airport. He wanted a new agreement negotiated because, he said, the Somali officials who had negotiated the current agreement did not have the authority to do so. Aidid threatened to expel the Pakistanis from the airport if a new agreement was not negotiated. If the Pakistanis remained, he said, the resulting bloodshed would be the responsibility of the United Nations. Aidid's threats immediately drew a sharp rebuke from UN Secretary-General Boutros Boutros-Ghali, who told Aidid that the Pakistani troops would not be withdrawn and that if there was bloodshed, he would hold Aidid accountable.[16]

The deteriorating situation continued to attract the attention of US representatives, who increasingly called on President Bush for robust US action in Somalia. On November 13, Representative John Lewis said, "We cannot stand by while thousands of people die." Senator Paul Simon and Senator Howard Metzenbaum spoke to Boutros-Ghali and acting Secretary of State Lawrence Eagleburger about Somalia.

The president's options were limited because overland routes into Somalia were dangerous and costly to use, while delivery by air was very expensive and had limited capacity. Mogadishu's harbor, controlled by a mix of militias, including Aidid's, was the key to getting the quantities of food required to feed the starving population. Huddled among a cove cut into the Horn of Africa, looking east upon the Indian Ocean, the harbor was vulnerable to shelling from high points controlled by Ali Mahdi Mohamed's forces. Overcoming these challenges was key to the food distribution effort. If it could not operate effectively, then the necessary food amounts would not get to the starving population.

With the harbor the key to the distribution effort, on November 14, Aidid escorted Johnston on a tour of the dock facilities to discuss potential improvements. Upon first glance, Johnston was stunned by the lackadaisical labor force, which further hindered the humanitarian relief effort:

> Even though there was docking space for three ships, the Somali workers chose to unload just one vessel at a time. If the Somalis had wanted to, they could have doubled, even tripled the amount of food off-loaded from incoming ships. Since they were not paid by the ton but by the day, they extended their effort as long as they could. Working faster to unload a second ship was not in their job description.[17]

During the harbor visit, artillery fire targeting the docking facilities came from the Mahdi position. Aidid informed Johnston that the firing was "just Mahdi sending a message." Afterward, he learned that three shells fired by Mahdi's forces had hit a relief ship carrying eleven tons of wheat, forcing it to return to Mombassa.[18]

That same evening—less than seventy-two hours after opening the airport—the Pakistani troops came under attack from Aidid's forces. Aidid had made good on his threat to retake the airport by raining mortars on the Pakistani positions. The sounds of shelling created pandemonium among international NGO personnel, who scrambled from their residences and offices and used their radios to call the Pakistanis for protection. Too busy trying to protect themselves from Aidid's forces, the Pakistanis were unable to help. Moreover, the NGOs had disregarded the Pakistani recommendations that NGOs house their personnel near one another for protection. Instead, their residences and offices were scattered throughout Mogadishu, making it difficult for the Pakistanis to keep track of NGO personnel. Subsequently, a group of French NGOs expressed their displeasure with the UN peacekeeping forces, while the Pakistanis expressed disappointment and disgust with the NGOs' unrealistic demands for protection. This episode solidified the wide divide and deep distrust between UNOSOM and the NGOs.

In early November, Undersecretary of State for Political-Military Affairs Robert Gallucci called a series of meetings among his staff to discuss options for alleviating the humanitarian crises in Bosnia and Somalia. At the time, Gallucci's staff was discouraged because members felt there was nothing more they could do about the situations, which were getting worse.[19] They were already providing logistical and diplomatic support for food and medical delivery to both Bosnia and Somalia, but Somalia was particularly bleak. The meetings all ended with the same conclusion about Somalia: militias and their warlord leaders would not work with peacekeepers to facilitate food deliveries. In fact, the militias would continue to loot the humanitarian aid unless faced with forceful opposition.

One of Gallucci's staffers, an Air Force fighter jock colonel nicknamed Melon Head who was Gallucci's former student at the National War College, suggested employing the military in both Bosnia and Somalia. "We can do it, so why don't we just do it?" he said.[20] State Department career personnel typically are more aggressive about using military force than Pentagon officials, who generally oppose the use of troops in humanitarian emergencies, especially those not central to US geostrategic interests. In the case of Somalia, Gallucci's political-military affairs office started promoting the idea of injecting US military forces into both Bosnia and Somalia.

Gallucci called Eagleburger's office asking how best to present his staff's Bosnia and Somalia military-intervention options. Since Bush had just lost the presidential election, Gallucci was wary about proceeding down a dead-end political trail.[21] He explained the proposal's content to Ken Jester, Eagleburger's assistant, and then said, "I know what happens after elections, and these policy proposals are not for transition." He asked Jester what would be the best way to push the proposals. Jester replied, "Don't send it with top and bottom identifications and not 'to' and 'from,' rather parse the arguments and send them to me and I will present them to Eagleburger."[22]

Gallucci's staff then worked on two toughly worded memorandums outlining two policy options that involved using the US military to spearhead humanitarian intervention in Bosnia and Somalia. The memorandums were then edited by Gallucci and sent to Jester, who gave them to Eagleburger. In the memorandums, Gallucci's staff argued the benefits of a US-run military operation in Bosnia or Somalia, or both. The Somalia paper said that intervening in Somalia was doable because there were no "real shooters and no real organization" as there were in Bosnia.[23] Moreover, the US military "had something to offer in Somalia. Our ability to land forces exceed[s] anyone else's in the world." The Somalia paper concluded that "a small professional force can take the place down and create an environment to feed people." It was "not talking about creating Athens in the Horn of Africa, but feeding people."[24]

On November 12, Gallucci received a call from Eagleburger telling him that he had read the memorandums but wanted to know what Gallucci was thinking. Eagleburger asked, "Do you know, Bob, did you notice, Gallucci, that we lost the elections?" adding that now "you are asking us to send in the military to two places where the US has no security interests?"

Gallucci said, "Yes."

"Come see me," Eagleburger replied.[25]

Based on the Gallucci memorandums and in the context of the prevailing political environment, Eagleburger wrote a briefing paper for Bush on Bosnia and Somalia intervention options. A few weeks later, Gallucci was told that Bush had decided that the United States was "going to do Somalia and not going to do Bosnia." When Eagleburger took both papers to the president, the president said that Bosnia would be too difficult. Opting for Somalia rather than Bosnia was an easy choice, according to Eagleburger:

> There was lots of pressure to get involved in Yugoslavia and some, but not as much, to get into Somalia. In Somalia, it was humanitarian aid, and in Bosnia, there was a real call for military intervention. After looking at Gallucci's proposals to intervene in both places, I decided that we could do something in Somalia but that under no circumstances would we get involved in Yugoslavia. I wrote a memo to the president that in Somalia there was a legitimate chance for success. The president reacted immediately and well to the memo.[26]

Asked what sparked the Somalia intervention, Eagleburger said, "It was the two memos from Gallucci that got me focused. Until that time, I was not really focused on it." Additional pressure came from Congress, especially "Senator Kassebaum and others wanting us to respond to the need in Somalia."[27]

By mid-November, American emergency-relief NGOs started coalescing around a single position on Somalia that would encourage the UN to deploy troops and use force without first seeking agreement and consent from the warlords. They began an advocacy strategy targeting the Bush administration and the UN for a stronger mandate and greater US support for relief operations in Somalia.[28] NGO representatives went to the UN to meet with the secretariat staff on November 16 and argued for more robust UN security to guard humanitarian operations. Boutros-Ghali was very receptive, having just read UN field reports discussing the horrible Mogadishu situation and outlining how the looting of humanitarian supplies had become the basis for the Somali economy.[29]

On November 19, Interaction's president and CEO, Peter Davies, sent two similar letters to Brent Scowcroft, national security advisor, and Frank Wisner, undersecretary of state for international security.

Cosigned by eleven large American NGOs, the letters "called on the United States to press the UN to empower its troops in Somalia to provide greater security for NGOs conducting humanitarian relief operations."[30] A copy of the letter was given to US Office of Foreign Disaster Assistance director Andrew Natsios, who delivered it to Walter Kansteiner, NSC's director of African affairs, saying "You guys need to read this."[31] Kansteiner then brought it to the attention of the National Security Council (NSC) Deputies Committee, which was "examining options and preparing proposals to the NSC adviser and the president."[32]

Meanwhile, Wisner discussed Somalia options with Boutros-Ghali, who requested greater US participation and support but did not request US troops. Wisner believed that the UN could help serve US interests, especially in the developing world, where he believed the United States should be more engaged.[33]

On November 18, Bush and President-elect Clinton met at the White House about a range of issues, including the disaster in Somalia. Bush tasked the NSC Deputies Committee to focus on a Defense Department paper that discussed the requirements for a US military–led humanitarian intervention in Somalia and then develop options. The committee met at the White House four times in five days from Friday, November 20, to Tuesday, November 24, taking off Sunday. The committee's mandate was to formulate an interagency policy option paper for presidential review.

Bush tracked intelligence related to the Somalia crisis and repeatedly asked his staff what the US government could do short of using a "heavy hand" to alleviate the famine. Bush had launched Operation Provide Relief several months previously in an attempt to use the US military to airlift relief supplies to isolated towns in the interior, and he had supported negotiations and meetings among the warlords. Bush had also utilized Marines to assist the Pakistani peacekeepers arriving in Somalia to implement the UN Security Council (UNSC) resolutions supporting a cease-fire. Yet the humanitarian crisis continued unabated. Traditional methods to alleviate the crisis had been attempted by the UN for more than one year with minimal success.

The chair of the NSC Deputies Committee was Admiral Jonathan Howe, the deputy national security adviser, who was considered to be a rising star and "wunderkind" by administration officials.[34] At the committee meetings, each deputy tried to bring his or her department's positions to the table, and Howe would try to put all those options together. Wisner, backed by Ambassador Herman Cohen, represented the Department of State, while the Joint Chiefs of Staff sent Admiral David Jeremiah, the four-star deputy to Powell.[35] Office of US Foreign Disaster Assistance

(OFDA) senior staff also attended the NSC Deputies Committee meetings, something they had been doing since the late 1980s.

The first NSC Deputies Committee meeting was held Friday, November 20 under the media and political spotlight, which is rare for such meetings. The day before the meeting, *The New York Times* ran a pro-intervention story by Leslie Gelb that featured sources who favored intervention. The Friday meeting was greeted by the morning's *New York Times,* which again carried a story favorable to a US military–led intervention in Somalia. The US Committee for Refugees sent out a media release urging Bush to make Somalia an immediate top priority because "at least 1,000 Somalis are dying daily, and at least 60,000 Somalis are likely to die in the sixty remaining days of the Bush presidency."[36] The meeting's discussion centered on how to deal with Somali militias and protect humanitarian supplies and delivery. The conversation did not get very far before the meeting was adjourned.

Yet, that same day, CENTCOM sent a warning to the First Marine Expeditionary Force (1MEF) at Camp Pendleton, California, to prepare for its central role in the Joint Chiefs–approved CENTCOM plan for sending a large-scale humanitarian force to Somalia.[37] The following day, 1MEF sent a team to Tampa's CENTCOM for two days of mission planning.[38]

On November 21 the Deputies Committee met for the second time. After initial discussion, everyone agreed that a threat of force was needed to turn the situation around in Somalia. Cohen told the committee that Aidid would do anything to claim the presidency, including sacrificing as many Somali lives as it took to attain his goal. Cohen also informed the committee that Aidid opposed any international intervention that did not support his leadership. During one of the meetings, Cohen replied in the affirmative when Howe asked, "Do you mean that we will have to clean Aidid's clock?"[39]

Jeremiah was frustrated with the Deputies Committee meeting because the policymakers could not make up their minds. He thought the meeting was getting nowhere. According to Jeremiah, the discussion was incrementally leading to US intervention because policymakers in the State Department and the White House wanted it, but the vehicle for that was the Deputies Committee. He "wanted them to get off the dime and do something. . . . Somebody wanted us to do that, but no one wanted to make a decision. Once you make a decision, do it . . . then this is easy and we'll do it."[40]

Jeremiah startled the people around the table when he said that "using the US military to alleviate the humanitarian suffering would be easy and they would do it if so ordered," but first if "you guys want to do this, say so. Make a policy decision, and then we will go do it."[41] Although he also expressed concern about the circumstances under which US forces could withdraw, Jeremiah's statement transformed the use of US ground troops from a nonoption to a strong likelihood. According to Howe, "When the military said they would be willing to do it, we said 'OK' and put it down as an option."[42]

The change in the Department of Defense's view on Somalia was influenced by an October trip to Somalia by Jeremiah. He traveled by C-130 from the Middle East to Kenya to assess the progress of Operation Provide Relief and view the situation in Somalia firsthand. He and Marine Brigadier General Frank Libutti, who coordinated the relief flight operations, traveled to Somalia's interior, where they met with village elders and chiefs. Although the humanitarian problem was intense, Jeremiah thought the problem of armed militias using food as a currency could be solved. His solution was "to create secure lines of communications from distribution points [that would entail] a lot of on the ground functions."[43] The US ambassador to Kenya, Smith Hempstone, briefed Jeremiah in Kenya, taking him "through 800 years of Somali history" and stating that he was "against US intervention in Somalia."[44]

Jeremiah reported to Powell what he had seen and heard while visiting Somalia. They agreed that "this can't go on, we were kicking the football and the US had to make up its mind and do something or not. Do we let a half-million people die? It was in our means to prevent that. That is what changed senior-level thinking about it."[45] As the chairman of the Joint Chiefs of Staffs, General Powell carried great influence. His position identified him as the president's principal military adviser and senior-ranking member of the Armed Forces. Although Powell preferred not to send US military forces to Somalia, he realized President Bush was leaning toward sending a force of undetermined size to Somalia.[46] Therefore, Powell pushed aside his own preference for staying out of Somalia. He also declined the SOLIC recommendation for US forces to play a supporting role to a UN force, in which he had little confidence. Instead, he argued that if US forces were going to go to Somalia, they should go in with overwhelming force.[47] Powell's thinking was shared by CENTCOM General Joseph Hoar, who would be in charge of the Somalia mission.[48]

The NSC Deputies Committee met for a third time, on November 23, to mull over alternatives for President Bush. The meeting determined that the only way to get the Somalis fed was to provide more international protection for relief workers. Three options, lettered A, B, and C, were developed and then forwarded to the president:

> **Option A:** Increase the current UNOSOM operation from 3,500 UN peacekeepers and provide heavier arms and equipment, coupled with the power to use deadly force if required.

Option B: Increase the current UNOSOM operation to more than 15,000 peacekeepers, backed by a US rapid-reaction force along with helicopter gunships based on ships off Somalia's shore. The expanded operation would be logistically supported by the United States, which would provide much of the transportation. It was conceptualized as a more muscular form of peacekeeping. Like the first option, troops would be equipped with stronger weapons and the authority to use deadly force.

Option C: Increase the current UNOSOM operation with US leadership in fashioning the operation, and then showing the way into Somalia and protecting the relief convoys. In addition to volunteering its leadership role, the United States would also include military forces on the ground. The idea was to unleash a massive show of US military force that Somali militias would not want to fight; they would be killed if they attempted to block or steal food aid deliveries. This concept was considered the "heavy option."

The fourth and final NSC Deputies Committee meeting took place on November 24, when it was called by Howe to review the three options and sharpen the language before sending them to President Bush. He also wanted to explore the possibility of the deputies recommending one of the three options.

At this final meeting, General Barry McCaffrey substituted for Jeremiah, who was unable to attend. Like Jeremiah's unexpected statement at the second Deputies Committee meeting, when he said that the US military could do the job if asked, McCaffrey also made a wholly unforeseen announcement. McCaffrey said that thousands of Somalis would die if their fate was left in the hands of the UN, which would require about six months of preparation before it could get on the ground and effectively secure food and medical aid for the needy population. This statement had a somber, yet disquieting effect on the deputies. McCaffrey was simply being realistic and honest when he said that it would take the UN months and that many people would die, but that the United States could do it successfully. The NSC's Richard Clarke said that the "UN couldn't do it because there was no place to land [with ports controlled by warlords] and the UN does not have an amphibious capability."[49] The State Department favored the second option, following Kissinger's advice that when bureaucracy comes up with three options, the B option is always preferred. Officials therefore "favored a robust operation without US forces on the ground."[50] The Deputies Committee cleared the options with no recommendation.

Meanwhile, negotiations between the UN and the Somali warlords continued to be meaningless. For example, on November 23 Mahdi promised the UN that he would open Mogadishu's port to allow food aid ships to dock. Yet the following day, a World Food Program ship was shelled by his forces as it attempted to enter the harbor. Later that day, CARE's Philip Johnston admitted that the UN's "100-day plan" was failing and sent a letter to Eagleburger informing him that the security situation needed to be addressed. He encouraged sending US logistical support for transporting the "3,500 UN peacekeepers already authorized."[51]

On the morning of November 25, Bush convened his senior advisers, including Powell, Cheney, Scowcroft, Clarke, and a few others to discuss the three options outlined by the Deputies Committee. In Clarke's briefing to the president, he made it clear that 700,000 people would die of starvation unless the US military intervened, because no one else would do it and no one else was capable. He presented two options to the president: let 700,000 people die or utilize America's unique capabilities to use amphibious resources, seize ports, brush technicals aside, secure distribution points, and save lives.[52]

Powell presented the military's preferred option; he had come to advocate full-scale intervention reluctantly, once it was clear in the days before the meeting that it was Bush's preferred course of action. He advocated using massive US military force based on the military's experience in the Gulf War. This plan was put together under General Hoar, who had recently replaced General Norman Schwarzkopf as CENTCOM commander. The plan under CENTCOM was titled Operation Restore Hope, which was designed to put "a substantial number of US troops on the ground to take charge of the place and make sure the food got to starving Somalis."[53]

After Powell's presentation and a wide-ranging discussion, Bush responded, "I like it. We'll do it." But he added, "I don't want to stick Clinton with an ongoing military operation." Scowcroft "looked uneasy" and said, "Sure, we can get in, but how do we get out?" After making eye contact with Powell, Defense Secretary Cheney commented, "Mr. President, we can't have it both ways. We can't get in there fully until mid-December. And the job won't be done by January 19."[54]

Bush brushed aside Cheney's comments and held firm to his selection of the heaviest, most extraordinary choice—Option C—calling for full-scale US military intervention. Bush agreed with the analysis that only the US military could act swiftly enough with ample force to turn the situation around quickly. The president probably thought, "What the hell? We've got nothing to lose. We might as well do the right thing."[55] When he looked at Somalia, it was clear that normal humanitarian intervention wouldn't work. The problem stopping food distribution was armed gangs, and the only way to protect the food was to take them out. Bush wanted enough military to control the two ports and enough troops to escort food to distribution points.

Bush's background also played a factor in his decision. Nearly a decade before, while serving under President Reagan, Vice President Bush and his wife, Barbara, had the opportunity to visit a CARE feeding center in the Horn of Africa during the Sahelian crisis. Bush said that he decided to send troops to Somalia in part because he and his wife remembered the massive loss of life during that trip.[56]

Other factors influencing Bush's decision were race and religion. Several Islamic governments, especially the Saudis, were urging for US military intervention in Bosnia for religious reasons. They criticized the United States, saying that when America is dealing with the slaughter of Muslims, especially by Christians, it does not get involved. One advantage of going into Somalia was that the United States could say to its Islamic friends that it cared about Muslims and would make enormous efforts to save Muslims.[57] Also, in a conversation at the White House the previous May, Boutros-Ghali had told Bush that Muslims were roused by the UN's failure to protect their co-religionists in Bosnia and Somalia. "Can't we do something about Somalia?" the UN chief had asked Bush plaintively.[58]

National Security Adviser Brent Scowcroft said there was pressure from guilt over the perception that the West cared little for the problems of black or Muslim populations. Scowcroft wanted to show that the US decision not to intervene in Bosnia was due to circumstances and not the Muslim faith. He said, "For me, Somalia gave us the ability to show they were wrong. . . . It was a Southern Hemisphere state; it was black; it was non-Christian, it was everything that epitomized the Third World."[59]

Immediately after making the decision, Bush formally created a full-time Somalia working group, appointing Ambassador Brandon Grove as director and Ambassador David Shinn as deputy director. He also sent Eagleburger to meet with Boutros-Ghali in New York City, where they agreed that force was necessary to provide food for starving Somalis. An agreement between them was quickly made concerning Bush's requirements before he would give the deployment order:

1. The UN would support a more robust operation led by the United States and that the UNSC would authorize the operation.
2. UN forces would replace the US military once food security was established.
3. A broad multinational military coalition would join the US forces.
4. The UN mandate would be strictly limited to humanitarian relief protection.

Boutros-Ghali agreed to the conditions after asking Eagleburger what would happen after President Clinton's inauguration on January 20, 1993. Eagleburger responded that if Clinton objected "all American forces would be withdrawn by January 19."[60]

Bush sent a team led by Admiral Jeremiah to Little Rock to brief President-elect Clinton and his senior advisers. The night before, at a White House USO dinner, General Powell told Jeremiah that "Clinton wants a briefing tomorrow on what we are doing in Somalia. I can't go, so you're going down to Little Rock."[61] Also on the team traveling to Little Rock was Gallucci, who was told by Eagleburger, "You're going to go to Little Rock and explain to Clinton why he has forces deployed in the Horn of Africa."[62]

In Little Rock, Jeremiah did the military operations briefing for Clinton, Vice President–elect Al Gore, future National Security Adviser Sandy Berger, and future Secretary of State Warren Christopher. Jeremiah stated that the operation did not entail nation-building because Bush was too smart for that. After Jeremiah finished his briefing, Clinton's first question was, "When will the kids stop dying?" Gallucci thought that was a good question to start with.[63] Clinton and his team were supportive of Bush's Somalia intervention decision.[64]

Bush's decision was viewed by the international community as honorable and disinterested, seen as part of a new era of world cooperation over humanitarian concerns (rather than the military and geostrategic factors involved with Iraq's invasion of Kuwait). At a time of a growing sense of a new world order with the demise of the USSR, Somalia leapt into the international headlines, and national newspapers ran articles praising Bush's Somalia intervention decision.

On November 27 Boutros-Ghali informed the UNSC that he supported Bush's decision and the deployment of US military forces under UN auspices because the current UNOSOM efforts were failing. He also wrote a letter to the Somali people to inform them that the UN was not their enemy, contrary to the claims of some warlords, including Aidid. Several days later, Boutros-Ghali informed the UNSC that the "extortion, blackmail, and robbery" imposed on relief agencies required the UN to move into Chapter VII force mode. He outlined five options for dealing with the humanitarian crisis, including Bush's offer to use US troops, who would resolve the immediate security problem and then be replaced by a UN peacekeeping operation as soon as the Somali militias had been "disarmed and the heavy weapons of the organized factions brought under international control."[65]

This last point represents one of the key disconnects between Boutros-Ghali and the US regarding the role of US military forces in Somalia.

Boutros-Ghali emphasized disarmament of irregular forces and gangs as its main purpose, while the US focused on securing delivery of humanitarian relief. At the same time Boutros-Ghali buried the disarmament remarks beneath thousands of words describing mundane details in long stretches of a rather dogged narrative to the UNSC. The Bush administration clearly reiterated its position that US military forces would be used to alleviate the short-term problem of securing food and medical aid and not anything more.

On December 1 Deputy Secretary of State for International Security Affairs Frank Wisner asked the US ambassador to Kenya, Smith Hempstone, for his opinion about inserting more than 30,000 US military personnel into Somalia in preparation for a transition to a UN follow-on peacekeeping force. Hempstone replied by cable, writing that he was "bemused, confused, and alarmed" by the US government's plan to enter "the Somali tar baby," noting that he failed to see "where any vital US interest is involved" and that foreign policy "is better made with the head than with the heart." Most importantly, he warned Wisner that Americans would face lethal and wily opponents:

> Somalis, as the Italians and British discovered to their discomfiture, are natural-born guerrillas. They will mine the roads. They will lay ambushes. They will launch hit-and-run attacks. They will not be able to stop the convoys from getting through. But they will inflict—and take—casualties. . . . If you liked Beirut, you'll love Mogadishu. . . . The Somali is treacherous. The Somali is a killer. The Somali is as tough as his country, and just as unforgiving. The one "beneficial" effect a major American intrusion into Somalia is likely to have may be to reunite the Somali nation against us, the invaders, the outsiders, the kaffirs who may have fed their children but also have killed their young men. . . . In the old days, the Somalis raided for camels, women and slaves. Today they raid for camels, women, slaves, and food."[66]

Wisner rejected the "tar baby" cable, as did Eagleburger, who thought that it probably exaggerated things substantially.[67] Subsequently, Hempstone responded that he supported the intervention, although he had doubts, which he expressed in a follow-up cable titled "Welcome to *jihad.*"[68]

On December 3 the UNSC approved Resolution 794, which authorized the use of "all necessary means to establish as soon as possible a secure environment for humanitarian operations in Somalia . . . [and that the] magnitude of the human tragedy in Somalia constituted a threat to international peace and security," referring to Chapter VII of the UN Charter. This "all necessary means" power was a dramatic, yet relatively unnoticed, departure from previous UNSC resolutions that sought the consent of the de facto Somali authorities for its activities. Typically, consent was included in all traditional UN peacekeeping practices. The Americans interpreted the resolution as a singular intention to, as quickly as possible, secure an environment for humanitarian relief distribution, while Boutros-Ghali viewed the resolution as a vehicle to disarm Somalis and control the whole county in order to rebuild it.

The following day, President Bush went on national television to say the US military intervention in Somali was morally correct and the right thing to do to save thousands of Somali lives. During his speech, Bush showed the November 19 InterAction letter that highlighted the massive suffering of the Somali people and said the only way to alleviate it was for the United States to take the moral imperative to lead.

Bush's intervention decision was generally popular with the public, while bipartisan reaction in Congress was predictably positive. For example, House Speaker Thomas Foley, a Democrat from Washington state, remarked that the "president [had] acted wisely, and in circumstances where he had very little choice without grave humanitarian consequences resulting."[69] InterAction members publicly thanked President Bush "for his historic initiative to protect the relief operation in Somalia through the United Nations."[70] Their support was essential to the mission's success because by December 2 there were thirty-two Interaction members working on humanitarian relief in Somalia, which was an increase from eighteen just four months earlier.

InterAction also had another reason to support President Bush's intervention decision. The Somalia fundraising effort by InterAction members raised significantly fewer donations than the Ethiopian famine of 1984–1985, trailing that effort by more than 90 percent. They believed that the difference was due to donor's fears that their contributions "would not be used effectively due to lack of security for relief supplies." For example, the International Rescue Committee (IRC) noted that "the relief effort is a bit of a charade without more security," while World Concern felt positive about the UNSC announcement "to provide additional security [and that it] feels that greater security will enhance our capability to touch a lot of people's lives." After President Bush announced the US intervention, an InterAction official said "we are confident that now that security has been restored, donations will pick up."[71]

Immediately after UNSC 794 passed, Bush lobbied other heads of state to support the resolution with troops and financial commitments, and made a series of appointments in order to implement the mission. The mission would be organized by CENTCOM's Joseph Hoar and led by Marine Lieutenant General Robert Johnston. He tasked Wisner's Africa Bureau to recruit countries for participation in the mission. The bureau successfully recruited more than eighteen countries, representing Africa, Asia, and Europe,—both Christian and Muslim. While the mission would include other branches of the military, including the transitioning to the Army, the Marines would remain in command. Initially designated as Joint Task Force Somalia (JTF Somalia), the UN renamed it Unified Task Force (UNITAF) as coalition members joined the mission, because "one of the main purposes of the intervention was to bolster the UN's peace enforcement reputation."[72]

Bush also announced the appointment of former Somalia ambassador Robert Oakley to serve as his special envoy to Somalia and head up the civilian side of the operation. Oakley had worked for Bush when the president was the US ambassador to the United Nations. Wisner called and offered the position to Oakley, who was already retired from the Foreign Service. Oakley accepted the appointment only after Powell promised Oakley's wife, Phyllis, "that he would come home for his daughter's wedding."[73] Oakley also requested that his former deputy chief of mission in Mogadishu, John Hirsch, be reassigned to Somalia as his top assistant from his position as consul-general in Johannesburg.[74]

Oakley was pleased with the clear direction and strong support he was getting from the administration, especially the State Department, which "for once, responded beautifully. They gave me a deputy and three political officers, all of whom had served in East Africa. Most of them had served in Somalia itself."[75] Oakley had read the Hempstone "tar baby" cable and was determined that Somalia would not become an American tar baby like Vietnam, where he had served as a Foreign Service officer:

> The true threat that Somalia will become a tar baby does not lie in a Vietnam or Beirut-type guerrilla war or terrorism. Rather it lies in an implied neo-colonial attitude, and in unrealistic/idealistic objectives and missions stemming from this attitude, which would require very considerable foreign involvement and major expense over a long period of time before there could be any hope of "success." Thus, arms reduction and control would be a positive element of a new mandate, whereas disarmament (i.e. total and forcible if necessary) would be decidedly negative.[76]

Oakley believed the civilian and military team that Bush put together had enough experience with previous American tar babies, such as

Lebanon and Vietnam, to avoid the same scenario in Somalia. He had worked with Powell at the NSC and State Department, while General Tony Zinni had significant experience in Vietnam and Marine Lieutenant General Bob Johnston had been a battalion commander in Lebanon and served as chief of staff for General Schwarzkopf during Desert Storm. They used their knowledge in discussions during the first week to determine the various traps that could be expected and how to avoid them.

The Monday after his appointment, Oakley flew to Ethiopia, where the UN was convening the Second Coordination Meeting on Humanitarian Assistance for Somalia, which lasted three days (December 3–5) in Addis Abba. The main thrust of this conference was Boutros-Ghali's decision to start the reconciliation process to coincide with UNITAF's launch.[77] The meetings involved the UN; various Somali groups, including 150 clan elders; and major donors, including the Japanese and Saudi Arabian governments, which donated $100 million and $10 million, respectively. That amount was more than enough to cover expenses for those contingents unable to pay their own way while participating in UNITAF.

After the conference, Oakley flew to Mogadishu, where he spent the next few days clearing a political path for the impending Marine arrival. He arrived ahead of the Marines by accident. He realized that if he returned to the United States after the UN-Ethiopia conference as planned, "everybody would be crossing paths." So he went to Mogadishu to see what he could do "to prepare the way."[78]

Oakley also quickly established the US Liaison Office (USLO) at the Conoco/Somalia compound in Mogadishu. He immediately focused on creating agreements among the warlords to get the food and medical aid flowing. He utilized the services of a seven-person team from the US Disaster Assistance Response Team (DART) that knew Somalia well.[79] They had been working with various relief organizations for more than six months, traveling all over the country.

UNITAF officials immediately began discussions with Oakley concerning the reduction of arms, but he was worried that disarming Somalis would further add to the chaos and suffering. And, most important, arms reduction was not part of the UNITAF mandate. One of the reasons that Oakley supported the US mission was that it was a clear and unambiguous mission to provide humanitarian relief, not an attempt to disarm Somalis:

> Three things are most important to a Somali: his weapon, his woman and his camel—and priorities change. . . . If you think the National Rifle Association has a fixation regarding weapons, it's nothing compared to the Somalis. It's part of

their manhood. And they learn how to use them. They also learn how to fight. Like the Chechens, if there's nobody else to fight they fight amongst themselves. But if there's a foreigner who comes in, everybody is perfectly happy to fight him and fight even harder because he's from the outside.[80]

Oakley warned the Somali leaders to stay away from the city's transportation facilities and the US troops when they arrived. They agreed that the debarkation of troops would be made on a beach south of Mogadishu. He talked to the warlords, especially Aidid, about fearing the overwhelming American military force that was already gathering off Mogadishu's shore. As a sign of strength to the Mogadishu warlords, two Naval F-14s would crisscross the city at 1,000 feet days before the US military landing. The dearth of Somali opposition to the US military landing could also be attributed the United States' success in defeating Saddam Hussein the previous year, which gave US forces an additional air of invincibility among the warlords.

Navy SEALs and Recon Marines launched UNITAF on December 9 with an amphibious assault by a Battalion Landing Team from the 15th Marine Expeditionary Unit landing on the southern beaches of Mogadishu as previously agreed by Oakley and the warlords, who had followed his advice and stayed clear of the landing area.[81] The next morning, Somalis awoke to American military forces on the Mogadishu beaches. The largest armed force ever to leave American shores to save another people had arrived. It was also the first time that military forces and international NGOs had worked together to bring humanitarian relief supplies to save a county from falling apart.

Although there was no official welcome for the arriving SEALs, the international media were there. According to Powell, who was tracking the landing from the Pentagon, the media presence, while temporarily dangerous, also had benefits: "The only resistance the SEALs encountered was from about seventy-five reporters and camera crews beaming spotlights on them, determined to broadcast a military operation live, increasing the danger to everybody. I was not all distressed, however, since I knew the Somali warlords seeing them would be impressed by the tough-looking SEALs."[82] Powell also "wanted the Somalis to see nasty, ugly-looking people coming ashore so they'd decide 'We'd better sit down and talk with Brother Oakley.'"[83]

The nighttime landing resulted in no casualties or Somali opposition. Oakley's main goal during his first forty-eight hours in Mogadishu had been successful: to facilitate a peaceful landing with the cooperation of the Mogadishu warlords. He had hosted meetings and negotiations, and whittled "them down gradually rather than confronting them." Oakley "never foreclosed long-term opportunity and said you can't be president [to Aidid and Mahdi], but we'll work on it."[84]

The following day, US forces, primarily the Marines—many of whom had desert experience in the Persian Gulf War or in extended Mojave Desert training—took control of Mogadishu's key transportation facilities. At the airport, "the Marines didn't realize the area had already been secured by Pakistani forces since a number of the Pakistanis couldn't speak English, it took some time for the US troops to understand who the uniformed people carrying guns really were."[85]

The US military landing was a success because of Oakley's efforts to gain the warlords' cooperation, and US military forces began to flow throughout Mogadishu, securing transportation facilities and routes. Within days, humanitarian relief supplies would be streaming into the countryside to thousands of Somalis on the verge of losing their lives. President Bush's UN experience and his knowledge of its specialized agencies influenced his thinking on Somalia. He had used precedent-setting military force in two recent previous humanitarian emergencies—Kurdistan and Bangladesh—and he now applied it in a more dramatic and overt way in Somalia. The president's decision reflected his own belief in US responsibility. His UN experience very much sensitized him to the UN and how he could use it for American and humanitarian interests. Unfortunately, President-elect Clinton did not have that same experience. He was soon to take office and, ironically, was to confront the greatest threat to the success of the American effort in Somalia—political neglect.

Notes

1. Richard A. Clarke (National Security Council, director, Office of International Programs, 1992; Department of State, assistant secretary of state for politico-military affairs, 1989–1992 and deputy assistant secretary of state for intelligence, 1985–1988), telephone interview with author, July 16, 2004.

2. Alberto R. Coll, "The Problems of Doing Good: Somalia as a Case Study in Humanitarian Intervention," Instructor Copy 518, Pew Case Studies in International Affairs (Washington, DC: Institute for Study of Diplomacy Publications, School of Foreign Service, Georgetown University, 1997), 4.

3. US Department of Defense official involved in UNITAF planning and implementation, interview with author, May 30, 2004. Conducted in confidentiality and name withheld by mutual agreement.

4. Ibid.

5. Coll, "The Problems of Doing Good," 4–5.

6. Clarke, interview.

7. US Department of Defense official, interview.

8. Clarke, interview.

9. The term "spontaneous distribution" was coined by NGOs to highlight the fact that diverted food to warlords and their militia was helping to reactivate local markets. John G. Sommer, *Hope Restored? Humanitarian Aid in Somalia: 1990–1994* (Washington, DC: Refugee Policy Group, 1994), 28.

10. Michael Maren, *The Road to Hell: The Ravaging Effects of Foreign Aid and International Charity* (The Free Press: New York, 1997); Alex De Waal and Rakiya Omaar, "Doing Harm by Doing Good? The International Relief Effort in Somalia," *Current History* (May 1993): 199–200.

11. Andrew S. Natsios, *U.S. Foreign Policy and the Four Horsemen of the Apocalypse: Humanitarian Relief in Complex Emergencies* (Westport, CT: Praeger Publishers, 1997), 62–63.

12. Philip Johnston, *Somalia Diary: The President of CARE Tells One Country's Story of Hope* (Atlanta: Longstreet Press, 1994), 57.

13. Peter Bell, "The Tragedy in Somalia Can't Wait for Clinton," letter to editor, *New York Times*, November 5, 1992, as printed in Johnston, *Somalia Diary*, 61.

14. Colin Powell with Joseph E. Persico, *My American Journey* (New York: Random House, 1995), 564.

15. Johnston's numerous bouts of sickness forced him to take repeated extended medical leaves from Somalia. Although he tried to direct humanitarian operations, his absences from Somalia for extensive periods of time limited his tenure.

16. UN Secretary-General Boutros Boutros-Ghali, letter to UN Security Council, November 27, 1992. S/24859. 2–3.

17. Johnston, *Somalia Diary*, 16–17.

18. Ibid., 63.

19. Ambassador Robert Gallucci (assistant secretary of state for political-military affairs, 1992), interview with author, Washington, DC, May 10, 2004.

20. Ibid.

21. Ibid.

22. Ibid.

23. Ibid.

24. Ibid.

25. Ibid.

26. The Honorable Lawrence Eagleburger (secretary of state, December 8, 1992–January 20, 1993; acting secretary of state, August 23, 1992–December 7, 1992; deputy secretary of state, 1989–1992), telephone interview with author, July 29, 2004. Eagleburger's view that something had to be done in Somalia was due in part to the fact that he actually helped create OFDA more than thirty years earlier and was known as the "Godfather of OFDA." As a young foreign service officer serving in the Belgrade embassy, Eagleburger witnessed the devastating effects and aftermath of the Skopje earthquake in Yugoslavia. Subsequently, he helped create OFDA and then supported its operations in order to help the US government respond more effectively to global disasters.

27. Eagleburger, interview.

28. InterAction "Somalia Strategy" memo, November 9, 1992.

29. UN Secretary-General Boutros Boutros-Ghali letter to UN Security Council, November 27, 1992. S/24859. 3.

30. Peter Davies, president and CEO Interaction, letter to Brent Scowcroft, National Security Advisor, November 19, 1992.

31. As quoted in Warren P. Strobel, *Late-Breaking Foreign Policy: The News Media's Influence on Peace Operations* (Washington, DC: United States Institute of Peace Press, 1994), 106.

32. Walter H. Kanstiner, "U.S. Policy in Africa in the 1990s," in *U.S. and Russian Policymaking With Respect to the Use of Force*, ed. Jeremy R. Azrael and Emil A. Payin (Santa Monica, CA: RAND, 1996), 112.

33. Coll, "The Problems of Doing Good," 9.

34. Admiral David Jeremiah (vice chairman of the Joint Chiefs of Staff for Generals Colin L. Powell and John M. Shalikashvili), interview with author, May 10, 2004.

35. At the end of January 1992, Frank Wisner moved from the undersecretary of state position in the Bush administration to the Defense Department as the new undersecretary for policy, succeeding Paul Wolfowitz. He and Anthony Lake, President Clinton's national security adviser, served as young foreign service officers in Vietnam.

36. US Committee for Refugees, "Immediately deploy 3,000 United Nations Peacekeeping Troops to Somalia," media advisory, November 20, 1992.

37. F. M. Lorenz, "Law and Anarchy in Somalia," *Parameters*, vol. XXIII, no. 4 (Winter 1993–1994): 27; Christopher L. Baggott, "A Leap Into the Dark: Crisis Action Planning for Operation Restore Hope" (Monograph, Army Command and General Staff College, School of Advanced Military Studies, Fort Leavenworth, Kansas, December 20, 1996), 14.

38. Baggott, "A Leap Into the Dark," 14.

39. Herman J. Cohen, *Intervening in Africa: Superpower Peacemaking in a Troubled Continent* (New York: Macmillan Press, 2000), 213.

40. Jeremiah, interview.

41. Ibid.

42. Admiral Jonathan Howe (deputy assistant to the president for national security affairs 1991-1992; special representative for Somalia to UN Secretary-General Boutros Boutros-Ghali, March 1993–February 1994), interview with author. Jacksonville, Florida, December 28, 2005.

43. Jeremiah, interview.

44. Ibid.

45. Ibid.

46. Coll, "The Problems of Doing Good," 5.

47. Ibid., 5.

48. Ibid., 5.

49. Clarke, interview.

50. Cohen, *Intervening in Africa,* 211.

51. Johnston, *Somalia Diary,* 66.

52. Clarke, interview.

53. Powell, *My American Journey,* 565.

54. Ibid., 565.

55. Clarke, interview.

56. As related in Natsios, *U.S. Foreign Policy,* 178, footnote 8.

57. Clarke, interview.

58. Dan Oberdorfer, "The Path to Intervention," *Washington Post,* December 6, 1992. A1.

59. As quoted in Samantha Power, *"A Problem From Hell": America and the Age of Genocide* (New York: Perennial, 2002), 293.

60. John R. Bolton, "Wrong Turn in Somalia," *Foreign Affairs* (January/February 1994): 59.

61. Jeremiah, interview.

62. Gallucci, interview.

63. Ibid.

64. Ibid.

65. Boutros-Ghali letter to UNSC, S/24868.

66. As quoted, Smith Hempstone, *Rogue Ambassador: An African Memoir* (Sewanee, TN: University of the South Press, 1997), 230.

67. Eagleburger, interview.

68. As quoted, Smith Hempstone, *Rogue Ambassador,* 230.

69. Harry Johnston and Ted Dagne, "Congress and the Somalia Crisis," in *Learning From Somalia: The Lessons of Armed Humanitarian*

Intervention, ed. Walter Clarke and Jeffrey Herbst (Boulder, CO: Westview Press, 1997), 195.

70. Interaction News Release, December 4, 1992.

71. Ibid.

72. Ken Menkhaus with Louis Ortmayer, "Key Decisions in the Somalia Intervention," case #464 (Washington, DC: Institute for the Study of Diplomacy, Georgetown University, and the Pew Charitable Trusts, 1995), 7.

73. Powell, *My American Journey,* 565.

74. Cohen, *Intervening in Africa,* 215.

75. Robert B. Oakley, "Urban Area During Support Missions: Case Study: Mogadishu: The Strategic Level," in *Capital Preservation: Preparing for Urban Operations in the Twenty-First Century,* ed. Russell W. Glenn, proceedings of the RAND Urban Operations Conference, March 22–23, 2000, 317–318.

76. Secret memorandum from Ambassador Oakley, US Liaison Office, Mogadishu, to secretary of state, "Ideas on the Next UN Phase for Somalia," December 1992.

77. UN Secretary-General Boutros Boutros-Ghali report on the Situation in Somalia. December 19, 1992, S/24992.

78. Oakley, "Urban Area During Support Missions," 319.

79. Ibid., 317–318.

80. Ibid., 311.

81. Confidential memorandum from secretary of state to chairman of the Joint Chief of Staffs and the National Security Council, "Getting Views From Somali Leaders on a Proposed Police Force," December 9, 1992.

82. Powell, *My American Journey,* 565.

83. As quoted in Sommer, *Hope Restored?* 33.

84. Ambassador Robert Oakley (ambassador to Somalia, 1982–1984; special envoy to Somalia for President Bush, December 1992–March 1993 and special envoy to Somalia for President Clinton, October 1993–March 1994), interview with author, Washington, DC, May 29, 2003.

85. Johnston, *Somalia Diary,* 74.

CHAPTER FOUR

ARMED HUMANITARIAN INTERVENTION

On December 10 the day after the US military forces landed, the United Task Force (UNITAF) military force commander, Marine General Robert B. Johnston, and the UNITAF director for operations, Marine General Anthony Zinni, arrived on a C-141 in Mogadishu after flying through the night from the United States. While being transported by helicopter from the Mogadishu airport to the US Embassy compound, Zinni observed out the windows the destroyed city below. Zinni said the city looked "devastated . . . like Stalingrad after the battle."[1] On the ground the city was even more troubled. Even though the hospitals were crude, they were "treating forty-five to fifty gunshot wounds on average per day; but these numbers sometimes reached one hundred fifty."[2]

On the morning of December 11, Johnson and Zinni met with Oakley and John Hirsch, who was a friend of Oakley's and an African expert, at the US Liaison Office (USLO) in Mogadishu. Oakley suggested that they proceed immediately to meet with the two key Mogadishu faction leaders, Aidid and Mahdi, whom he had invited to the USLO office in southern Mogadishu. Each of the warlords was accompanied by a contingent of ten to twelve guards and staff. Although Mahdi had always played up to Americans and the UN to encourage international intervention as a buttress against Aidid's greater firepower, he feared attending the meeting because the USLO office was in territory controlled by Aidid. To ease his doubts, Oakley told him that it was his compound and therefore US territory, and thus he would be escorted and protected by US security forces.[3]

At the meeting, Oakley outlined his political strategy. He said that if they worked together in establishing UNITAF logistical bases, they then could propel UNITAF military forces to get out of the city more quickly and help broader Somali political reconciliation efforts; there were more than fifteen faction leaders and militias competing for power in southern Somalia. Oakley specifically encouraged Aidid and Mahdi to accept a seven-point agreement that included a truce, road-block removals, heavy-weapon clearance from the streets, and an agreement not to carry arms on the streets. Once Aidid and Mahdi agreed, Oakley would then present it to the other faction leaders.

Discussion and negotiations continued over a meal of goat and pasta. After lunch Aidid and Mahdi said they needed to talk privately and asked Oakley, Johnston, and Zinni to go downstairs. Since the Barre regime collapse and civil war two years earlier, Aidid and Mahdi had not met face to face, making Oakley's resourcefulness all the more impressive in bringing the two sides together on US property. After waiting for several hours, Johnston complained to Oakley that he had more important things to do. Oakley replied that these discussions were fundamental to getting a cease-fire and heavy weapons off the streets. In his mind, one of the most important things for the Americans to do was to build understanding with the Somalis in order to reduce the likelihood of violence. Inter-Somali discussions, he believed, should be encouraged because then they wouldn't be fighting one another or Americans. In order to encourage discussion and keep open communication with Aidid and Mahdi, Oakley never told Aidid and Mahdi "you can't be president."[4]

Immediately after the meeting, Aidid and Mahdi came downstairs and made their joint public debut to a skeptical audience of media and Somalis. They said that the agreement sealed their reconciliation and that they would support international humanitarian relief efforts. Oakley thought this initial Aidid-Mahdi get-reacquainted meeting turned out "very well" because the two sides continued to meet and have lunch on a regular basis at the USLO. It was "a good place to talk as it reduced tension" and "every day they received a free lunch."[5] Knowing that Somalis feared attack by aircraft, Oakley ordered F-14A Tomcat fighter aircraft from the USS Ranger and AH-1W Super Cobra attack helicopters from the USS Tripoli to conduct flyovers and show-of-force maneuvers during his meetings with Aidid and Mahdi.[6]

Most importantly, the meetings produced an Aidid-Mahdi signed agreement, proposed by Oakley, which with US pressure compelled the factions to implement its conditions within ten days, bringing calm to Mogadishu.[7] Aidid gave Oakley and the US generals security advice, which they followed:

> If the militias and gangs know you are coming, they will get out of the way and won't cause trouble. And make sure that the first troops arrive with food and medicine to give directly to the people. In this way they won't see you as just another armed band to be feared but will associate you with good things.[8]

US military officials also met with UN and NGO leaders to coordinate relief operations, including the establishment of a Humanitarian Operations Center (HOC) that would coordinate relief operations and a Civil Military Operations Center (CMOC) to coordinate the HOC operations with US military efforts. The meetings quickly produced results; humanitarian aid convoys with international protection got under way and the first relief ships to enter Mogadishu's port since October 14 were successfully unloaded.

As a result of the successful meetings with Somali, NGO, and UN leaders, the US forces achieved their objectives within seven days rather than the anticipated thirty days. Also contributing to mission success were American military officers who had gained experience from recent military relief operations, such as Operation Provide Comfort in Iraq the year before, and applied the lessons learned to the Somalia mission.[9] The US military's primary mission was humanitarian aid delivery, which was a new experience for most of its soldiers. That led to some coordination problems with NGOs.

In many ways UNITAF was like old times for its American leaders. Even a very cursory glance at this list of UNITAF participants revealed noticeable, if intriguing, fault lines. The Vietnam connection was strong among Oakley, Johnston, and Zinni. Hardened by their experiences in Vietnam, they did not support nation-building from the top down. Rather, they wanted to understand local dynamics before acting. Facing a familiar post-Vietnam predicament, Oakley, Zinni, and others were determined to de-emphasize local Somali politics while vowing to relieve the humanitarian crisis.

US military forces quickly secured Mogadishu's main transportation facilities, such as the airport and harbor, in order to facilitate arrival of additional forces and equipment with the goal of bringing in humanitarian aid faster. Helicopters and off-road vehicles gave UNITAF forces the ability move quickly into the interior without using the main roads.[10] They also launched a psychological operations (PYOPS) campaign, which included radio broadcasts to help educate the Somalis on the humanitarian relief effort and, especially important, alleviate their fears about rumors that foreigners were taking over the country.

As part of the operations, American officers identified military personnel with unique skill sets to manage the facilities. A former civilian manager of the Port of San Francisco and now a US Naval Reserve captain was assigned the Port of Mogadishu, and the airport was assigned to a US Air Force lieutenant colonel with air traffic control experience.[11] In addition, UNITAF leaders organized deployment of coalition forces based on their capability or operating instructions, because some national forces were reluctant to be placed in dangerous situations, and, in most cases, the US military also had to provide deployment and transport support to other national forces arriving in Somalia.[12]

In addition to the arrival of other international coalition forces, international media and NGOs started flooding Somalia. They brought in lots of money and their own host of demands on the NGOs and UNITAF military personnel. The journalists also helped push up the prices of rental housing, vehicles, security services, and Somali employment wages, further increasing the cost of humanitarian relief operations. According to estimates by relief workers and CNN reporters, CNN spent more on its Somali coverage than the CARE International's Baidoa food relief distribution program, which was one of the largest programs of its kind in the country.[13] The flood of journalists became a "nightmare" for many relief workers living in Mogadishu. For example, ABC outbid Save the Children for a Mogadishu rental house, and CBS spent more than $2.5 million in Somalia during the first three weeks of UNITAF's arrival, including a $3,000 per day reporter logistical allowance.[14]

The UN believed that the journalists' safety concerns and reliance on their Somali security guards may have affected the way they covered Somalia. In the UN Lessons Learned report on Somalia, it noted that some media may have given more positive coverage to those militia leaders that controlled the neighborhoods where the journalists lived.[15]

Some media tired of the starvation story and started focusing on other issues. According to reporter Jonathan Stevenson, who covered Somalia for *The Economist* and *Newsweek*, "The press tired of on-scene horror—'You've seen one starving child, you've seen 'em all'—and instead looked summarily to a cadre of certain in-country relief gurus they dubbed 'dial-a-quote.'"[16]

One UN staff person working with international and local media commented later that the international media preferred covering violence, or in the case of no violence, the warrior society of Somalis, rather than political progress or the enormous progress made in alleviating starvation.[17] Westcott, of the US Office of Foreign Disaster Assistance (OFDA), recalls the following exchange with a journalist:

> I suggested to one well-known reporter a trip to northern Somalia, where he could do a contrast story about how it makes much more sense to focus on rehabilitation efforts in the north compared to the south given the better security situation there. He said that the only reason that he and other reporters were still hanging around Mogadishu was because they "were just waiting for another US soldier to get killed." That makes news, not success stories in the north.[18]

The immediate arrival of dozens of NGOs also brought in a host of challenges. Some NGO relief personnel were a lubberly crowd and appeared to have not an inkling of organizational skills.[19] One international aid worker in Somalia, Michael Maren, argued that the relief NGOs in Somalia were self-serving and negatively affected the ability of Somali society to recover.[20] According to OFDA's Tom Dolan, many NGOs in Somalia believed "that the military was 911—that whatever instability or security issues the military would take care of it."[21]

The security services provided by the Somalis to the NGO community created one of the greatest threats to UNITAF's efforts to protect humanitarian aid operations and encourage reconciliation attempts. Many NGOs opposed the disarming of their Somali guards by UNITAF forces, who wanted to create a secure environment. NGO officials wanted "UNITAF to solve all their problems, or were resistant to breaking the self-imposed cycle of paying fees to security guards in what amounted to extortion."[22] One of the problems of the NGOs hiring great numbers of Somali gunmen at generous contracts was that it created and sustained a strong market for small arms and light weapons. The fees paid to Somalis by NGOs were large and progressively escalated as Somalis played NGOs against each other. Numerous NGOs were paying their Somali security guards more than $100,000 per month.[23] They were also paying about $2,500 per month per vehicle, which came with driver and guards.[24]

Yet many NGOs remained opposed to UNITAF's request that they centralize their locations for their own protection. Throughout Mogadishu, NGOs had 585 facilities, including housing compounds, offices, and clinics that needed UNITAF protection.[25] According to President Bush's envoy to Somalia, "some of the anarchy in Somalia was undoubtedly caused by inappropriate security measures that complicated the task of the US military when it eventually arrived."[26]

The flood of guns and other weapons into the hands of gunmen hired to protect international media and NGOs further heightened insecurity, not only among the Somali factions competing for contracts but also between the Somalis and the UN military forces. For example, a US Marine patrolling Mogadishu's streets observed a pickup truck flying a "Feed the Children" banner and careening around a corner a block away. As it accelerated toward the Americans, the dozen or so armed Somalis waved their rifles and cheered as they passed. The armed men were security personnel for a relief NGO, and thus, they were allowed to openly carry guns in the Mogadishu streets. "It's not a policy everybody agrees with," angrily commented one of Marines.[27] Some UNITAF commanders feared that NGO security guards doubled as nighttime bandits. That, if true, meant that NGOs "were unwittingly contributing to a system that rewarded extortion and made banditry profitable."[28] Some UNITAF soldiers also believed that some NGO Somali guards were nighttime bandits, and during the daytime they had difficulty distinguishing bandits from NGO Somali guards.[29]

Somalia was the first time that the politically neutral International Committee of the Red Cross (ICRC) hired armed forces to protect its relief supplies and convoys. It did so out of necessity in trying to serve vulnerable populations, and this instance did not represent a change of ICRC doctrine. According to its policy of neutrality, the ICRC tried but failed to get agreement from the warlords in its area of operations. Not only did the warlords not cooperate, but Somali gunman, especially teenagers and children, also paid little heed to authority from outsiders. Before Somalia, ICRC operating procedures assumed that there was an authority figure controlling military forces who could allow safe passage and delivery of humanitarian relief. In Somalia this presumption did not apply because of central authority collapse. During a drive near Mogadishu, an ICRC staffer discussed the organization's anti-military stance with US military officials, yet she needed the military protection to get around Somalia.[30]

NGO hiring and firing practices also led to rising violence against NGOs, including several incidents that resulted in attacks on NGO staff, some of them fatal. NGOs needed protection to fulfill their humanitarian operations, so they hired guards, who were already armed. As a result, they "would entrench and perpetuate an immoral system of shameless banditry."[31] Somalis fought among themselves for the large contracts, such as personal security or truck transportation services. Natsios writes a blistering critique of the NGO role in exacerbating the conflict and lessening chances of peace in Somalia:

> The efforts of NGOs, the United Nations, and the International Committee for the Red Cross to provide their own private armies of security guards to protect relief commodities and infrastructure in Somalia not only failed but also exacerbated the violence racking the country. By creating a demand for weapons and ammunition far beyond what the warlords ever caused, humanitarian organizations inadvertently encouraged the importation of weapons.[32]

National Geographic reported the following:

> Somalia was one big extortion racket. Laborers, truck drivers, and armed security men all demanded huge sums of money and a share of the cargo to let the relief agencies deliver the

food. . . . Every agency had to hire its own private army of technicals and armed men, but many of these guards were the same young Somalis high on khat who stole, often from their own employers, and terrorized the city.[33]

NGOs were also in disagreement concerning whether US intervention was in the best interests of Somalia. In general, European NGOs opposed the US action, whereas more than two dozen large American NGOs endorsed it. Some NGOs even disagreed internally—and publicly. For example, when President Bush announced his deployment of US troops to Somalia, Save the Children/United Kingdom criticized the US effort, even as Save the Children/US endorsed it, and, compounding the confusion, both made their views known to the media simultaneously.

Save the Children was not the only NGO to have internal disputes. The US Office of Human Rights Watch had been pressing the US government to intervene militarily, but when Bush announced the intervention, the British office berated it. The criticism led to the dismissal of two members of the British office staff and Human Rights Watch endorsement of the intervention but not without embarrassment over this contradiction of its own position. Overall, those NGO and UN personnel working on the ground in Somalia were pleased to see US military forces. James Grant, director of UNICEF, recalled his "exhilaration" over the event and the fact that the decision for military intervention was made for humanitarian reasons and was also considered good politics.[34]

Ironically, as some NGOs criticized the US military intervention, the US military itself was making an unprecedented outreach effort to NGOs. Somalia marked the first situation in US military history that its military officers reached out to NGO leaders to work in coordinated fashion. They invited the NGO leaders "to its war room for extensive briefings by senior commanders on its operations in Somalia" and "later it held similar, after-action briefings for NGOs on lessons learned."[35]

As the relief situation stabilized, the US delegation at the UN started pressuring the UN to begin preparations for taking over the UNITAF mission. The United States wanted the follow-on mission to be a more robust peacekeeping operation with a broader mandate. At the same time the Department of Defense wanted its forces, which formed the significant bulk of UNITAF's forces, to operate within tighter guidelines and withdraw as soon as possible. Assistant UN Secretary-General for Peacekeeping Kofi Annan agreed with this concept, but Boutros-Ghali had reservations and wanted to see UNITAF's results, including a disarmament program, before making such a commitment.

The UN Security Council (UNSC) Resolution 794 authorization for the US-led mission clearly did not include a disarmament program. Although Boutros-Ghali called for disarmament in his alarming Somalia relief reports to the UNSC, it was not included in the resolution. In fact, disarmament was specifically left out of the original humanitarian proposal because of administration fears that members of Congress would oppose the mission on the grounds that it was a police action rather than humanitarian in nature. Moreover, there was also concern that US Central Command (CENTCOM) and the Joint Chiefs wanted a narrow directive to prevent placing additional responsibilities on the military. The administration continued to fend off UN demands for further intensifying US involvement, including disarmament, throughout the next few months.

Another issue with UNSC 794 was clarification on who would ultimately decide that the mission "to create a secure environment for humanitarian relief operations in Somalia" had been achieved.[36] Article 18 of the resolution "requests the Secretary-General and, as appropriate, the States concerned" to report on the resolution's implementation "and the attainment of the objective of establishing a secure environment so as to enable the Council to make the necessary decision for a prompt transition to continued peacekeeping operations."[37] Yet President Bush believed that "US Armed Forces will remain in Somalia only as long as necessary to establish a secure environment for humanitarian relief operations and will then turn over the responsibility of maintaining this environment to a UN peacekeeping force assigned to Somalia."[38]

Congressman Robert Andrews of New Jersey wanted confirmation that the United States would make the decision for determining the establishment of a secure environment. On December 17 at a congressional hearing on the Somalia crisis, he and Assistant Secretary of State for African Affairs Herman Cohen had the following exchange:

> Mr. Andrews: It is my understanding that when coalition forces have created or succeeded in moving toward the creation of an environment for safe delivery of humanitarian assistance, that it would be our intention to depart, that that decision would be made by the United States and by the leader of the ground forces; is that correct?
>
> Mr. Cohen: The United States, by virtue of the resolution, is in command of that operation, so when the commander informs Washington through his channels that he feels that it is safe now to turn it over to a UN peacekeeping operation, we will

then talk to the UN and say we think it is time for the UN to
start phasing in.

On December 8, the eve of the American landing, Boutros-Ghali wrote
Bush telling him that US forces must disarm Somalia before he would
order the UN to take over from UNITAF. In the letter, Boutros-Ghali
rejected the US position that the intervention did not include disarmament. Bush responded to Boutros-Ghali's letter by restating that the US
mission in Somalia was limited and specific: to create an environment in
which assisting Somali's vulnerable populations was possible and then to
transfer responsibility to the UN.

During a December 17 House hearing on the crisis in Somalia, representatives pressed administration officials on disarmament and the differing interpretations between the secretary-general and the president.
Congressman Lee Hamilton and Cohen had the following exchange concerning Boutros-Ghali's December 8 letter to Bush:

> Mr. Hamilton: But it is our view that the US forces there will
> disarm the Somalis only in relationship to its mission, which is
> the creation of a secure environment; is that correct?
>
> Mr. Cohen: That is correct; that is not part of their mission.

In mid-December Bush sent Eagleburger and Undersecretary of State
for International Organizations John Bolton to New York to meet with
Boutros-Ghali to work out a smooth transition from the US to the UN
phase. At the meeting, US officials explained to Boutros-Ghali that disarmament was not required by UNSC Resolution 794 and that UNITAF
was concerned primarily with providing security to protect relief shipments. They also pressed for immediate transition planning, whereas
Boutros-Ghali said that it would be difficult to discuss transition details
until the success of UNITAF's ability to establish a secure environment
was determined.

Boutros-Ghali also informed the American officials that he had come
to a separate understanding with President Bush that had been defined in
an exchange of letters between himself and the president at the beginning
of December 1992. On December 8 he sent Bush a letter outlining two
conditions for the UN to take over the mission from the US: 1) Disarming
all Somalis is necessary for national reconciliation; and 2) The US military
must establish control throughout Somalia. Without these actions,
Boutros-Ghali told Bush, he did "not believe that it will be possible to
establish the secure environment called for by the UNSC resolution or to

create conditions in which the United Nations' existing efforts to promote national reconciliation can be carried forward and the task of protecting humanitarian activities can safely be transferred to a conventional United Nations peacekeeping operation."[39]

The day after his meeting with Eagleburger, on December 19, Boutros-Ghali wrote a letter to the UNSC stating that it was too soon to consider a UN follow-on force. He wrote that UNITAF needed to disarm all the Somali militias, control the whole country, and establish a police force before he could begin planning for UNOSOM II.[40] Even though UNSC 794 did not include these tasks, Boutros-Ghali continued to insist that they be done.

Five days later, on December 22, Boutros-Ghali received support for his disarmament demands from members of Congress. Representatives Dan Burton of Indiana and Donald Payne of New Jersey sent a House Committee letter to Secretary of State Eagleburger calling for "broadening the terms of engagement for US forces in Somalia" to include disarmament. They made the following arguments in favor of disarmament:

> It is difficult to understand the wisdom of merely allowing the warlords and technicals to retreat in the countryside until our forces withdraw. . . . Relief agencies have already suffered casualties among their national personnel because in some instances our troops were ordered to turn their heads when coming upon large caches of arms and ammunition. . . . We firmly believe that the disarming of warring factions wherever noticed should be added to the terms of engagement. UN Secretary-General Boutros-Ghali should be supported in his request that the United States grant more latitude to our troops in order to confiscate weapons of warring factions. Only then will UN peacekeeping forces have the opportunity to maintain a peaceful environment conducive to relief rehabilitation and development.

The major reason food was getting through to vulnerable populations was that Oakley had met with many Somali militia leaders and solicited their support and cooperation in laying the groundwork for relief operations. He warned them to keep their militias clear of US and UN forces, whose rules of engagement (ROE) were designed to protect troops and Somalis. It was "forward-leaning ROE exercised by backward-leaning troops because they understood . . . that by showing restraint we were going to be less endangered than by shooting every time we had a chance."[41] The ROE stating that US military personnel could shoot if threatened by a Somali with a weapon had a psychological impact on the

Somalis. UNITAF forces also employed offensive air support (OAS) operations as a psychological weapon to serve as a credible deterrent to Somali
militias.[42] During the first stages of the UNITAF landing, more than 2,500
sorties per day were recorded.[43] UNITAF warnings to militias not to be
hostile, coupled with UNITAF's show of force, made the Somalis less
prone to take on UNITAF forces, which led to fewer casualties on both
sides and contributed to the operation's initial success.

One of these first violent incidents between American military forces
and Somali fighters occurred three days after the US forces landed. Two
Somali militia technicals fired on two US helicopters, which returned fire
and immediately destroyed the technicals. After such incidents, Oakley
would talk with Aidid and Mahdi, telling them, "I assume that these were
not your people, and I'd appreciate it if you'd go on the air with your
radios and tell everybody that this was not done by you, that you're not
having a war with us. Otherwise, it's going to be very dangerous for you."
They did so.[44]

UNITAF would follow similar procedures after every UNITAF-Somali
incident. Oakley or his staff would

> go around and talk personally to the faction commander who
> was responsible and say, "Okay, let's go over what happened
> here." They would come back and say, "They weren't my men
> at all." So we avoided building up the most dangerous thing in
> operations of this kind—an adversarial mentality, the idea that
> you're enemies . . . we wanted to maintain it at the original low
> level. Part of it was due to how we handled the civilian diplo-
> matic and political side. We never broke off dialogue. No mat-
> ter how outrageous they might seem, we wanted to maintain
> the dialogue until and unless we got into a state of actual war.
> It reduced the chances of greater danger later on.[45]

Compounding Oakley's challenges in getting Somali militias on board
with the relief was the Somali leadership vacuum. As in most civil wars,
there was a large migration of elites, especially those associated with the
Barre regime, out of Somalia to other countries. Numerous Somali elites
had fled to Canada, Finland, the United Kingdom, the United States, and
neighboring countries, such as Kenya and Saudi Arabia. Many of these
migrants had governing experience, which most of the remaining leaders
or warlords did not have. Many of the migrants also had financial
resources and advanced educations that could have helped alleviate the
situation, whereas the warlords based their authority on the application
and threat of violence.

As Mogadishu became more secure for unloading humanitarian relief at the airport and port and its streets become more secure for transporting the relief, NGOs continued to pressure the US military to do more, more quickly. The day after the US military landed on Mogadishu's beaches, InterAction urgently requested military forces for Baidoa, where relief workers felt that they were in extreme danger.[46] Other NGOs also pressured the US military to expand its operations outside of Mogadishu by "roaring" their complaints: "We need the military now!"[47] Adding to the sense of urgency was a December 14 ICRC call for US and UN military forces to expand out of Mogadishu as soon as possible to secure the remaining parts of the country. ICRC stated that "although the international forces would appear to have restored the calm in certain parts of Mogadishu, a concerted effort must now be made to do likewise in other parts of the country, where violence continues to ravage the everyday lives of the Somali people and to hamper humanitarian action."[48] The ICRC request was in reaction to their personnel and facilities being attacked in Baidoa and Kismayu.

Five days after the UNITAF landing, seventy trucks carrying 670 US Marines and French Legionnaires rolled into Baidoa on December 14. After the airfield was secured, more Marine and French military units were flown in from Mogadishu, eventually securing Baidoa by December 16. The day before the military units arrived, Oakley went to the city to meet with local clan, military, and religious leaders in order "to establish dialogue with the people in control rather than relying only on firepower."[49] Oakley told them "that no one should be in the vicinity of the Baidoa airport after midnight tonight. Any technicals seen will be 'made invisible.'"[50] Oakley stressed UNITAF's firepower as a way to pre-empt violence, which proved effective in Baidoa and elsewhere where he went out in front of UNITAF forces and international NGOs laying the groundwork for peaceful military and humanitarian operations in the area.

During the meeting with elders, a Muslim sheik expressed his concern that the United States was coming to Baidoa to destroy Islam. Oakley told him that "we are not coming to destroy Islam" and that there were a lot of Muslims in the United States, so Americans understood other religions. Oakley then sent a Muslim Lebanese-American Marine to find the old sheik and learn his needs, which included building a mosque. Interestingly, the mosque was built soon after by the American relief NGO Catholic Relief Services.[51]

After meeting with the leaders, Oakley met with representatives of the seven international NGOs operating in Baidoa to brief them on the movement of UN forces into the city. He told them that the instruction to the soldiers was that no disarming of Somalis was to occur "unless they pose a threat to the troops or to the humanitarian efforts of feeding the starving." The World Vision Baidoa-based representative stated that he was "very pleased" with Oakley's announcement.[52] The CARE team leader in Baidoa also had positive comments about the arrival of the US Marines because that meant "more food can get to Baidoa, and 100 percent of it gets distributed to the needy."[53] Many Somalis were also pleased with the arrival of UNITAF forces. For example, on December 19—ten days after the Mogadishu beach landing—US military forces and Belgian paratroopers conducted an amphibious landing in Kismayu to the cheers of thousands of Somalis.[54]

Oakley continued traveling in southern Somalia, utilizing the same process for educating Somalis on the UNTIAF presence. He would visit each site before US troops moved in to speak to local leaders and explain the mission. Sometimes, leaflets would be dropped explaining the UNITAF presence, and in some cases, US military aircraft would circle the city as a signal to armed groups to stand down.

At a Christmas Eve press conference, General Johnston informed the international press that the UNITAF operation was more than three weeks ahead of schedule and that the operation was preparing to transfer the relief effort to a multinational force under UN control. UNITAF finished deploying throughout the major relief centers of famine-stricken southern Somalia.

A major part of UNITAF's quick success was its emphasis on PSYOPs to reduce conflict. The operations were designed to alleviate the concerns of Somalis who might think of US and other UNITAF forces as an invading and occupying force. PSYOP personnel created leaflets and posters, some of which entailed crayon drawings, such as American troops waving and shaking hands with Somalis. PSYOP also produced radio shows that each day started with a different verse from the Qur'an to appease the Islamists. Every two weeks, Oakley met with the moderate Islamic Higher Council, some of whom he'd known ten years earlier, to explain what UNITAF was doing and to get their views. Oakley listened to their criticism, which he shared with UNITAF, who in turn adopted more religiously sensitive practices.

During the four-month UNITAF operation, PSYOPs hosted 750 news media representatives, wrote more than 250 stories, and filed more than fifty radio reports on Armed Forces Radio. UNITAF had a Somali-language radio station to disseminate the UNITAF message of peace. Although there were plenty of news sources for Somalis, most of them were inaccurate and propaganda. To counter misinformation and Aidid's inflammatory radio broadcasts, UNITAF established a radio station that was called "Rajo"—"hope" in Somali. UNTIAF radio broadcasts

overwhelmed warlord broadcasts, especially Aidid's, which were provoca-
tive and inflammatory. As a result, US forces didn't have to "take them
down." Aidid and other warlords tried to get UNITAF radio off the air
but they couldn't do it; UNITAF was too well organized.[55]

UNITAF radio broadcasts did not make Aidid happy, and he complained to Oakley, who told Aidid that UNITAF would tone down its
broadcasts when Aidid toned down his own inflammatory rhetoric.
Aidid agreed, and Oakley considered it "another victory for nonviolent
engagement."[56]

PSYOPs also oversaw the production of other counter-communication
measures, which included publishing a Somali-language paper called
Maanta, which means "today" in Somali. The paper highlighted successful economic and political stories. The paper also carried Somali poetry
and Islamic religious stories.

Before leaving office Bush decided to visit Somalia to view the results
of his last major military decision. The Somalia diversion gave Bush the
distinction of possibly being the first US president since Lincoln to visit
a hostile-fire area. On the morning of December 30, Bush visited southern
Somalia, including a clinic and school in Laffole, located thirty miles
southwest of Mogadishu, and Baidoa, where he greeted US troops.

Bush spent the evening on the USS Tripoli, a Navy amphibious assault
ship, rather than staying overnight in Mogadishu. The following day,
Bush paid another visit to the troops on the ground in Somalia, where he
received many greetings. He also received a gift from Aidid. It was a large
cake, which was decorated with Aidid's face sandwiched between
the Somali and American flags.[57]

President Bush informed Zinni and other UNITAF leaders that the UN
still had not agreed to take over the mission. Two days after Bush
departed Somalia, Boutros-Ghali visited Mogadishu on January 3. As
Boutros-Ghali was visiting a feeding center outside of Mogadishu,
Undersecretary-General Jonah visited UNOSOM headquarters, but his
convoy was repulsed by Aidid supporters throwing stones and rotten
fruit to protest Boutros-Ghali's visit. Jonah's convoy ended up taking
hours to return to the Mogadishu airport. In the meantime, Boutros-
Ghali monitored the situation via radio from UNITAF headquarters and
decided to avoid visiting Mogadishu and continue on to Addis Ababa.
Jonah's experience with the anti-UN crowds in Mogadishu helped
Boutros-Ghali conclude that the UNITAF mission had not established a
secure environment.

The day after leaving Somalia, Boutros-Ghali participated in a Somali
national reconciliation and unity conference January 4–15 in Addis
Ababa, where fourteen Somalia factions and groups participated. He said

time was a factor because there was a narrow window for support before the international community lost patience with Somalia.

On January 15 the Addis Ababa agreements were finalized and included a step-by-step blueprint for disarmament and demobilization. The militias agreed to place their heavy weapons in storage sites they would disclose to UNITAF, together with inventories of all weapons stored. UNITAF then would carry out routine inspections of these sites. The importance of the Addis Ababa meetings is that they created the political and security environment for UNITAF to implement cease-fire and disarmament polices.

In early January 1993 US officials believed that they had achieved their mission and had created a secure environment for the conduct of the humanitarian effort. At the same time, they remained under pressure from Boutros-Ghali's demand that they forcibly disarm Somali militias, which they themselves thought impossible without escalating the violence with warlords at the expense of humanitarian relief operations.

> Since such a huge undertaking could require a year or two and lots of resources to create jobs and to support disarmed men during the transition to another job, UNITAF said that they would start the process but that they would be leaving so it must eventually be a UN responsibility. The UN refused, so there was no disarmament.[58]

Unfortunately, the transition to UN required the UN's help, which was not forthcoming quickly, if at all. Boutros-Ghali's insistence on disarmament and the resulting dispute with the Bush administration filtered to Somalia on-the-ground tension between UNITAF and UN leaders. Further compounding the UNITAF mission's increasing duties beyond relief was lack of financial and political support from the UN itself. Ismat Kittani, the UN Special Representative to Somalia, had already informed US military officers on December 12 that the US would be on its own.[59] He reportedly didn't have the charisma or the high energy level of his predecessor Sahnoun, and as a twenty-five-year UN bureaucrat, was more concerned with UN public relations.[60] Although Kittani was empowered to direct UN operations, Oakley directed the real power—US military forces. This led to tension between the two sides, especially because the Somalis knew where the real power was. Moreover, UN peacekeeping staff in Somalia, already minimal, was not augmented as the secure environment was being created in Somalia.

The peak of US military forces in Somalia was reached on January 15, five days before President Bush left office, when there were 25,426 US troops committed to UNITAF. It was sadly ironic that as US forces in Somalia grew, Somalia itself was soon lost amid the Bush-Clinton transition. Powell commented that the "waning hours of the Bush era were not particularly pleasant" for him because they were "full of strangers. . . . And we had several loose ends still flapping . . . Haiti, Bosnia, Somalia, and Iraq."[61] President Clinton and his administration were overwhelmed with pressing international issues and crises, such as the implosion of Liberia and relations with China, and Somalia was not a top priority.[62] Clinton opined that when he took office, he "had a whole kennel full of barking hounds, with Bosnia and Russia howling the loudest, and several others, including Somalia, Haiti, North Korea, and Japan's trade policy, growling in the background."[63] The Somali mission was soon adrift among Clinton administration officials overwhelmed by other international events and exasperated by dealing with the UN's cumbersome bureaucracy.

After taking office, Clinton appointed Anthony Lake as his national security adviser (NSA). Before taking his position, Lake received a Somalia briefing on the telephone by the exiting NSA Brent Scowcroft, who said, "By the time you guys show up on the 21st, this will be over."[64] Meanwhile, Richard Clarke, the National Security Council's (NSC) International Organization bureau chief looked at the Bush administration's flow plan and realized that not all troops would be back by then. They still would be going into Somalia. So Clarke went to the transition office and told Lake, who was surprised to hear it.[65] Lake said later that "There was no internal plan about withdrawing by 1/20 and if there was, I never saw it."[66] As Lake took charge, American troops were in the midst of the UNITAF operation, which most American officials called Operation Restore Hope, in Somalia, the largest humanitarian intervention in history. The Marines had secured the ports, airports, and roads leading to distribution sites, and the starving populations were being regularly fed for the first time in months.

Clinton had also been told the US troops would be out of Somalia by the time he took office. According to Clinton, Scowcroft told Sandy Berger, Clinton's Assistant Transition Director for National Security and Senior Foreign Policy Advisor during the campaign, that the US military forces would be out of Somalia by the January 20 inauguration.[67] In response Bush later said that "withdrawals had begun by January 20. . . . I had no understanding of any sort with President Clinton. I simply told him the first time we met that I planned to begin withdrawals as soon as possible."[68] Powell commented that he had said "from the beginning we can't do this by January 20; we'll barely be in by then."[69]

Complicating the American Somalia policy was the fact that the new Clinton security team was "leaderless" according to Powell: "Lake did not drive meetings, Christopher passive, Aspin, when he took issue . . . took it onto tangents to skirt immediate issue." The result was that at meetings, "the discussions continued to meander like graduate-student bull sessions or the think-tank seminars in which many of my new colleagues had spent the last twelve years while their party was out of power . . . [and Clinton] was not well served by the wandering deliberations he permitted. He had an academic streak himself and seemed to enjoy these marathon debates."[70]

Powell was also most disappointed in Clinton's choice of Les Aspin, who "had been a miscast as secretary of defense."[71] Aspin's first priority was to conduct a "Bottom Up Review" of military, which took nearly one year to complete. During this time the Somali mission quickly got out of control and off the secretary's radar. According to Powell,

> Aspin had a management style that was the complete opposite of Cheney's. He was as disjointed as Cheney was well-organized. We never knew what time Les was coming to work in the morning. Staff meetings were sporadic. When meetings were held, they turned into marathon gabfests, while attendees for subsequent meetings stacked up in the hallways. . . . Aspin's immediate problem, from the day he took over the department, was the image he projected . . . rumpled tan suits, sounded inarticulate, resisted seeing foreign leaders . . . not good to inspire confidence in armed forces.[72]

In the meantime, Boutros-Ghali and the UN continued to drag their feet in taking over UNITAF from the Americans, and at that same time Boutros-Ghali demanded that the American forces do more before he would allow the UN to take over. On January 26 Boutros-Ghali wrote to the UNSC that the UNITAF-to-UN transition was "proceeding smoothly in close cooperation and consultation with the Command of UNITAF."[73] This is a surprising statement considering the challenges and problems that US military officials on the ground in Somalia were having getting UN support in the field. Boutros-Ghali also congratulated UNITAF for "rapidly and successfully securing major population centers and ensuring that humanitarian assistance is delivered and distributed without impediment," but he concluded that general security remained dangerous.[74]

On January 28 Powell met Clinton for the first time to discuss military issues. Powell was disappointed in the meeting and with Clinton. He wrote that he "figured the commander in chief's first meeting with his top military advisers ought at least to raise purely military issues. As soon as I finished, however, we spent the next 105 minutes solely on homosexuals in the armed forces."[75] Powell "felt increasingly disappointed that this issue had been allowed to become the new administration's first priority."[76]

Like Powell, Oakley was also not impressed with the leadership of the new administration's foreign policy team. He compared the team's experience to that of the Bush administration:

> Here you had a wonderful contrast between administrations. An administration came in with no previous international experience at the top. The experienced Bush national security team recognized that the operation in Somalia needed to have a civilian political/humanitarian component as well as a military side.[77]

On January 29 the US Senate Armed Services Committee reviewed the UN request to disarm Somalia and said no.[78] It supported the US military leaders in Somalia; they were eager to exit Somalia and turn over the mission to the UN. They believed that the US military had achieved UNITAF's mission objectives and that the intervention was effective in staving off starvation and improving the security environment. In their opinion, the humanitarian mission that President Bush ordered was accomplished.

On the first of February, Madeleine Albright flew to New York City to assume her post as US ambassador to the United Nations. Albright liked Boutros-Ghali, especially since they had much in common. Both were former professors, so they enjoyed discussing their individual transitions from academic to diplomatic life. They had met seven years earlier, when Boutros-Ghali represented Egypt at a conference on democracy sponsored by the National Democratic Institute.[79] Albright's instructions on Somalia were clear and her challenges were many in trying to get the UN to take over the mission:

> Instructions were to negotiate the rapid handover of principal responsibility from the US to the UN. The Pentagon was eager to call its mission a success and bring our soldiers home. Boutros-Ghali resisted, arguing that the world body was neither staffed nor equipped to take on another major new operation. . . . The NSC was relentless, calling me nearly every day to ask, 'What's taken so long?' New on the job and eager to earn my place as a full member of our foreign policy team, I told the Secretary-General he had no choice, US troops would leave whether the UN was prepared to take their place or not.[80]

Despite Albright's stance, Boutros-Ghali would not allow the UN to accept the hand-off from the United States until the Americans committed to a new deal, which included a 4,000-member US logistics military force, a 1,300-member Quick Reaction Force (QRF), and UNITAF remaining after UNOSOM II took over. American officials understood that in order to exit Somalia they would have to commit significant resources, including some US military participation, to the follow-on UNOSOM II mission. Thus, they agreed to many of Boutros-Ghali's requests.

The reality was also that Albright and other US officials had to compromise with Boutros-Ghali in order to get the bulk of US troops out of Somalia and transfer the operation to the UN.[81] Compounding the transition difficulty was an escalation of violence among the major warlords. On February 21 and 22, Barre's son-in-law, Hersi Morgan, took the important southern port city of Kismayo by force from Aidid's main ally, Colonel Omar Jess. Morgan had used women and children to disguise the infiltration of weapons into Kisamayo and drive Jess out of Kismayo. Morgan's attack violated his agreement with other warlords at the January Addis Abba meeting to halt all force movements until a national reconciliation peace plan could be negotiated.

Aidid protested Morgan's attack and Jess's expulsion, asking UNITAF to force Morgan out of the city. Aidid's Mogadishu supporters believed that UNITAF forces declined to force the locally backed Morgan out or let Aidid support Jess with a counterattack. As a consequence, Aidid sponsored violent anti-US and anti-UN demonstrations near the US Embassy and UN headquarters. The rioters were prompted by Aidid complaints of American favoritism toward Morgan and other clans in his radio broadcasts.[82] Even if Aidid's allegations were not true, it was a good tactic to scapegoat his enemies.

UNITAF used force to put down the riots, which further fueled Aidid's propaganda and violence. The day after the riots, an Irish NGO, Irish Concern, convoy from Afgoi to Baidoa was attacked, which resulted in the shooting of their staff, including Valerie Place, who was shot in the head.[83] Violence also escalated throughout Mogadishu despite UN claims that stability had been restored. For example, several days after the riots, on February 26, the Italian commander informed the international media that Mogadishu was calm and secure, but during the briefing smoke poured into the room from a nearby firefight.[84]

On March 3 Boutros-Ghali further delayed the transfer to the UN, saying the UNITAF mission was not complete and providing further suggestions for disarming Somali militias. He told the UNSC that his letter to President Bush in December had provided an outline of the mandate for the UN mission and that it must cover the whole territory of Somalia and include disarmament. He also set May 1, 1993, as the target transition date for UNITAF to be handed over to the UN and renamed UNOSOM II.[85]

At the same time Department of State officials wanted a broader intervention in the form of an expanded UNSC mandate. They feared that if US forces prematurely departed, the sources of Somalia's problems—too many armed militias and lack of national government—would continue. In contrast the Bush administration resisted UN attempts to expand the mission from the clear mission of food relief to end mass starvation. According to John Bolton, President Bush's assistant secretary of state for international organizations, Clinton administration officials "set about pioneering 'assertive multilateralism' and efforts at nation-building that led to the violence and embarrassment that ultimately ensued."[86]

Boutros-Ghali had no illusions about the UN's ability to disarm and rebuild Somalia. He was well aware that the Americans had the power to disarm—not to mention the capability to lead a nation-building effort. The Clinton administration was well aware of the UN's agenda, trying various efforts to assist Boutros-Ghali's goals, but its own agenda was more subtle and complex. Clinton officials in the State Department and NSC were trying to adjust from the Gulf War success in building an international coalition under UN auspices to nation-building also under UN auspices. In the administration's view, if the UN effort in Somalia succeeded in re-establishing it as a functioning state with possibly a democratic government, then the UN could be used to help enhance US security.

On March 26 the UNSC passed Resolution 814, which authorized UNOSOM II to take over from UNITAF. The resolution was a compromise between the US desire to get out of Somalia and the UN desire to avoid carrying most of the operation's weight. It dramatically expanded the size and mandate of the original UNOSOM I and UNITAF missions from protecting humanitarian relief supplies and staff to disarming militias and rebuilding Somalia economically and politically. The main purpose was to lessen the likelihood that concluding the UN operation would result in the recommencement of widespread famine and violence.

The Clinton administration enthusiastically endorsed UNSC 814, especially since they drafted significant portions of the resolution.[87] Albright's speech to the UNSC announced that the resolution was a "historic undertaking. We are excited to join it and we will vigorously support it."[88] Powell's feeling was more tepid and foreboding:

> It was now up to the UN force to maintain that order. But UN Secretary-General Boutros-Ghali reasoned that the catastrophe had been provoked by feuding fourteenth-century-style warlords,

the solution was a dose of twentieth-century-style democracy. The UN approved a resolution shifting the mission from feeding the hungry to "nation-building," the phrase I had first heard when we went into Vietnam.[89]

At the State Department policy level there was agreement with the UN on what it would take to fulfill the expanded UN mandate, including the use of US troops. The strong, but calculated, nation-building resolution was a State Department effort to help rebuild Somalia with the help of US military forces. According to David Shinn, a member of the Somalia Task Force at the State Department, UNSC 814 was "far more carefully worded than most people give anyone credit for." He takes exception to criticism that the resolution was too broad. Rather, he said, it gave flexibility to the UN to do what it could in Somalia to make the situation better. The resolution "doesn't say, thou shalt create a national government or thou shalt recreate an economy. It says that the international community should do what it can to help the Somalis recreate a government."[90]

The new UN mission was designed to help the Somalis rebuild their country economically and politically. UNSC Resolution 814 was far-reaching in scope and new in practice, as UN nation-building had never been attempted. It had three parts: 1) political reconciliation and economic rehabilitation, which included establishing councils of local leaders; 2) security issues linked to Chapter VII peacemaking powers, including expanding UNOSOM to a five-brigade force and forcibly disarming the warring factions; and 3) a trust fund established for Somalia to help it rebuild.

Boutros-Ghali recognized the significance of UNOSOM II:

> [Resolution 814] would be the first operation of its kind to be authorized by the international community. It would be an expression of the international community's determination not to remain a silent spectator to the sufferings of an entire people for no fault of their own. It would also be an answer of the international community to the universally shared concern that the situation in Somalia, though primarily of a domestic nature, could affect the peace and stability of the entire region of which Somalia forms an integral part, unless energetic and timely action is taken to avert a major humanitarian and security disaster.[91]

Meanwhile, among the upper-level Clinton appointees there was little discussion on UNOSOM II's implications. One of the reasons was that many mid-to-upper-level Clinton appointees not yet been confirmed, so foreign policy decisions lacked depth.[92] Even though most of the State Department nominees, such as Albright, had been confirmed, many of the Defense Department nominees, especially at the higher and mid-levels, were still in the confirmation process; with no one in the positions, the Pentagon "salutes the leadership to political matters and moves on."[93]

According to Shinn, to the best of his knowledge "there was no one in the administration who thought #814 was a mistake or badly done or anything else."[94] In response to the question of why the Department of Defense did not weigh in on the resolution, a Department of Defense official involved with the Somalia missions said, "I was not standing on the roof yelling no."[95]

There was a sense among Department of Defense officials, however, that the new administration wanted to use the military for nontraditional purposes, such as peacekeeping operations. The Clinton administration was reorganizing the Pentagon, including considering a proposal for creating an undersecretary position titled "peacekeeping."[96] A noted proponent of multilateral arrangements, Mort Halprin, was considered for the position, but the administration determined he was not confirmable.[97]

As part of the new deal and to further American involvement in UNOSOM II, Boutros-Ghali offered to appoint an American in the special representative post to replace an ailing and ineffective Kittani. Lake nominated Admiral Jonathan Howe, who had chaired the four November 1992 NSC Deputies Committee meetings that had prepared the Somali intervention options for President Bush. Lake and Howe had worked together in the NSC in the 1960s and had met again when Lake was briefed by Bush's National Security Adviser Scowcroft and Howe, who was still at the NSC during the Bush-to-Clinton transition period. Lake believed that Howe was an excellent choice for the position because of his professional experience in US government with the UNITAF mission. Lake called Howe, who had retired to Florida to take over a private foundation, asking him to come back.[98]

Robert Gosende, who had been serving as Oakley's public affairs officer in Somalia and was then teaching at Georgetown University, received a telephone call from a State Department official in late January with the message, "Congratulations. The president has appointed you a special envoy to Somalia."[99] Gosende was familiar with Africa, especially Somalia, where he had served in 1968–1970 as the cultural affairs and English teaching officer for the United States Information Service. Oakley had worked to lay the groundwork for UNITAF operations, and Gosende's duties were to implement the US strategy of ramping up the UNOSOM II mission, ensure a successful transition, and diminish UN and Somali dependence on US resources.

The administration also suggested General Çevik Bir, a Muslim from Turkey, as the commanding officer for UNOSOM II. Bir would officially report to Howe, who was responsible for both the military and civilian aspects of the operation. Howe, in turn, would report to Boutros-Ghali and the UN headquarters.

The United States actively and aggressively lobbied governments to contribute men, material, and/or financial commitments to UNOSOM II in order to make the transition from UNITAF smoother. The United States feared that UNOSOM II could lose the security gains made by UNITAF if there was not an adequate international military presence in place after the departure of the majority of US armed forces. Its concern was justified. Despite the passage of UNSC 814 and the Bir and Howe appointments, the UN persisted in slowing the transition. According to Oakley, it was still "unclear to everybody who was in charge."[100] Zinni complained that "the UN proved extremely reluctant to assume the mission . . . the UN command was slow to form and take charge, and in general dragged its feet."[101]

A few days after the resolution's passage, Howe flew to Somalia, reading UNSC 814 on the plane. From the moment he arrived in Somalia, Howe was adversely struck by the appearance of the country's people. First, the Pakistanis and other UN troops held a nice ceremony to welcome him. Afterward, as he was driving in a motorcade into town, where he would be living, his convoy got held up to let another motorcade go by. It was US Seabees heading to Mogadishu's port to return to the United States. Howe remembered asking himself the following:

> Why are they leaving here in March? They are exactly what UNOSOM II needs. These are the people to build things. I really got mad.[102]

The UNITAF to UNSOM II transition was not working well. There was increasing tension between US and UN officials, including Howe. In late March, after nearly three months of uninterrupted food delivery, the food convoy escorts by UNOSOM II forces were reduced. Johnston had started the transition process, which he had hoped to launch two months earlier. By this time US troop strength had already been cut almost in half to about 13,000 from a peak of more than 25,000 in January. It did not help UNOSOM II prospects for success when a combination of Boutros-Ghali's tepidness in taking on the mission and US eagerness to leave converged.

The military transition from UNITAF to UNOSOM II took longer than expected. The slow transition and the UN-United States cleavages

emboldened Aidid and other Somali warlords to forcibly challenge
UNOSOM II. In purely military terms, the UNITAF intervention had
been a huge success, with few hostile casualties to US and UN forces.[103]
But the prospects for long-term peace in Somalia seemed dubious as long
as the warlords continued to jockey for power and hold up reconstruction
efforts.

The focus on guarding food had obscured broader problems that began
well before the famine arrived, namely, the destruction of key components
of Somali society and the political implosion of a central government.
What the UN was soon to experience was that its excessively grand design
at nation-building was to be undermined by local Somali leaders threatened by an external authority and by a historical Somali dislike of outsiders. It was a formula for catastrophe and tragedy.

Notes

1. Tom Clancy with General Tony Zinni (Ret.) and Tony Koltz, *Battle
Ready* (New York: G.P. Putnam's Sons, 2004), 239.

2. Ibid., 240.

3. Ambassador Robert Oakley, (ambassador to Somalia, 1982–1984;
special envoy to Somalia for President Bush, December 1992 to March
1993 and special envoy to Somalia for President Clinton, October
1993–March 1994), Washington, DC, May 29, 2003.

4. Ibid.

5. Ibid.

6. General Libutti interview as quoted in Major Eric F. Buer, USMC,
"United Task Force Somalia (UNITAF) and United Nations Operations
Somalia (UNOSOM II): A Comparative Analysis of Offensive Air
Support," Master Thesis, United States Marine Corps, Command and
Staff College, AY 2000–2001, 14.

7. Robert B. Oakley, "Urban Area During Support Missions: Case
Study: Mogadishu: The Strategic Level," in *Capital Preservation:
Preparing for Urban Operations in the Twenty-First Century,
Proceedings of the RAND Urban Operations Conference,* ed. Russell W.
Glenn, March 22–23, 2000, 324.

8. Clancy, Zinni, and Koltz, *Battle Ready*, 246–247.

9. Zinni served as the chief of staff and deputy commanding general
of Combined Task Force Provide Comfort during the Kurdish relief
effort in Turkey and Iraq and as the military coordinator for Operation
Provide Hope, the relief effort for the former Soviet Union.

10. The area of responsibility was around 15,000 square miles
throughout southern Somalia. Major Michael J. Curry, "21st Century

Combat and the Operational Logistics Link," Monograph, School of
Advanced Military Studies, United States Army Command and General
Staff College, Second Term AY 98-99, 19.

11. Colonel Pete Dotto interview, December 16, 1996, quoted in LTC
Christopher L. Baggott, "A Leap Into the Dark: Crisis Action Planning
for Operation Restore Hope," Monograph, Army Command and
General Staff College, School of Advanced Military Studies, Fort
Leavenworth, Kansas, December 20, 1996, 22.

12. Ibid., 21.

13. Mark Huband, *The Skull Beneath the Skin: Africa After the Cold
War* (Boulder, CO: Westview, 2001), 296.

14. Ibid., 293.

15. "Comprehensive Report on Lessons-Learned From United
Nations Operation in Somalia April 1992–March 1995," Lessons-
Learned Unit of the Department of Peace Keeping Operations,
December 1995, 20.

16. Jonathan Stevenson, *Losing Mogadishu: Testing US Policy in
Somalia* (Annapolis, MD: Naval Institute Press, 1995), 40.

17. Helen Fogarassy, *Mission Improbable: The World Community on
a UN Compound in Somalia* (Lanham, MD: Lexington Books, 1999),
189–190.

18. Jan Westcott, "The Somalia Saga: A Personal Account
1990–1992," Refugee Policy Group, November 1994, 40.

19. Stevenson, *Losing Mogadishu*, 38–39.

20. Michael Maren, *The Road to Hell: The Ravaging Effects of Foreign Aid and International Charity* (New York: The Free Press, 1997).

21. Interview conducted by Anita Parlow for a discussion paper on
"Formalizing Relations between DoD and OFDA in Complex Humanitarian Crises," Conference on "Civil-Military Relations in Complex
Humanitarian Crises 'Forging Peace'" at Harvard University, March
13–18, 1998.

22. F. M. Lorenz, "Law and Anarchy in Somalia," *Parameters*, vol
XXIII, no. 4 (Winter 1993–94): 39.

23. Ibid., footnote 10.

24. Jonathan T. Dworken, "Restore Hope: Coordinating Relief Operations," *Joint Forces Quarterly* (Summer 1995): 17; Lorenz, "Law and
Anarchy," footnote 10.

25. UNITAF, "Civil-Military Operations Cell," as sourced in
Dworken, "Restore Hope," 17.

26. Andrew S. Natsios, *US Foreign Policy and the Four Horsemen of
the Apocalypse: Humanitarian Relief in Complex Emergencies*
(Westport, CT: Praeger Publishers, 1997), 125.

27. David Bowne Wood, *A Sense of Values: American Marines in an Uncertain World* (Kansas City: Andrews and McMeel, 1994), 180.

28. Lorenz, "Law and Anarchy," 32.

29. Dworken, "Restore Hope," 17.

30. US Department of Defense official involved in UNITAF planning and implementation, interview with author. May 30, 2004. Conducted in confidentiality, and the name withheld by mutual agreement.

31. John Drysdale, *Somalia: A Tale of Tragic Blunders* (London: HAAN Associates, 1994), 46.

32. Natsios, *US Foreign Policy*, 106.

33. Robert Caputo, "Tragedy Stalks the Horn of Africa," *National Geographic* (August 1993): 102.

34. Quoted in John G. Sommer, *Hope Restored? Humanitarian Aid in Somalia: 1990–1994,* (Washington, DC: Refugee Policy Group, 1994), 33.

35. Natsios, *US Foreign Policy*, 112.

36. UNSC 794, Article 7, December 3, 1992.

37. UNSC 794, Article 18, December 3, 1992.

38. President Bush letter to Representative Tom Foley, Speaker of the House of Representatives, December 10, 1992. This was the same message given to Congress by Deputy Secretary of Defense Donald Atwood, designating Operation Restore Hope as a contingency operation. Memorandum from Deputy Secretary of Defense Donald Atwood for Secretaries of the Military Departments, Chairman of Joint Chiefs of State, et al., December 8, 1992.

39. UN Secretary-General Boutros Boutros-Ghali letter to President George Bush as quoted in the UN Secretary-General report on the Situation in Somalia. December 19, 1992. S/24992.

40. Ibid.

41. Oakley, "Urban Area During Support Missions," 324–325.

42. Major Eric F. Buer, USMC, "United Task Force Somalia (UNITAF) and United Nations Operations Somalia (UNOSOM II): A Comparative Analysis of Offensive Air Support," Master Thesis, United States Marine Corps, Command and Staff College, AY 2000–2001, 6 and 14.

43. Ibid., 29.

44. Oakley, "Urban Area During Support Missions," 325.

45. Ibid., 325–326.

46. "Relief Workers in Extreme Danger: Urgently Request UN Troops to Baidoa," InterAction Press Release, December 10, 1992.

47. Philip Johnston, *Somalia Diary: The President of CARE Tells One Country's Story of Hope* (Atlanta: Longstreet Press, 1994), 81.

48. ICRC Update No. 9 on ICRC Activities in Somalia. December 14, 1992.

49. Oakley, "Urban Area During Support Missions," 322.

50. Oakley, interview.

51. Ibid.

52. World Vision interoffice memo from Russ Kerr to Relief Distribution.

53. Caputo, "Tragedy Stalks," 112.

54. Theo Farrell, "United States Marine Corps Operations in Somalia: A Model for the Future," *Amphibious Operations: A Collection of Papers,* The Occasional, Number 31, Geoffrey Till, Mark J. Grove, and Theo Farrell, The Strategic and Combat Studies Institute, October 1997, 48.

55. Oakley, "Urban Area During Support Missions," 327–328.

56. Ibid.

57. Clancy, Zinni, and Koltz, *Battle Ready,* 268.

58. Oakley, "Urban Area During Support Missions," 339.

59. Clancy, Zinni, and Koltz, *Battle Ready,* 251–252.

60. Stevenson, *"Losing Mogadishu,"* 47; Jonathan Stevenson, "Hope Restored in Somalia? *Foreign Policy,* no. 91 (Summer 1993): 148.

61. Colin Powell with Joseph E. Persico, *My American Journey* (Random House: New York, 1995), 567.

62. Ambassador Jim Bishop (deputy assistant for Africa, 1981–1987; US ambassador to Somalia 1987–1990), interview with author, Washington, DC, May 28, 2003.

63. Bill Clinton, *My Life* (New York: Alfred A. Knopf, 2004), 502.

64. Anthony Lake (national security adviser, 1993 to 1997), interview with author. Washington, DC, May 10, 2004.

65. Richard A. Clarke (National Security Council, director, Office of International Programs, 1992; Department of State, assistant secretary of state for politico-military affairs, 1989–1992 and deputy assistant secretary of state for intelligence, 1985–1988) telephone interview with author, July 16, 2004.

66. Lake, interview.

67. Clinton, *My Life,* 550.

68. President Bush written responses in Sommer, *Hope Restored?* 32.

69. Powell interview as quoted in Sommer, *Hope Restored?* 31–32.

70. Powell, *My American Journey,* 577.

71. Ibid., 580.

72. Ibid., 578–579.

73. UN Secretary-General Boutros Boutros-Ghali, report on the situation in Somalia, January 26, 1993. S/25168.

74. Ibid.

75. Powell, *My American Journey*, 571.

76. Ibid., 572.

77. Oakley, "Urban Area During Support Missions," 321.

78. Senators John Warner (R-Va). and Carl Levin, (D-Mich), *Warner-Levin Report*, "Review of the Circumstances Surrounding the Ranger Raid on October 3–4, 1993," United States Senate Committee on Armed Services, October 2, 1995, 16.

79. Albright, *Madam Secretary*, 136.

80. Ibid., 142–143.

81. Clancy, Zinni, and Koltz, *Battle Ready*, 241.

82. Stevenson, "Hope Restored," 140.

83. Brigadier General Ed Wheeler (USA-Ret) and Lt. Colonel Craig Roberts (USAR-Ret), *Doorway to Hell: Disaster in Somalia* (Tulsa, OK: Consolidated Press International, 2002), 80.

84. Lorenz, "Law and Anarchy," 37.

85. UN Secretary-General Boutros Boutros-Ghali, Further Report of the Secretary-General Submitted in Pursuance of paragraphs 18 and 19 of Resolution 794 (1992). March 3, 1994. S/25354.

86. John R. Bolton, "Wrong Turn in Somalia," *Foreign Affairs* (January/February 1994): 56.

87. Ambassador Robert Gosende (President Clinton's special envoy to Somalia, 1993; public affairs officer for President Bush's Special Envoy to Somalia Ambassador Robert Oakley, 1993–1994), interview with Author, New York, New York, October 22, 2007.

88. Foreign Policy Bulletin 3, no 6, (Jan–April 1993), 48.

89. Powell, *My American Journey*, 580.

90. Ambassador David Shinn (State Department deputy director of the Somali Task Force), interview with author, Washington, DC, April 8, 2004.

91. Further Report of the Secretary General G Submitted in Pursuance of paragraphs 18 and 19 of Resolution 794 (1992). March 3, 1993. S/25354.

92. William J. Durch, "Introduction to Anarchy: Intervention and 'State-Building' in Somalia," in *UN: Peacekeeping, American Policy and the Uncivil Wars of the 1990s*, ed. William J. Durch (New York: St. Martin's Press, 1996), 327.

93. US Department of Defense official, interview.

94. Shinn, interview.

95. US Department of Defense official, interview.

96. The Clinton administration also created an Office of Peacekeeping at the State Department.

97. Highlighting the differences between the administration's focus on using the military for nontraditional security operations and the Department of Defense, Chairman of the Joint Chiefs of Staff Colin Powell exploded at a security meeting when Madeleine Albright, Clinton's US Ambassador to the UN, said, "What's the point of having this superb military that you're always talking about if we can't use it?" "I thought I would have an aneurysm. American GIs were not toy soldiers to be moved around on some sort of global game board." Powell, *My American Journey,* 576.

98. Lake, interview. Howe had actually returned to Washington, DC, the previous month to accept the National Security Medal at a White House ceremony with President Bush on January 13.

99. Gosende, interview.

100. Oakley, interview.

101. Clancy, Zinni, and Koltz, *Battle* Ready, 241.

102. Admiral Jonathan Howe (deputy assistant to the president for national security affairs 1991–1992; special representative for Somalia to UN Secretary-General Boutros Boutros-Ghali, March 1993–February 1994), interview with author. Jacksonville, Florida, December 28, 2005.

103. UNITAF incurred eight killed in action, twenty-four noncombatant related deaths, and twenty-four wounded in action. Clancy, Zinni, and Koltz, *Battle Ready,* 267.

CHAPTER FIVE

ARMED NATION-BUILDING

As the United Task Force (UNITAF) wound down operations and prepared for the May 4 turnover date, the mission's success was evident and measurable. The US military forces did an excellent job in leading UNITAF to reverse the famine, lower the death rates, and even raise the price of weapons. For example, four months after the US military forces landed in Somalia, the number of deaths per day in Bardera dropped from more than 300 in November 1992 to fewer than five in April, and in Mogadishu the price of an AK-47 went from under $50 to almost $1,000 because of weapon searches and confiscations. Many Somalis expressed their gratitude to the American forces as they withdrew from Somalia to make way for the follow-on UN Operation in Somalia (UNOSOM) II forces. For example, Kismayo citizens presented a live goat and a petition asking Alpha Company of the 24th Marine Expeditionary Unit to remain.[1]

After nearly three months of uninterrupted food delivery, the food convoy escorts by UNITAF forces were reduced in preparation for the May 4 turnover to UNOSOM II. Among Clinton administration officials there was a growing recognition that the mission to save Somalia included not only food but also implementation of a means of disabling factions. Otherwise, the international community would have to return in a few months. One Clinton official made the following comments:

> We need to do Somalia right and not necessary to sweep it under the rug. People ask did we try to do nation building? Absolutely. It was nation building. We recognized going forward that the mission needed to be a multifaceted one by necessity. For it to be successful and sustainable it had to deal with other aspects of the food problem, such as security and institution building."[2]

Others within the administration had high expectations for the UNOSOM II operation. They predicted that it boded well for a new era in international cooperation. According to one enthusiast, US Ambassador to the UN Madeleine Albright called UN Security Council (UNSC) Resolution 814, which authorized UNOSOM II, an example of "multilateral assertiveness" in the new post–Cold War world. Albright and others thought sincerely that the UN could handle Somalia. A Department of Defense official, who disagreed with the administration's support of UNSC 814 and its nation-building philosophy, visited Somalia several times and said that the administration wanted to "turn Somalia into Maryland."[3]

Yet why did the Clinton administration push the strong UNSC Resolution 814 to rebuild, disarm, and establish a functioning political system in Somalia yet not support it with the required resources? According to the Special Representative for the Secretary-General to Somalia (SRSG), US Admiral Howe, the truth lies somewhere among three possible answers: no one was paying attention, they did not know any better, and they kept the mindset of the Bush administration in terms of defining success by getting out.[4]

The major challenge confronting UNOSOM II forces was disarming Somali militias, who had made most of their money by shaking down international humanitarian assistance operations. Boutros-Ghali continued to argue that UN political and humanitarian operations were not possible without effective disarmament of all the factions and warlords. But managing a disarmament program in Somalia, a relatively large country with vast empty spaces in which to conceal weapons, would be difficult. Without an organized military or police force, Somalis would intuitively feel more comfortable carrying guns to protect themselves and their families. Another disarmament challenge would be eliminating or at least regulating the small arms and light weapons commerce.

Although UNITAF's success was acclaimed, an undercurrent of rising tensions among Somali warlords gave several US officials trepidation about UNOSOM II's success. They hoped that the UN could handle the new operation, but its expanded mandate to include disarmament and the slow transfer gave some American officials, including Oakley, pause about UNOSOM II's chances for success.[5]

From its inception, UNOSOM II faced major challenges different from those confronted by UNITAF. First, UNOSOM II was a radical change in vision of a typical UN peacekeeping mission. The battlescape in Somalia was half war and half political. The political engagement required of UNOSOM II was far higher than that in UNITAF's mission, which primarily required securing humanitarian relief supplies, routes, and distribution. The UNSC mandated that UNOSOM II achieve democratization objectives that were unrealistic considering the lack of personnel and resources it provided to the mission and the ongoing dynamics of the militias. Moreover, UNOSOM II was trying to bring clans together under a form of representative government, which was foreign to the Somalia political experience.

UNITAF was conceived and implemented by the Bush administration with a limited mission that measured success by leaving when Somalis were feeding regularly, whereas the Clinton administration wanted to ensure a fully functioning country, including political and economic stability. The Clinton administration's support for UNOSOMI II changed the American interest in Somalia from a simple feeding operation to a large mandate to nation-build. Unfortunately, Clinton officials, such as Albright, held an idealistic view that the UN would be able to achieve the mission with less US support than that it had provided UNITAF. According to Howe, "UNOSOM II kept the Bush mindset in the Clinton administration. We're getting our troops out and there was no sense of responsibility for doing the job. There was some naiveté that UN could do it. Here, expectations changed. We had to develop a strategic plan for doing this, and the UN was weak in terms of responding quickly."[6]

Like other peacekeeping operations, UNOSOM II was confronted with the challenge of troop flows into the operation at its start and the quality of those troops. Moreover, once troops arrived they required cultural, military, and political familiarization time, especially considering the inner conflicts in Somalia. For example, although the United States and forty-one other governments had committed 28,598 troops to UNOSOM II, only 14,898 of those were deployed in Somalia at the time of the turnover.[7] To overcome this shortcoming, immediately upon arriving in Somalia, Howe did his best to encourage UNITAF troops to participate in UNOSOM II. One of his first actions was to build up UNOSOM II forces, including requesting in his first correspondence from Somalia to Boutros-Ghali that the secretary-general encourage UNITAF-participating nations, especially Australia, to keep their forces in Somalia under the UNOSOM II mission.[8] According to Howe,

> We lost the Australians and Canadians and most of the Americans. The Australians knew how to do it well. They established justice system, etc. Canadians had some problems with a few of their troops but were very good. The US was occupying south Mogadishu and replaced with Pakistanis. Italians were questionable. They were asked by me to leave Mogadishu. We were losing very capable units and sent to cover larger and larger chunks of territory.[9]

Another challenge facing Howe was working for effective results with the UN bureaucracy; his position as UN special representative carried little power at the dysfunctional UN. For example, a post-UNOSOM mission report produced by the UN Department of Peacekeeping Operations (UNDPKO) Lessons-Learned Unit discovered that "the responsibility for different aspects of the operation was splintered across different departments of the Secretariat. The result was 'stove-pipe' communication between the field and New York. For example, the chief administrative officer would report to one department, the SRSG [Howe] to a second, and the Humanitarian Coordinator to a third. . . . Since it took time for coordination to develop, the right hand did not know what the left was doing."[10]

Unfortunately, Howe also found himself short of qualified civilian and military personnel to help put into action the massive UNOSOM II mandate required by UNSC Resolution 814. He made many requests to Boutros-Ghali for more staff, but for the most part they remained unfulfilled. Howe believed it was critical to mission success "to establish momentum by going in Somalia and delivering."[11] Howe made more appeals to the in-country UNITAF personnel but met with little success because those troops and personnel were ready to go home. Howe said he "was going around, pushing very hard on getting humanitarian, political, and security resources and we weren't delivering for the Somalis. We lost momentum."[12]

The UN also failed to give Howe the material and personnel resources required to achieve "a relatively secure environment, good local cooperation, and adequate resources."[13] For example, many of the military troops lacked proper equipment, such as armored personnel carriers (APCs) for protection from the fire of small arms and light weapons.

From UNOSOM II's beginning, the Pentagon tried to fend off continuous efforts by Congress and the UN to get the US military to do what they felt should be left to the UNOSOM II forces. There was also concern that substantial involvement in such activities could further broaden and intensify US military participation in UNOSOM II.

Despite the Pentagon's concerns, the US-UNITAF handover to the UN was given an assist from the US government, which included an in-force package of US military resources to facilitate UNOSOM II's military objectives. The package was a two-edged sword: although its soldiers and equipment added needed teeth to the expanded operation, the United States encouraged the UN to select General Çevik Bir, a Turkish general, to command UNOSOM II but then induced a command structure that made certain US armed forces report to US Army General Thomas Montgomery, appointed as deputy commander, rather than Bir. The US armed forces reporting system was similar, in various forms, to other international forces in Somalia that did not report through the UN but directly back to their home countries. These command arrangements and communications eventually led to misunderstandings among the national military forces and between the civilian and military leaders. Sadly tragic was that the UN personnel and forces needed to be on the same page to accomplish the mission of disarming the Somali militias and carefully rebuilding the political system, which was required under UNSC Resolution 814.

In addition, key military assets enjoyed by UNITAF forces were stripped away from UNOSOM II forces. For example, UNITAF was able to effectively utilize a range of air operations to fly over militia positions as a show of force and provide intelligence.[14] However, a majority of the fixed and rotary wing aircraft left with UNITAF. Because of limited air assets, UNOSOM II air support operations became reactive, thus leaving ground personnel vulnerable to increasingly hostile Somali militias that no longer feared air attacks.[15]

This may also be due to the fact that many air attack operations were based from Mogadishu's airport, which bordered a heavily urbanized area. The missions were easily compromised by observant Somalis near the airport who would use radios to warn potential targets in the city, thus eliminating the element of surprise.

But even if the Somali factions were disarmed by UNOSOM II forces, there remained the challenge of developing a functioning political system. As a first step, from March 14 to 27 the UN hosted a national Somali political meeting in Ethiopia's capital, Addis Ababa. The new civilian UN leadership attended, including Howe and his deputy, Guinean Permanent Representative to the UN Lansana Kouyate. They were joined by nearly 300 Somalis representing militia groups, Islamic leaders, clan elders, and women's groups. On March 27 Somali political leaders signed a comprehensive agreement covering disarmament and security. The "Addis National Reconciliation Conference" was designed by the UN to move the Somali political development process forward because UNOSOM II had political reconstruction in its mandate.

The Addis Ababa agreements established the Transnational Council (TNC) and a framework for district and regional councils to help jumpstart the development of a national government.[16] UNOSOM II would help facilitate creating community assemblies to elect traditional leaders, such as clan elders and religious leaders, to participate in national politics. Many Somalis and foreign officials, including those representing the United States and the UN, hoped that the conference would legitimize the reconciliation process and eventually lead to a national government. It was also designed to attract the Somali people and help justify a new leadership that incorporated Somalia's traditional leaders—the elders—

and warlords. Previously, the Somali clans had primarily unified in opposition to a larger threat, such as Barre's rule. The agreement provided a tenuous political balance with a scheduled phase-in electoral process supported by economic development and infrastructure rehabilitation projects.

On March 30, three days after the conference officially ended, a second agreement document outlining the specific choosing of the TNC members was signed by fifteen faction leaders in Addis Ababa but without the participation and support of UNOSOM II officials. The March 27 and 30 agreements differed significantly in the TNC selection process. For example, whereas the March 27 agreement reserved seats for women and provided a long timeframe for the selection process, the March 30 agreement did not reserve seats for women and narrowed the selection process to only forty-five days. UNOSOM II gave a positive response to the March 27 agreement, but it never supported the March 30 agreement because it disagreed with the agreement's more prominent role for factions in Somalia's political reconstruction. The resulting dispute contributed to the foundation for military conflict between UNOSOM II and particular Somali factions.[17]

The UN and US support for the more inclusive March 27 agreement, which included leaders of Somali traditional society, was no match for the armed warlords and their militias. The UN was inexperienced in nation-building, and the national development process was captured by ambitious warlords and their militias, who did not represent the broader community. The UN and US leaders could not exploit the March 27 agreement for Somali reconciliation. Besides not supporting the warlord-driven March 30 conference and agreement, another major difficulty was the high turnover between and among UNITAF and UNOSOM II staff. Its leaders were in the midst of transferring responsibility and therefore focused on the transition rather that what was going on at the Addis Ababa Conference. When the UNOSOM II forces and leaders came in, they needed time to learn the lay of the land and understand the dynamics of Somali warlord politics. The result was that political momentum generated by the Addis Ababa conferences was not exploited by the UN.

As the Addis Ababa talks were continuing, US Representative Benjamin Gilman of New York offered a substitute for Senate Joint Resolution 45 as House Joint Resolution 152 to limit UNOSOM II to six months, saying the US had "done its share."[18] Possibly in reaction to Gillman's resolution, the following day (March 17), Howe asked the White House for more time to organize UNOSOM II before the UNITAF scheduled departure date of May 4. The White House rejected Howe's request, noting that the May 4 official transition date had been fixed only as a technical accounting date when the UN would start paying the operational costs.

Despite the lack of UN preparedness and willingness to support the requisite resources to the UNOSOM II mission, it became apparent to Howe that the United States was sticking to its position that the military command was going to be transferred out in early May. In fact Marine General Johnston already was implementing orders to get US troops and equipment out by the May 4 deadline, which required starting to send people out of Somalia in February. Among his troops there was a huge psychological expectation to get home.[19]

In late April Howe left the region for the first time since arriving in order to return to UN headquarters and brief Boutros-Ghali. Howe expressed uncertainty about the transition's progress:

> General Bir came to see me to say that he had agreed to May 4th US pullout. I went back to Boutros-Ghali and said here are the circumstances. "The Commander thinks we can do it, and I don't think we can." I explained the situation to Boutros-Ghali quite frankly. He picked up the phone and called, I think, Albright, requesting another month. He requested the US to remain in Somalia one more month. The US did not agree.[20]

Howe was later told by Boutros-Ghali that one of the reasons the United States did not agree to postponing the withdrawal was that it believed "its small Quick Reaction Force (QRF), which was remaining behind as an emergency reserve, provided sufficient insurance for unforeseen developments."[21] Howe did not believe this. He did not know the exact reasons but believed it had something more to do with the Department of Defense not getting reimbursed for its involvement in UNITAF.[22]

On May 4 the UNITAF turnover to UNOSOM II occurred despite Boutros-Ghali's and Howe's appeals to the United States to extend the UNITAF mission order to give UNOSOM II more time to ramp up its operation. Among the many dignitaries attending the turnover ceremony was General Colin Powell, who was also celebrating his fifty-sixth birthday.

After a traditional Somali ceremony, UNITAF Gens. Johnston and Zinni drove in two Humvees through Mogadishu's narrow streets to the airport to return to the United States. Johnston ordered the vehicles to stop near a group of children, and according to Zinni they

> got out of the vehicles, and he gathered all our pens and pencils and gave them to the kids (who all seemed pleased to get them). After his little act of charity, he slowly swung his gaze

around. Something was obviously weighing on his mind. "What are you thinking about?" I [Zinni] asked. He looked up at the bright sunny sky. "I give this place thirty days," he said, "and then it's all going to go to hell.[23]

Aidid and other Somali faction leaders correctly calculated that UNOSOM II was not as strong as UNITAF, which had entailed a multinational force of some 30,000, including more than 20,000 American troops. In comparison, on the first day of its operation, UNOSOM II was composed of a feeble mix of small military forces of about 16,000 troops. The Pakistanis formed the largest contingent at 4,000 but were still lacking much of their equipment. As a result Aidid's aggressive anti-UNOSOM II actions increased after the departure of a majority of the American forces, whom he feared. It was also believed that Aidid had been told by fundamentalist Muslims to stir up trouble against the United Nations and the United States.[24]

After the transition the UNITAF principal group based at the National Security Council (NSC) was relocated to the State Department, which, in turn, disbanded its Somalia Task Force on April 1 because there was not enough work to justify its continued existence.[25] However, its Africa Bureau argued that although it didn't need the Somalia Task Force, the job was too big for its Somalia Desk officer to handle alone because the US still had troops in Somalia. So David Shinn, who was the State Department's deputy director of the recently disbanded Somali Task Force, was asked to come back as the State Department's point person for Somalia and was given a small staff. For the Clinton administration, the move changed Somalia to a lower bureaucratic level because it "was not top priority and it could not be a top priority."[26]

Despite the fact that Somalia was the only place in the world where Americans were being shot at and UNOSOM II would end up being more complicated and dangerous for US military forces than UNITAF, the Somalia mission was lowered on the Clinton administration's list of priorities.[27] The NSC provided oversight during the final weeks of UNITAF, but both the Pentagon and State were devoting less high-level attention to the operation, as a consequence both of the anticipated hand-off and of turnover as the Clinton administration sought confirmation for its new political appointees.

Further complicating the transition was that US leaders in UNOSOM II were told to lower their profile to make it a non-US looking mission and to separate it from UNITAF, which was perceived by Somalis as American. For example, Ambassador Robert Gosende, who replaced Oakley as the US adviser in Somalia, was ordered not to go into the countryside, even though he wanted to meet with Somali leaders based there. He had seen Oakley do it and had seen that it had worked.[28]

Also impeding UNOSOM II's implementation of the Addis agreement was an outbreak of intense fighting in Somalia's second-largest city, Kismayo, 200 miles south of Mogadishu. On May 6, two days after the official UNITAF turnover to UNOSOM II, Aidid's warlord ally Jess and his militia, who had been ousted from Kismayo in February, launched a new attack on the city in an effort to wrest control from clans loyal to the pro-Barre warlord Morgan. It was an egregious violation of the cease-fire agreement hammered out several weeks before in Addis Ababa.

Jess's attack was repulsed by the Belgian troop component of UNOSOM II. Aidid and Jess were upset that UNOSOM II forces supported Morgan and his faction, whereas a few months earlier UNITAF forces did not assist Jess and his faction when Morgan's forces kicked them out of Kismayo. Aidid accused the Belgians and UNOSOM II of not being impartial. Aidid did not distinguish between UNITAF, which was in charge of Kismayo in March, when Morgan took it away from Jess, and UNOSOM II, which strongly intervened to protect the city from being taken over.[29] UNOSOM II had hoped to establish its credibility by helping Morgan's forces repulse Jess's attack, but it actually widened the political cleavage between Aidid and UNOSOM II.

Aidid especially feared UNOSOM II's robust military response in inter-Somali fighting and feared that he was being cut out of UNOSOM II's political process to develop a Somali national government. He was also very concerned that UNOSOM II's attack against his ally Jess was part of a broader UN plan to marginalize him and prevent him from taking the Somali presidency. The expansive UNOSOM II mission threatened Aidid and his prospects to maintain his power base, which was the south side of Mogadishu, where UNOMSOM II was establishing its operational headquarters.

The high priority that Boutros-Ghali gave to disarmament as part of UNOSOM II's mission also generated the hostility of Aidid, whose power relied on brute military force. Aidid believed that Boutros-Ghali's disarmament focus was directed against him and disarming his militia in order to appoint a Somali president of Boutros-Ghali's choosing. Also, because Howe continued pushing Boutros-Ghali to support the disarmament program, Aidid's suspicions about UNOSOM II's true intentions were further magnified.[30]

Actually, Boutros-Ghali alarmed most Somalis, including other warlords and leaders, by incessantly calling for disarming all Somalis. Without the protection of a central government, many Somalis armed themselves for protection. In addition, disarmament by a foreign entity raised the ire and suspicion of many Somalis, who, in general, were hyper-sensitive to the intentions of outsiders. Somalis historically were known to be hostile toward foreigners, especially those trying to control their country. The disarmament and political development components of the UNO-SOM II mandate struck at the heart of Somali sovereignty. Aidid used the Somali distrust of foreigners in order to rally Somali support to fight and resist UNOSOM II forces.

It did not help Aidid's relationship with UNOSOM II that he had always been suspicious of Boutros-Ghali. During the Barre reign Boutros-Ghali was Egyptian foreign minister and good friends with Barre, who had imprisoned Aidid. Also, many Somalis believed Egypt fostered Ethiopian-Somali hostilities as part of its Horn of Africa Nile strategy to retain influence in the region.[31]

Under UNITAF's American leadership, the tensions between Boutros-Ghali and the Somalis, especially Aidid, was insulated. This was greased by Oakley's proactive cross-cultural efforts to secure cooperation from Aidid and other warlords before moving UNITAF troops. In addition, UNITAF's relatively smooth relations with Aidid were facilitated by the fact that UNITAF did not consider disarmament a key component in its mission. In sum, Aidid felt comfortable working with Oakley toward clearing paths for humanitarian relief. He did not feel good about the UNOSOM II mandate because it authorized UN forces to use military force to disarm uncooperative militias, a policy that was pushed by the Egyptian Boutros-Ghali.

In May Aidid began inviting a selection of Somali warlords and leaders to participate in a national reconciliation conference that he was planning for later that month in the central Somali city of Galcayo. On May 13 Aidid sent a letter to UNOSOM II headquarters requesting financial support for his conference. Although the UN initially agreed to financially and logistically support the conference, it quickly withdrew because of disagreements with Aidid about who would be in charge of the agenda and sponsor the conference. Acting in place of the deputy special representative of the secretary-general, Ambassador Kouyate, who was on leave, Ambassador April Glaspie, the former US ambassador to Iraq and a career American Foreign Service officer seconded to UNOSOM II, "became suspicious of Aidid's intentions" and wanted broader Somali participation, including some of Aidid's antagonists.[32]

The UN reversal of committing financial support to the conference frustrated Aidid. He had wanted UN support, in part, to help legitimize him as the Somali national leader. It also reinforced Aidid's suspicions that Boutros-Ghalis's intentions in Somalia were to undermine his pursuit of the Somali presidency. Aidid held the conference anyway and began using his radio station to broadcast anti-UN propaganda.[33]

Aidid's anger at UNOSOM II stemmed from his perception, real or imagined, that UNOSOM II was interfering in the Somali political process and attempting to marginalize his role. The rise of Aidid and UN differences regarding sponsorship of the conference and its agenda highlighted their different philosophies of how best to develop a unity national government. Aidid thought he was the country's natural leader because he led the major military forces that ousted Barre, was from Somali's largest clan, and currently controlled most of Mogadishu, including its airport and port facilities. In comparison, the UNOSOM II officials wanted a political system in place to have free elections. Aidid viewed Howe and Gosende as vehicles for his foreign adversary Boutros-Ghali.[34]

Aidid and his supporters resented the new procedures, which further alienated Aidid from UNOSOM II's mission.[35] Aidid saw UNOSOM II as a threat to his survival because he didn't have the votes under its proposed formula for selecting judges. Howe tried to make him think he was missing out by not joining the process, but Aidid did not buy into the UNOSOM II judicial reform process.[36] The changes in judicial selection procedures, coupled with a different agreement that he had with UNITAF for developing and selecting a Somali police force, further inflamed Aidid's antagonism toward UNOSOM II.[37]

In light of Aidid's differences with UNOSOM II, Jess's fighting in Kismayo, changes in the selection of judges and police, and a lack of UN support for the Galcayo Conference, the tension between Aidid and the United Nations increased. For example, in a May 11 broadcast, Aidid radio accused UNOSOM II of trying to colonize Somalia and establish a trusteeship under UN control. The radio broadcasts continually spoke of the rich Somali history of resisting foreign domination. Aidid's radio station continued broadcasting anti-UN messages that eventually escalated in mid-May to threats to kill UN peacekeepers, including Americans, and became xenophobic in tone. This was the first public hint of broad threats to Americans and, as a result, the State Department sent out a warning via Voice of America and the BBC that Americans in Somalia might be targets.[38]

In Mogadishu, Aidid's pan-Somali and anti-UN propaganda was particularly successful among many Somalis, especially those from his clan. Because of the country's low literacy rate, cheap, portable radios provided the main source of information for Somalis. As a result UNOSOM II felt the radio broadcasts gave Aidid an "unfair advantage over political rivals."[39] The anti-UNOSOM II radio diatribes accused the UN of "interference in the internal affairs of the Somalia" and accused UN military forces of "murder, rape, and pillage against Somali citizens." In the US opinion, these radio broadcasts contravened the spirit and letter of the Addis Ababa agreements.[40]

UNOSOM II's radio station could not effectively counter Aidid's radio rhetoric because it was only on for forty-five minutes per day.[41] Howe thought Aidid's Radio Mogadishu was not a threat because it had limited broadcasting range. He wanted to exploit this weakness and broadcast the UNOSOM II message "to the whole country and really get the word out."[42] At a cost of only about $1 million, Howe thought funding would not be an issue, especially because he had been told by UN personnel that one of their mistakes in Cambodia was not getting a radio started.[43]

Unfortunately, the UNOSOM II radio staff was hindered by the same lack of resources and qualified personnel that plagued the rest of the mission.[44] Howe eventually convinced the UN secretary-general that UNOSOM II needed a radio system, and it finally got into the UN budget,[45] but at a subsequent UN General Assembly budgetary committee meeting, the group declined funding to set it up.[46]

Unable to effectively counter Aidid's radio propaganda campaign with its own, UNOSOM II started to explore other options. Soon thereafter, the US policy adviser to Somalia, Robert Gosende, began asking Montgomery and other UNOSOM II and American officials to shut down Aidid's radio station. On May 21 he cabled State Department and NSC officials, declaring that, "if the US wants to help the UN to implement the Addis Abba accords, it's clear to us that that will only be possible if Aidid is taken off the scene."[47] The culmination of Aidid-UN disagreements produced an antagonistically edgy atmosphere in Mogadishu. It was a flashpoint for potential violence that could be easily be triggered by the slightest provocation on either side.

Montgomery approved verification inspection for the Radio Mogadishu weapons site and, in anticipation of violence, on June 3 he requested additional troops for Somalia. Since the Pakistanis were responsible for southern Mogadishu, where Radio Mogadishu was located, Montgomery ordered them to begin preparations to inspect the site on June 5. UNOSOM II officials gave differing views on whether the weapons inspection was genuine or was merely a cover-up for reconnaissance and subsequent seizure of Radio Mogadishu.[48]

The Pakistani inspection plan, which was developed by UNOSOM II military staff, entailed giving twelve hours' notice of the visit to Aidid's militia at the site.[49] The Pakistanis knew that Aidid feared a UNOSOM II seizure of his radio station, and Pakistani officers recommended to UNOSOM II commanders "that either no notice be given or if given, that no inspection be carried out until the Somali National Alliance's (SNA) reaction was communicated to them."[50] Neither Pakistani request was fulfilled.

During the late afternoon of Friday, June 4, Lieutenant Colonel Kevin McGovern, UNOSOM II deputy chief of intelligence, and Timothy Byrne, chief of the Ceasefire and Disarmament Division, UNOSOM II Force Command, were ordered to deliver a letter from Montgomery to Ambassador Alim, an adviser to Aidid, at Aidid's residence. The letter gave notice of the inspection the following day. Since Alim was not present, McGovern and Byne informed Mohamed Hassan Awale Qaibdid, one of Aidid's closest acquaintances, that the designated weapons site would be inspected on the following day. Qaibdid, a member of Aidid's SNA security council, indicated that the SNA needed time to respond and that if UNOSOM II insisted on conducting the inspections as planned, it would lead to a war.[51]

McGovern noted the objections in a memorandum, which was signed by Colonel Giuseppe Pirotti, the UNOSOM II chief of intelligence, and then delivered it to Montgomery.[52] Howe said that he was never told of the "this is war" response.[53] A subsequent UN report regarding the weapons inspection stated that "UNOSOM II officials decided to proceed with the planned inspections despite the SNA's strong objections because they felt that they had the mandate to use force to execute their tasks and that, therefore, there was no need to discuss or negotiate with SNA on the matter."[54] The notification also took place on the Islamic Sabbath—Friday, which probably led to speculation among Aidid supporters that UNOSOM II was planning to take down the radio station rather than conduct a legitimate weapons inspection.

The following day, Pakistani troops inspected the radio station and were attacked by Aidid loyalists. The Pakistanis fired warning shots but were quickly overwhelmed by enraged Somali mobs who believed the auto-mounted loudspeakers "screaming that the Pakistanis had massacred women and children during the capture of the radio station."[55] Twenty-four Pakistanis were killed and more than fifty-five injured. The Somalis viciously tore apart the bodies of the Pakistanis, some troops were disemboweled or had their eyes gouged out by Somali mobs. In addition, six Pakistani soldiers were taken prisoner. One of them was killed in Somali captivity, and the five others were released to UNOSOM II officials two days later by an official of the SNA. During the fighting, one Italian and three US soldiers were wounded while coming to the aid of the Pakistanis.

The high casualties on one day of fighting forced UNOSOM II to face up to the tremendous stumbling blocks in attempting to disarm Somalia by force.[56] Opportunities for reconciliation between Aidid and UNOSOM II forces were dealt a setback when, early the following morning, Aidid broadcast a pan-Somali message recognizing the citizens who fought the "foreigners," as well as an anti-UN message on Radio Mogadishu.[57]

On June 6, the following day, at the urging of Pakistan's Permanent Representative to the UN Jamsheed Marker, the UNSC met in emergency session and passed Resolution 837, which was drafted primarily by US officials, condemning the attacks on the Pakistani forces and singling out the United Somali Congress (USC) and SNA for using Radio Mogadishu to encourage the attacks. It was passed unanimously; "with little debate and no dissent, the council condemned the assault and called for the apprehension of those responsible."[58] The resolution also upheld UNOSOM II's mandate and the endorsement of retaliatory action against the SNA leadership.[59]

Punishing Aidid and his faction was not a hotly debated question. "It was a relative no-brainer," according to one Clinton official involved in drafting the resolution.[60] According to Albright, the strong punishment language in UNSC Resolution 837 was deliberate in order to protect and sustain ongoing and future UN peacekeeping operations. The UNSC felt "that if UN peacekeepers could be killed with impunity in Somalia, they would become targets everywhere. Aidid's attack was a test of whether UN peacekeeping had indeed entered a new era."[61] Undersecretary of State for Political Affairs Peter Tarnoff supported Aidid's capture and sending US Special Forces to do the mission. "We didn't want to put too much daylight between Howe and us," he said.[62]

Walter Clarke, the deputy chief of mission for the US Embassy in Somalia during Operation Restore Hope, believed that the

> US and UN officials faced the practical consideration that, around the world, thousands of peacekeepers were in vulnerable situations. Failure to act against a direct attack in Somalia, the Clinton Administration felt, would put those forces in jeopardy. Finally, the US and UN decision makers recognized that, given Somali culture, a forceful response was needed to stave off additional attacks.[63]

On the other hand, Joint Chiefs Chairman Powell commented that "this action was taken without any serious discussion among senior US policymakers over expanding the Somalia commitment from nation-building to hunting down Somali chieftains."[64] Central Command (CENTCOM) General Joseph Hoar also opposed attempts to eliminate Aidid because he thought that there was only a 25 percent chance of success and that even if he was removed, his clan members would continue the fight against the UN.[65]

National Security Adviser Lake favored the resolution, but it was not discussed at a gathering of the Principals at the NSC, nor was there opposition among administration officials.[66] Lake recalls that he discussed it with Powell, Christopher, and Aspin and that they all agreed that the UN resolution "should be the response but that we should try to avoid turning this into an us-versus-[Aidid] struggle as we tried to apprehend [Aidid] and his lieutenants—that we shouldn't hype it."[67] A senior Clinton administration official noted that the decision to eliminate Aidid did not include a clear order to kill him, "but the president knew that if something fell on [Aidid] and killed him, no tears would be shed."[68]

This is the kind of decision that normally would require the NSC to closely examine what happened and consider whether to support a different level of commitment. According to Howe, such consideration "would be a time when you could've recorded what was needed, for example rebuilding, police, etc. So what do you do? We did it half-way again. Just not make a quick decision. You just don't drop the ball and then go back to business as usual."[69]

As a result of the June 5 violence and the passage of UNSC Resolution 837 to bring Aidid to justice, Mogadishu became a tense battleground between the UN and Aidid's SNA armed forces. For the first month Aidid restricted his militia's attacks, and UNOSOM II forces took the offensive. Howe focused the UNOSOM II mission on three objectives over the next few hectic days. First, he moved a majority of the UNOSOM II civilian staff to Kenya and bunkered down the remaining personnel in the UN military compound. UNOSOM II military patrols became less aggressive and were in force-protection mode. As a result, they did not garner as much constructive and effective street intelligence because UNOSOM II soldiers in armored vehicles weren't chatting as much with Somalis on Mogadishu streets.

Second, he wrote letters to Aidid and other Somali leaders urging them to comply with UNSC Resolution 837. On June 8 Howe sent Aidid a letter reminding "him, *inter-alia*, of the prohibition against the display of weapons and the requirement to cooperate fully with the disarmament programme in Mogadishu."[70] He also sent a letter to chairmen of the eleven other Somali political factions giving notice "that no group or individual should seek to take advantage of the current tension in Mogadishu."[71]

Finally, Howe and UNOSOM II officials requested more US military equipment and trained forces to help with implementing UNSC Resolution 837 to capture Aidid. The day after the "Pakistani massacre," Howe started asking for greater US military assistance to augment UNOSOM II forces in order to take Aidid. He realized that UNOSOM II did not have the intelligence mechanisms for pinpointing Aidid's location or the trained professionals necessary to make an arrest while minimizing the risk to Somalis and UN troops involved.[72]

UN Undersecretary for Peacekeeping Kofi Annan called Howe to ask him to compile a list of ten things he wanted because Boutros-Ghali was going to meet with Secretary of State Warren Christopher in Paris on June 8 or 9. After conferring with Montgomery and Bir, Howe wrote a list that included attack helicopters, armored personnel carriers, tanks for the Pakistanis, and specially trained forces.[73] Boutros-Ghali then presented the list to Christopher.

Howe wanted American Special Forces because they were a small force capable of arresting Aidid and his officers without killing lots of Somalis.[74] From the beginning, the Pentagon tried to prevent the effort to use US Special Operations Forces for this purpose. On June 9 US Defense Secretary Aspin rejected Howe's request for a team of commandos to get Aidid. The Pentagon opposed the request because it felt that fulfilling it would create a slippery slope of intensified US involvement. Also, according to a Pentagon staffer involved with the Somalia mission and Special Forces, the request was opposed because it was a

> looking for Elvis mission. . . . Every year, US police depart-
> ments receive on average 25,000 calls of live sightings of Elvis.
> We don't have human intelligence to find Third World yahoos.
> The US military's dilemma in these kinds of missions are, if
> we're successful, we capture or kill a Third World yahoo, and
> then he becomes a hero. If we're unsuccessful in capturing or
> killing him, he becomes a bigger hero. He becomes invisible,
> and enters into lore. We essentially aggrandize these guys
> beyond what they deserve.[75]

Howe's requests had more backing from UNOSOM II and American officials in Somalia than at the Pentagon and administration. Howe personally pushed on his request for Special Forces through his Washington, DC, contacts, including accessing his Navy links at the Pentagon and connections at the NSC, where he still had friends.[76] As Scowcroft's deputy national security adviser, Howe knew the inner workings of the US security agencies, especially the NSC and Defense Department. He was also a retired US Navy admiral and could get attention and action. Howe knew what form his requests should take. According to Richard Clarke, who was at the NSC during the time and working the Somalia portfolio,

> Howe was asking everyone to help provide stuff to him in
> Somalia and to do things in support of that mission. He was
> going to NSC rather than up and down. It would have been
> hard for someone else to do same thing, based on Howe's
> knowledge and NSC connections.[77]

Under continually increasing pressure from UN and US administration officials, as well as from Montgomery, who was both the commander of US forces in Somalia and the deputy United Nations commander, the leadership in the Pentagon yielded and reluctantly recommended deployment of Special Forces.[78] Powell supported Howe's requests based on what he had learned from his Vietnam experiences, but he also questioned the package requested by Montgomery.

> [He] asked for US helicopter gunships and AC-130 strike planes to attack Somali strongholds. . . . I supported the request, and the president approved. But when the UN command further pressed us to send in our elite counterterrorist Delta Fore to capture Aidid, I resisted, as did Aspin and Hoar. Finding Aidid in the warrens of Mogadishu was a thousand-to-one shot. Worse, we were personalizing the conflict and getting deeper and deeper into ancient Somali clan rivalries. I tried to get our spreading commitment reviewed, but was unsuccessful.[79]

Although it was not announced publicly, a group of Army Rangers and Delta Force were ordered to begin training for a mission in Somalia the day after the Pakistani ambush and on the same day that UNSC Resolution 813 passed.[80] In the early morning hours of June 12, the first UNOSOM II military action since UNSC Resolution 837 occurred. Recently arrived American AC-130 gunships destroyed several Aidid facilities, including his radio station and selected SNA weapons and ammunition sites that were investigated June 5. UNOSOM II gave the Pakistanis "the task of dismantling the largest site and did so very effectively, so that "by late afternoon this well-executed first military initiative had been successfully completed."[81]

The following morning, Aidid loyalists staged a protest in front of a UN checkpoint manned by Pakistanis near a Mogadishu hotel where many international media stayed. The protesters marched toward the UN position nearly engulfing the Pakistanis, who, fearing for their safety in light of the ambush the week before, responded with gunfire that killed Somali civilians, including women. Witnesses stated that armed Somalis nearby fired into the crowd, confirming that it was a carefully staged incident calculated to create casualties before the world press and try to weaken the UN's effectiveness in dealing with organized mobs in the future.[82] In addition, women and children were used by Aidid's forces "as human shields to screen attacks on UNOSOM II fixed guard spots and strong points."[83] Some of the civilians were also paid or threatened by Aidid "to participate in 'rent-a-crowds' that would cover his militiamen."[84]

An angry Howe called Aidid a "murderer" and announced a reward of $25,000 for information leading to his capture. According to Howe, "We thought it important at that juncture for the Somali people, and especially his own sub-clan, to realize that the UN did not consider him to have a political future in Somalia unless he was first cleared through a judicial process."[85]

Although the Aidid arrest and reward edict was cleared by UN headquarters, it caught Defense Department officials by surprise, but there was little they could do.[86] Posters proclaiming "WANTED Aidid for REWARD of $25,000" were displayed in Mogadishu, whereas in southern Mogadishu posters and T-shirts proclaiming Aidid as president were everywhere, but it seemed his popularity was regionally limited at this time.

UNOSOM II made its next raid on Aidid's headquarters complex, resulting in another lethal fight between Aidid and UNOSOM II forces. Before the raid the Aidid enclave was cordoned off before sunrise by Moroccan and Italian forces. Then Pakistani forces carried out the weapons search while French troops were held in reserve. The Moroccan forces came under intense fire by Somalis trying to block the UNOSOM II search and had to be rescued by the French. After five of their soldiers were killed, the Moroccans complained that they lacked accurate intelligence about the composition and strength of Aidid's forces, the element of surprise was lost because of several rehearsals conducted nearby, and the vulnerable location of the cordon contributed to the high casualties.[87] As a result, UNOSOM II never again carried out any multinational search operations of this magnitude.[88]

The fighting that started June 12 was to be the first of eight firefights resulting from UNOSOM II attempts to capture Aidid over the next four months. Two days later Boutros-Ghali asked the US government to deploy to Somalia, "on an urgent basis," Special Forces specialists to track and capture Aidid and "a Marine Amphibious force capable of rapidly deploying air and ground forces."[89] In early October, after a bloody firefight between Aidid and US forces—known subsequently as the Black Hawk Down battle—resulted in hundreds of casualties on both sides, Aidid declared a unilateral cease-fire and President Clinton called off the raids and ordered the US military to engineer a stunning withdrawal of US forces from Somalia.

The UNOSOM II staff was overwhelmed by mutually reinforcing problems of sequencing political reconciliation and development. For example, "a police force could not function without a judicial system, which in turn could not function without a secure environment guaranteed by a police force."[90] As the humanitarian situation stabilized, Aidid took an increasingly tougher stance against UNOSOM II, whose leaders did not believe or realize Aidid's attempts to derail the process would be successful.

Notes

1. David Bowne Wood, *A Sense of Values: American Marines in an Uncertain World* (Kansas City: Andrews and McMeel, 1994), 191.

2. State Department official involved in UNITAF and UNOSOM II planning and implementation, interview with author. Conducted in confidentiality, and the name withheld by mutual agreement. Washington, DC, July 6, 2004.

3. US Department of Defense official involved in UNITAF planning and implementation, interview with author. Conducted in confidentiality, and the name withheld by mutual agreement. May 30, 2004.

4. Admiral Jonathan Howe (deputy assistant to the president for national security affairs 1991–1992; special representative for Somalia to UN Secretary-General Boutros Boutros-Ghali, March 1993–February 1994), interview with author. Jacksonville, FL, December 28, 2005.

5. Ambassador Robert Oakley (ambassador to Somalia, 1982–1984; special envoy to Somalia for President Bush, December 1992–March 1993, and special envoy to Somalia for President Clinton, October 1993–March 1994), interview with author, Washington, DC, May 29, 2003.

6. Howe, interview.

7. Data on troop pledges were supplied by the Office of Regional Affairs, Bureau of African Affairs, US Department of State, as quoted in Herman J. Cohen, "Intervention in Somalia," in *The Diplomatic Record: 1992–1993*, ed. Allan Goodman (Boulder, CO: Westview Press, 1995), 74, fn. 60.

8. Jonathan T. Howe, "Relations Between the United States and United Nations in Dealing with Somalia," in *Learning From Somalia: The Lessons of Armed Humanitarian Intervention*, ed. Walter Clarke and Jeffrey Herbst (Boulder, CO: Westview Press, 1997), 164.

9. Howe, interview.

10. UN Department of Peace-keeping Operations, Lessons Learned Unit," report of the seminar (June 19–20, 1995, New York) Lessons Learned from the United Nations Operation in Somalia at the Strategic and Operational Levels, August 1995.

11. Howe, interview.

12. Ibid.

13. As a trivial example, when Howe arrived in Mogadishu the only office telephone was on his desk, but it could not be answered by his secretary, "who was in the other room out of sight." Howe, "Relations Between the United States and United Nations," 163.

14. Under UNITAF, US air operations could conduct surprise flights over Mogadishu. In contrast, when UNOSOM II aircraft did attack, it led to massive collateral damage, which lowered Somali public support for the mission. Major Eric F. Buer, USMC, "United Task Force Somalia (UNITAF) and United Nations Operations Somalia (UNOSOM II): A Comparative Analysis of Offensive Air Support," Master Thesis, United States Marine Corps, Command and Staff College, AY 2000–2001, 32.

15. Ibid., 32–33.

16. Addis Ababa Agreement of the First Session of the Conference on National Reconciliation in Somalia.

17. Commission report S/1994/653, 16–17.

18. John G. Sommer, *Hope Restored? Humanitarian Aid in Somalia: 1990–1994* (Washington, DC: Refugee Policy Group, 1994), B-4.

19. When they did get home, there was big celebration at the White House, which made Howe feel that UNITAF commanders defined victory by getting out, not getting the job done. Howe, interview.

20. Ibid.

21. Howe, "Relations Between the United States and United Nations," 164–165.

22. Howe, interview.

23. Tom Clancy with General Tony Zinni (Ret.) and Tony Koltz, *Battle Ready*, (New York: G.P. Putnam's Sons, 2004), 270.

24. Wood, *A Sense of Values*, 195; Yossef Bodansky, *Bin Laden: The Man Who Declared War on America* (New York: Forum, 1999), 83.

25. Ambassador David Shinn (State Department deputy director of the Somali Task Force), interview with author, Washington, DC, April 8, 2004.

26. Ambassador Robert Gosende (President Clinton's special envoy to Somalia, 1993; public affairs officer for President Bush's special envoy to Somalia, Ambassador Robert Oakley, 1993–1994), interview with author, New York, October 22, 2007.

27. Ibid.

28. George Fredrick (State Department political officer in Somalia, February 1993–July 1994), interview with author. Washington, DC, May 30, 2003.

29. Commission Report, S/1994/653, Page 18.

30. Shinn, interview.

31. Hussein Adam, professor of political science, Holy Cross College, testimony at a hearing on "The Recent Developments in Somalia"

before the Subcommittee on Africa of the Committee on Foreign Affairs, House of Representatives, February 17, 1993.

32. Commission Report S/1994/653, 18–19.

33. Attending Aidid's conference in Galyco were leaders from the Somali National Alliance (SNA), Somali National Front (SNF), Somali Salvation Democratic Front (SSDF) and Somali National Democratic Union (SNDU).

34. Patrick J. Sloyan, "The Secret Path to a Bloodbath: How US Policy in Somalia went from bad to worse," *The Washington Post National Weekly Edition*, April 18–24, 1994, 24.

35. Commission Report S/1994/653, 17.

36. Howe, interview.

37. Commission Report (S/1994/653) 17.

38. Confidential memorandum, secretary of state to secretary of defense, US Information Agency and other US embassies and missions, "Threat Against AMCITS in Somalia," May 1992.

39. Commission Report S/1994/653, 20.

40. Confidential memorandum, secretary of state to US Mission at the UN. "Somalia Policy on Aidid and SNA," June 1993.

41. Further report of the SG submitted in pursuance of paragraph 19 of resolution 814 (1993) and paragraph A 5 of Resolution 865 (1993), 10/12/93 SG report S/26738 9.

42. Howe, interview.

43. Ibid.

44. When UNITAF departed, the Americans took their very effective PSYOP (psychological operations) units with them.

45. Howe, interview.

46. UN Department of Peace-keeping Operations, Lessons Learned Unit, "Report of the seminar." Howe found out later at a February 1994 UN meeting in New York that the Americans vetoed it. Howe, interview.

47. Susan Rosegrant, "B 'Seamless' Transition: United States and United Nations Operations in Somalia–1992–1993," Kennedy School of Government Case Program (Cambridge, MA: President and Fellows of Harvard College, 1996), 5.

48. Commission Report S/1994/653, 22.

49. Ibid., 21.

50. Ibid., 22.

51. Ibid., 23; UN Secretary-General Boutros Boutros-Ghali Report on the 5 June 1993 Attack on UN forces in Somalia. 5. August 24, 1993. S/26351.

52. Commission Report S/1994/653, 23.

53. Quoted in Sommer, *Hope Restored?*, 40.

54. Commission Report S/1994/653.

55. Helen Fogarassy, *Mission Improbable: The World Community on a UN Compound in Somalia* (Lanham, MD: Lexington Books, 1999), 47.

56. Commissioner's Report, S/1994/53, 24.

57. Report of the Secretary General on the Implementation of UN Security Council Resolution 837 (1993). S/26022, July 1, 1993. 4.

58. Madeleine Albright, *Madam Secretary*, (New York: Miramax Books, 2003), 143.

59. Commissioner's Report, S/1994/53. 25.

60. Author interview, former Clinton NSC official, Washington, DC, July 6, 2004.

61. Albright, *Madam Secretary*, 143.

62. Elizabeth Drew, *On The Edge: The Clinton Presidency*, (New York: Simon & Schuster, 1994), 321.

63. Walter Clarke and Jeffrey Herbst in "Somalia and the Future of Humanitarian Intervention," *Foreign Affairs,* vol. 75, no. 2 (March/April 1996): 80.

64. Powell, *My American Journey*, 584.

65. Sloyan, "The Secret Path," 24.

66. Drew, *On The Edge,* 319–320.

67. Ibid., 320.

68. Sloyan, "The Secret Path," 24.

69. Howe, interview.

70. UN Secretary-General Boutros Boutros-Ghali, report on the Implementation of UN Security Council Resolution 837 (1993), July 1, 1993. S/26022.

71. Ibid.

72. Howe, "Relations Between the United States and United Nations," 169.

73. Howe, interview.

74. Ibid.

75. Department of Defense official, interview.

76. Clarke, interview; Sloyan, "The Secret Path," 24.

77. Clarke, interview.

78. Montgomery interview, quoted in Warner-Levin, 24.

79. Powell, *My American Journey,* 584.

80. Quoted in US Senate, Committee on Armed Services, US Military Operations in Somalia, testimony of Major General William Garrison, Commander, US Joint Special Operations Command, 103rd Congress, 29th session, S Hr 103-84, May 12, 1994, 2.

81. Howe, "Relations Between the United States and United Nations," 169.

82. UN Secretary-General Boutros Boutros-Ghali Report on the Implementation of UN Security Council Resolution 837 (1993), July 1, 1993. S/26022.

83. Ibid., 6; Norman L. Cooling, "Operation Restore Hope in Somalia: A Tactical Action Turned Strategic Defeat," *Marine Corps Gazette*, September 2001, 97.

84. Cooling, "Operation Restore Hope in Somalia," 97.

85. Howe, "Relations Between the United States and United Nations," 171.

86. Senators John Warner (R-Va) and Carl Levin, (D-Mich), *Warner-Levin Report* "Review of the Circumstances Surrounding the Ranger Raid on October 3–4, 1993 in Mogadishu, Somalia," United States Senate Committee on Armed Services, October 2, 1995, 23.

87. The nationality of the five dead are in some dispute. A State Department official involved with the Somalia policy at that time, thinks that Aidid's forces killed one Pakistani and four Moroccan soldiers, including the Moroccan force commander. Woods, 162.

88. Commissioner's report, S/1994/53, 28.

89. Confidential memorandum, secretary of state to USLO Mogadishu, "UN Secretary-General Requests Logistical Support from US," June 1993.

90. UN Department of Peace-keeping Operations, Lessons Learned Unit, "Report of the seminar," 11.

CHAPTER SIX

THE MISSION FALLS APART

The UN faced several challenges in overcoming Aidid's intransigence. First, the UN Operation in Somalia (UNOSOM) II mission did not have the same psychological assets and capability that the United Task Force (UNITAF) had to counter Aidid's propaganda, whose anti-UN rhetoric became reality for many Somalis. Second, UNOSOM II military operations were hindered by its careful planning to avoid civilian casualties and property damage. In many cases, UNOSOM II staff warned civilians of an impending military action in order to allow evacuation. Although this humanitarian-inspired policy was good for Somali citizens, it hurt the UN's military operations by exposing troops to greater risk. As a result, UN military personnel reduced coordination and communication with civilian personnel regarding attack planning. The communication breakdown eventually caused dissension and confusion among UN officials because one group did not know what the other group was doing.

A third challenge for UN military force planning was the lack of a Somalia government with which to coordinate actions or engage in international relations. Instead, UNOSOM II forces were required to seek consent from multiple competing militias and individual Somali leaders, which slowed down the implementation process.

The biggest challenge for the UN was a weak unity of command system. The UN military leaders directed a wide assortment of international troops that mostly consulted with their own governments before deciding whether to follow the UNOSOM II commander's orders. According to the UN's after-mission report,

> Some contingents that were ostensibly part of UNOSOM were in fact following orders from their respective capitals; this made them unreliable in the mission area and reduced the mission's effectiveness. . . . A fundamental cause of the failure of

UNOSOM II's coalition force to maintain a secure environment in Mogadishu after the departure of UNITAF was the failure of individual contingents to respond consistently to the direction of the Force Commander except where that direction fitted national imperatives and agendas.[1]

Many times troops were hesitant to back forces from another country or strengthen another area, which led to increased tensions among national officers and UNOSOM II military and political leaders. Kofi Annan, UN undersecretary for peacekeeping operations, remarked about the UNOSOM II military forces, "I have wondered if we are one force, or even a friendly force, willing to go to the aid of one another when attacked."[2]

Lacking unity, the UNSOSOM II troops were putting themselves at greater than necessary danger while at the same time putting missions at risk. For example, in early May a Belgian commander, believing that he was outgunned and outmanned and whose troops had to engage a large Somali militia force in the dangerous Kismayu region, requested US quick-reaction forces to help maintain security. His request was turned down by American officials based in the United States, who said that the assigned Quick Reaction Force (QRF) mission would only allow deployment for emergencies.[3] The main point is that UNOSOM II military officers, including its American deputy commander, Thomas Montgomery, did not have command over the QRF forces. As a result, the Belgian forces became less aggressive in maintaining security and effectively removed themselves from the UNOSOM II chain of command.[4] In other cases, Zimbabwe troops refused the UNOSOM II commander's orders to be deployed to Mogadishu because of "uncertainty and violence of the capital," Indian forces refused to operate near Pakistani troops,[5] French forces refused UNOSOM II orders to transfer troops from Baidoa to Mogadishu,[6] Saudi Arabian forces refused to follow UNOSOM II orders without first clearing them with Riyadh,[7] and Egyptian soldiers contributed to UNOSOM II's military inefficiency by accepting bribes from Somalis to fake resistance while thievery occurred under their guard.[8]

The Italian troops were also uncooperative with UNOSOM II commanders' wishes on some key missions. Certain UNOSOM II forces alleged that that Italians were paying and bribing Somalis and thus were partially responsible for stymieing UNOSOM II's efforts to capture Aidid.[9] UNOSOM II commanders wanted to teach Aidid and the Somali National Alliance (SNA) a lesson, but the Italians' actions of breaking off from UNOSOM II command and control boosted SNA morale and further complicated apprehending Aidid.[10] Italian troops also conducted unilateral actions that highlighted possible incongruities between Italian and US or UN political objectives.[11]

The performance of Italian troops is particularly important because, as the former colonial power in southern Somalia, Italy was looked to for leadership by many Somalis. On June 22 a decisive change in UNOSOM II and Italian relations occurred when a US quick-reaction-force sweep of an SNA weapons site in an Italian-controlled sector of Mogadishu generated Italian anger. The Italian commander, General Bruno Loi, was incensed because the operation took place without his permission and also because an Italian newspaper reported that the mission was actually an attempt to catch Aidid.[12]

A diplomatic storm erupted when the Italians lodged protests with UNOSOM II officials in Mogadishu that the operation was done without prior consultation.[13] "In no democratic country," the Italian ambassador to the UN said, "could parliamentary and public opinion accept heavy casualties in operations carried out without its own participation in the planning."[14] The Italians also protested at UN Headquarters and with State Department officials in Washington, DC. The State Department responded that the only weapons used were smoke grenades to disperse an unruly crowd of Somalis and, more importantly, that "the UNOSOM II force commander informed the Italian liaison officer of the mission of the US forces."[15]

The operation itself was launched from a Navy ship, the USS Wasp, off Mogadishu's shore with troop helicopters and Cobra gunships. The mission was to catch Aidid. According to the Marines on the ship, it was a "flawless mission," but the target escaped.[16] Nevertheless, as a result of the Italian diplomatic protests, the Marine snatch team was never used again in Somalia. Later, when asked why the Marines had been removed from the hunt for Aidid, the Joint Chiefs authorized a spokesman to convey this answer: "What you saw happen, did not take place."[17]

The day after the attempted Aidid snatch, June 23, 1993, the Senate approved a $1.2 billion supplemental appropriation for the Defense Department, of which $750 million was for Somalia.[18] At the same time, Undersecretary of Defense for Policy Frank Wisner was warning Aspin that the failure of the UN in Somalia would hurt US national interests.[19] Thus, by early July, Joseph Hoar, Commander in Chief, U.S. Central Command (CENTCOM), believed that US policy was to catch or kill Aidid.[20]

In early July US Ambassador to the UN Albright and Rick Inderfuerth, who was the US representative for special political affairs to the UN, visited Mogadishu and Kismayo. In Kismayo they met with local clan leaders, who Albright believed were "eager to organize themselves and resume normal economic activity" and "fully backed measures to eliminate or marginalize Aidid."[21] In Mogadishu, Albright and Inderfuerth met with UNOSOM II officials, including Howe, who told Albright that he was frustrated with the non-American UNOSOM II troops' "lack of functioning coherently" and asked Albright to pressure the Department of Defense (DOD) for more troops.[22] Albright thought that the transition was going well except for the Mogadishu area, so she agreed to carry Howe's request back to Washington, DC.[23]

Meanwhile, Boutros-Ghali called Aidid an enemy of the UN in his July 1 report to the Security Council. He said that Islamic fundamentalist fighters were supporting Somali factions opposed to the UN because they considered it a "foreign force" in Somalia.[24] In the following weeks, Howe noticed more capability in Aidid's forces, including trainers and weapons. Although he had no evidence, Howe thought some of the trainers were al-Qaida operatives who trained Aidid's forces to mine roads and bring down Black Hawk helicopters.[25] The US Special Envoy to Somalia, Robert Gosende, also noted that "from February to March 1993, Aidid was out of country in Libya and Sudan, where he was meeting with Saudis, so Bid Laden's [Al Qaida leader] current claims about Al Qaida fighting the US in Somalia are not entirely opportunistic."[26] By August 10, 1993, US Army helicopters flying over Mogadishu were coming under fire more frequently.[27] During that period UNOSOM II intelligence gathering was considered corrupted and inadequate.[28]

Recognizing his vulnerability to the US military helicopters, Aidid had "brought in some fundamentalist Islamic soldiers from Sudan who had experience downing Russian helicopters in Afghanistan to train his men in RPG [rocket propelled grenade] firing techniques."[29] Iranian and Sudanese Islamic fundamentalist interests also supported Aidid as part of a long-term Islamic International plan to use "all the Islamic forces, in a major operation intended to transform Mogadishu into a 'second Kabul' or a 'second Beirut' for the Americans."[30] Foreign Islamists also considered the UN an enemy as it was headed by Boutros-Ghali, an Egyptian Coptic Christian, whom they considered as partial to the United States.[31]

In a series of July meetings in Washington and Rome, the Italians expressed their dissatisfaction with the increasingly aggressive nature of UNOSOM II operations in Mogadishu and their desire to appoint an Italian officer to a senior military position in UNOSOM.[32] Italian Ambassador Biancheri said that he was being pressured by the Italian government, which in turn was being pressured by Italian domestic public opinion and Italian military, especially after the deaths of three Italian soldiers in Mogadishu, where they were conducting a house-to-house weapons search.[33] The Italians believed that Aidid's support among

Somalis was increasing rather than waning, whereas the United States expressed hope that the Italian forces in Somalia would cooperate more fully with UNOSOM II commanders.[34] Also, the Italian government wanted more political options emphasized in relations with Aidid rather than solely focusing on military tactics. Clinton did not agree. At a July 4 luncheon with reporters at the White House, Clinton remarked about Aidid that "he'll continue to cause problems until and unless we arrest him."[35]

On July 7 six UN Somali employees hired to deliver the UNOSOM II newspaper *Maanta* around Mogadishu were killed.[36] Their deaths effectively put a halt to the distribution *Maanta* and instilled fear in other UN Somali employees working at Radio Maanta. Further death threats forced UNOSOM II to consider alternative ways of combating Aidid's propaganda war, including Somali contractors to deliver the news, some of whom were based in southern Mogadishu and loyal to Aidid.

After being ordered by the UNOSOM II commander on July 9 to occupy Point 42 in SNA-controlled downtown Mogadishu, Italian military officials negotiated with SNA officials. The following day, the Italians peacefully occupied the position, which led some UNOSOM II officials to believe that the Italians had cut a deal with Aidid rather than take the risk of possible military action.[37]

On the same day that the Italians retook Point 42, Howe met with Somali elders to discuss reconciliation attempts. Many of the Somali elders who met with Howe died three days later, on July 12, when US forces launched Operation Michigan, which destroyed the compound where they were meeting. The attack occurred without warning and in reaction to SNA violent attacks on UNOSOM II personnel, especially the UN Somali staff distributing the *Maanta* paper. Operation Michigan was intended to eliminate the SNA command and its occupants. Rather than Aidid's forces, the compound is reported to have been hosting a meeting of "Habre Gedir clan elders at the house of one of Aidid's lieutenants," who were discussing ways to resolve the Aidid-UNOSOM II conflict.[38] Ironically, one of the purposes of the attack was to compel Aidid to participate in peace discussions with UNOSOM II.

The attack resulted in a large number of Somali casualties. Immediately after the attack, four foreign journalists arrived to cover the story but were chased by enraged Somali mobs. Three were stoned and hacked to death. From the date of this attack, the SNA closed its ranks and many Somalis stopped giving information to UNOSOM II, which became more cautious in its operations. The SNA increased both the number and aggressiveness of its attacks over the next three months, whereas UNOSOM II forces became increasingly bunkered down, limiting their operations to "a few search-and-sweep operations conducted mainly by the QRF."[39] It carried out a string of ambushes that employed varied methods against UN personnel and vehicles that branched out around Mogadishu. The SNA also released a statement to the international media claiming, among other things, that UNOSOM II troops "imprison and torture innocent civilians and rape both male and female citizens," and that "America deployed a force of homosexuals in Somalia."[40]

Boutros-Ghali's UNOSOM II mission and Aidid's SNA forces were now at war. The problem was that UN Security Council (UNSC) Resolution 837 required arresting Aidid, which foreclosed political reconciliation avenues. A senior UN official said, "We can't talk to him, because he's a wanted man. We dare not go after him until the city is awash with troops, because of the backlash. And we can't beat him, because urban guerilla wars are unwinnable."[41] It might have also violated international law, thus giving Aidid an international legal recourse to fight UN forces. According to the UN report written one year later concerning the Somali fighting,

> the US QRF and later the ranger operation, all of which had connotations of war, were not under UNOSOM's control. If these operations were not under UNOSOM II, the question arises as to whether they were authorized by the UN. If they were not, then the SNA's right to defend itself was even more appropriate, and hence the evolution of the entire situation into a war.[42]

Congress became increasingly concerned about US military forces in Somalia after reading reports about Operation Michigan and the casualties caused. Senator Robert Byrd, a West Virginia Democrat, took the opportunity to persist in his objections to keeping US forces in Somalia. Besides having reservations about US involvement in Somalia, he also believed that the costs were too high.[43] One week later, on July 27, Congressman Sherrod Brown, an Ohio Democrat, introduced Resolution 227, urging US armed forces to be withdrawn from Somalia as quickly as possible.[44]

Despite Byrd's opposition, there was strong bipartisan Senate support for a continued US military presence in Somalia. For example, on July 16, Paul Simon of Illinois quickly responded to Byrd's opposition by taking the Senate floor and defending the mission, saying that it would be unfair to the twenty-two-nation coalition for the United States to pull its troops out.[45]

Also the State Department Somalia coordinator lead a ten-member interagency assessment team to Somalia on July 20–27 that concluded that UNOSOM II was making considerable progress but that "Aidid's campaign of urban guerrilla warfare is putting the entire mission at risk."[46]

On August 6 David Shinn, the State Department deputy director of the Somalia Task Force, and some members of the US interagency assessment team on Somalia briefed Senior UN officials. The team noted that except for Mogadishu, which is the "one setback for UNOSOM," "remarkable progress" had been made throughout the country since UNOSOM II had taken over the mission.[47]

Two days later, on August 8 four American military personnel were killed in their Humvee by a landmine detonated by Somalis. A British reporter who witnessed the aftermath of the accident wrote, "Such was the force of the explosion that by the time correspondents arrived, youths gathering at the scene had only bits of flesh and burned combat fatigues to hold up for the cameras. I remember how one youth picked up a strip of bloodied meat from the dust and ripped at it with his teeth."[48]

As a result of the mine casualties, Howe and Montgomery again asked the Clinton administration for more military help. Foot dragging in Washington, DC, concerning Somalia policy came to an abrupt halt in light of the deaths and took a dramatic turn toward more assertive military action, including the sending of more armed assets.[49] The Defense Department, which had held out on sending Special Operations units to Somalia, changed its position. Immediately after the killings, staff at the Joint Chiefs sent a recommendation for sending Special Forces to Powell.[50] The staff was concerned with the sophistication of the attack and the possibility of future casualties if something was not done. During a visit to Washington, DC, on August 9–11, General Hoar suggested that the administration reconsider the idea of trying to get Aidid.[51]

Meanwhile, Undersecretary Wisner realized that more American deaths were likely if Aidid was not quickly neutralized. He thought that the United States should deploy American Special Operations Forces immediately to Somalia because it was "the least objectionable of a series of options."[52] Wisner also thought that Hoar, despite suggesting the Aidid search should cease a few weeks previously, "was in favor of the deployment, or at least, had acquiesced in it."[53]

After the killing of the four Americans by the remote-controlled mine, the administration also sent a working-level interagency team, headed by Shinn, to Somalia to review how people were being killed on a humanitarian mission, which, intuitively, is not supposed to happen.[54] On August 19 Shinn submitted his report, which carried Howe's and Montgomery's request that US Special Operations be included in any subsequent reinforcement package.[55] Shinn's report also noted that UNOSOM II commanders had "an insufficient military presence in south Mogadishu to maintain order and arrest [Aidid]."[56]

Specifically, the interagency assessment team recommended that "the US should provide additional special operations forces to enhance QR direct action urban warfare capability . . . until [Aidid] is captured."[57] Shinn also conveyed an Ethiopian government official's suggestion that the best way "to deal with the [Aidid] problem, one has to gather friends of Aidid to encourage him to exile."[58] The interagency assessment team reported that there was an Ethiopian and Eritrean initiative to place Aidid under house arrest in a third country.[59] On August 21 Shinn briefed Powell and relayed the reinforcement request from Howe and Montgomery. According to Powell, after the Shinn briefing and a push by General McCaffrey, "who had a representative on the Shinn team that recently returned from Somalia," and "since Garrison, Montgomery, the UN and Shinn all are pushing us to do this," he said, "I will go along since as a general principle, I believe in supporting the Commander in the field."[60]

Besides the Special Forces request, Montgomery also asked US Central Command (CENTCOM) for tanks, Bradley Fighting Vehicles, mine-removal equipment, more helicopters, and additional troop support. One of the main reasons for his mechanized vehicle request is that Montgomery was increasingly concerned about remote-controlled mines. Ambassador Gosende, the US special envoy to Somalia, supported the appeal for reinforcements by writing a compendium to Montgomery's cable for the tanks, Bradley Armored Personnel Carriers, and other resources. He believed that it was only a matter of time before a US helicopter would be shot down and when that happened "we're in trouble because we don't have a fire department to rescue helicopters if downed."[61] Montgomery and Howe also knew that the chances for a helicopter being successfully taken down were increasing, especially "since they could see Somalis practicing on how to shoot recoilless rifles, standing on walls so the RPB burn does not go to their butt."[62]

Undersecretary of Defense for Policy Frank Wisner responded to Gosende's cable by informing him that he "never wanted to see another message like that from your embassy." Gosende asked, "You're telling me not to report?" and Wisner replied, "You've stuck yourself in military business." Gosende's response was that "this isn't a military operation. It is a military-political operation and that is why I sent that message. There is political background to Montgomery's report and request."[63] During a brief visit to Somalia, where he met with Gosende, the CENTCOM Commander General Hoar also told Gosende to keep his "nose out of military business."[64]

Montgomery modified his request after Hoar told him it was too large, but except for some additional combat engineers, the request, which went all the way to Aspin, was never approved.[65]

On August 22, six American servicemen were injured by a remote-controlled mine in Mogadishu, the second mine attack on American forces in Mogadishu in two weeks. On his first vacation since becoming president, Clinton had just finished golfing on Martha's Vineyard when he was informed of the casualties. Clinton and National Security Adviser Lake decided that the time had come to send Special Forces. According to Howe, Clinton approved the sending of Special Forces in late August as a result of the American mine deaths.[66] Lake remembers a Powell call "on the weekend saying that he saw no alternative to sending Delta Force . . . and I also said that I didn't like it but agreed."[67] Lake thought that "we would be dammed if we did and we certainly would be dammed if we didn't."[68]

The mine attacks and Shinn's report, which argued that "security is unlikely to improve dramatically while he [Aidid] remains on the scene," helped change the Department of Defense's mind on sending Special Operations Forces to Somalia.[69] Powell told President Clinton "we have to do something or we are going to be nibbled to death."[70] The mission took more of a political focus after Shinn's report. According to Aspin, he and others at the Defense Department

> were being influenced by command control mines killing Americans. I was on vacation in Wisconsin and received a telephone call from Powell on Sunday, August 21. He said that he had had a long discussion with General Hoar and thought that we ought to deploy Special Ops forces for this mission. I said OK. I thought General Hoar had changed his mind. General Powell and I did.[71]

Powell did in fact support the Special Forces request in light of the mine attack.

> We started to take American casualties. In late August, I reluctantly yielded to the repeated requests from the field and recommended to Aspin that we dispatch the Rangers and the Delta Force. It was a recommendation I would later regret.[72]

The US informed an appreciative Boutros-Ghali that it would soon send the Special Forces that Howe and Montgomery had originally requested in early June. On August 21 Powell called Hoar and said, "It is a go." Hoar later said Powell had lots of pressure from Boutros-Ghali,

Montgomery, and Howe, whereas Powell said that people involved in the decision included Aspin, Wisner, and Lake.[73]

Aspin might have been more receptive to the US field military commanders' request for more equipment had his domestic worries over reforming the Department of Defense not intensified in the last days of May and June—which also was when some of his key appointments were just coming into office after their unusually late confirmations.

Interestingly, American officials came to another conclusion in late August: The US Somali policy needed a new direction and it should be to engage Aidid politically. Wisner says that "the single most serious flaw in our policy was that we tried to accomplish political objectives solely by military means"; Oakley had previously reached the same conclusion independently.[74]

The policy to approach Aidid politically rather than militarily started July 21 when Italian Ambassador Biancheri met with the State Department's Peter Tarnoff to stress the importance of the political process in Somalia. He said the "UN's efforts in Somalia are important for future peacekeeping missions elsewhere and how the UN responds to new challenges."[75]

On August 17 Boutros-Ghali sent another report to the UNSC that stressed increased disarmament efforts and highlighted his goal of controlling south Mogadishu and targeting Aidid because he was responsible for the violence and loss of life.[76] He said that "there are reliable indications that increased activity by UNOSOM forces is having an effect on the United Somali Congress/Somali National Alliance militia operations in south Mogadishu" and therefore instructed UNOSOM II "to maintain a forceful disarmament programme in South Mogadishu as long as resistance continues. More active patrolling, weapons confiscations, and operations against USC [United Somali Congress] /SNA militia depots have been undertaken."[77]

On the day of Boutros-Ghali's report, Hoar was informed of actionable intelligence to get Aidid.[78] Five days later Clinton secretly ordered Delta Force and Rangers to Somalia, but they were not informed of the president's decision. Instead, the Rangers were ordered to fly back to Texas from Fort Bragg, where they were training with Delta Force and AC-130 gunships for the Somali mission.[79] One week later, on August 24, a UN investigative team found Aidid guilty of the June 5 attacks on the Pakistanis.[80] The Pentagon then announced that it was reinforcing the American QRF in Somalia with a task force composed of the 75th Ranger regiment and other elements of the US Special Operations Command. The task force would consist of approximately 400 troops. Although the US government did not know how long the troops would remain in Somalia, it stated that they "will be there as long as they are needed."[81] The deployment of the task force was a result of increasing violence in Mogadishu that was impeding UNOSOM II's focus on "other aspects of its mission, particularly the continued development of its political and economic infrastructures."[82]

The following day, the 3rd Ranger Battalion was resummoned from Texas to Fort Bragg. This time, they were told to take only two companies totaling 450 men, so Company A, who had trained with the others at Fort Bragg, was left in Texas.[83] In addition, the AC-130 gunships, on which the Rangers had trained in early August, were also omitted from the Ranger package and would not go to Somalia.[84] Ranger Lieutenant Colonel Danny McKnight asked himself, "Who is the idiot who made these decisions?"[85] In response to McKnight's inquiry, General Downing, commanding general of the US Army Special Operations Command at Fort Bragg, said the mission needed to be low-profile to avoid a Vietnam impression.[86] Approximately 440 US Rangers and Special Operations personnel deployed to Somalia with a mission to capture Aidid and his principal lieutenants.

Task Force Ranger and Delta personnel arrived in Somalia on August 26 but at a reduced strength. Although Howe was extremely pleased with the reinforcements, which he had wanted in early June, he believed that the forces arrived too late to be effective in capturing Aidid. According to Howe, "Such a force was requested within several days of the attack, but it was not until the American Rangers arrived more than two months later in late August that we finally had the appropriate means. By then, probabilities of capture decreased."[87] Moreover, the Special Forces would not report to Howe but to a new joint Special Operations Command headed by Maj. General William Garrison, who in turn reported to CENTCOM in Tampa, Florida.

After arriving in Mogadishu, the Rangers and Delta Force personnel found their strength further depleted as they devoted limited manpower and resources to securing and strengthening their base, located at Mogadishu's airport. Base protection was not one of their original mandates, yet it had to be done.

> One weak area that we found was our airfield. We took rounds in some of our Cobra helicopters while they were sitting at the airfield. We found that there was an old factory building overlooking the airfield from which a sniper could hit the aircraft. We didn't have enough people to maintain a watch over every possible situation from which an enemy could engage the airfield. What we did was take a lot of sea cargo containers. We stacked them as high as we could, six high, and put them around the airplanes and helicopters to block a sniper's field of fire.[88]

While the Special Forces were arriving in Somalia on August 27, the administration for the first time publicly articulated the new US role in Somalia in a speech by Aspin at the Center for Strategic and International Studies. After laying out the 12-month history of US involvement, he outlined criteria for measuring success in Somalia.[89] His speech was optimistic about the US role in Somalia, and he argued along lines similar to Albright's August 10 *New York Times* op-ed piece, which had highlighted positive developments, such the development of village councils, as steps toward the formation of a national government.[90] In his speech, Aspin also called for a renewed effort to find a political solution with Aidid because of concerns about the political costs of military escalation. So it was a contradictory policy: chasing Aidid yet also trying to give him a political way out.[91]

Meanwhile, Albright still supported catching Aidid and said the snatch efforts of the US Special Forces "would pay off." Also, she was "being told by those on the ground that Aidid was all that prevented success" and "that Aidid's own clan would cooperate in persuading the renegade general to leave Somalia. Certainly Aidid's capture would have lent momentum to the political process and restored cohesion to the UN force."[92] Albright's analysis was based on the Shinn interagency team's recent Somalia report, which argued that "[Aidid's] eventual demise will send a powerful message to the other warlords not to cross UNOSOM."[93] In her August *New York Times* op-ed, Albright expressed her disdain for Aidid and supported the UN's attempts to capture, detain, and try him:

> Unlike other Somali warlords, Mr. Aidid has obstructed UN efforts to end the violence and rebuild the country. He violated commitments made to the UN as soon as he realized that he could not operate in a society governed by law. For him, piracy meant prosperity. His aim is to return Somalia to anarchy.[94]

By early September, Clinton was worried about getting into a war situation in Somalia and kept asking Christopher for an update on the political settlement progress in Somalia. Clinton did not want to escalate the hunt for Aidid, as he still considered Somalia a humanitarian operation and thought it would look bad if there were heavy military operations resulting in casualties. Clinton also wanted to go to Congress to request forces for Bosnia to help implement an agreement, and he knew that if Somalia was perceived to be out of control, his request would be denied.[95]

The problem for the United States in trying to negotiate with Aidid was opposition by Boutros-Ghali, who continued to emphasize a military solution that would result in Aidid's arrest and prosecution. Boutros-Ghali responded negatively to Christopher's diplomatic outreach efforts to Aidid:

> The fact that UNOSOM has been able to achieve the progress that it has in different parts of the country, despite the armed hostility that it faces almost daily from Mohammed Farah Aidid and his militia, is testimony to the Somali people's as well as UNOSOM's resolve not to be deterred by such obstacles as well as to the desire of the Somali people for peace and normalcy. But the fact remains that the country will not enjoy complete stability unless and until the criminal elements have been apprehended and brought to justice as demanded by the Security Council in its Resolution 837.[96]

After the arrival of the Rangers and Delta Force, a few attempts were made to capture Aidid in Mogadishu. Their first operation occurred on August 30 and was a political fiasco. The US forces rappelled from helicopters onto a villa roof that was occupied by UN Development Program (UNDP) staff. They were arrested, but later released, thereby drawing unwanted negative media and political attention. What the UNDP staff didn't know was that the building had been declared off limits by UNOSOM II staff, and thus the Americans were not expecting to find UN employees in the villa. This communication blunder highlights one the many problems that Admiral Howe and other UNOSOM II leaders faced. They did not have "operational control over the independent UN relief organizations" and the NGOs. In fact, the leader of the UNDP group captured by the Americans later stated that Howe did not have authority over his operations.[97]

On September 8 Senator Byrd recommended his opposition to US participation in UNOSOM II by introducing an amendment to cut off Somali funding for the mission unless Congress approved it. He argued that "the United Nations mandate to disarm the warlords and rebuild a civil society in Somalia, approved by the UN Security Council, was never addressed, never debated, or never approved by this [Senate] body, even though it sought to establish a new era for UN peacekeeping." Indeed, the Senate never debated US participation in UNOSOM II. It passed Senate Joint Resolution 45 in early February before the UNSC created UNOSOM II.[98] The House, however, debated and included the new mandate for UNOSOM II in its version of the resolution. But the two resolutions never made it to conference in order to reconcile the differences between the two chambers.

Rather than supporting the mission, members of Congress began increasing pressure on the administration by compromising between Byrd and the Senate leadership, who continued to support, albeit tentatively, the president's policy. A compromise was reached when both the House and the Senate agreed to a version of Byrd's original amendment and incorporated it into what was called the Byrd Amendment, which called on the president to report to the Congress by October 15 a description of the mission, command arrangements, and the anticipated period that American forces would remain in Somalia. Additionally, it expressed the sense of Congress that by November 15, Clinton should receive congressional authorization for US forces to continue being deployed in Somalia. On September 9 the Senate passed the Byrd Amendment by a vote of 90 to 7.[99]

That same day, a large number of Somalis were killed in an attack on American engineers and Pakistani soldiers in Mogadishu. US Army helicopters were used to protect the American and Pakistani soldiers, and although great care was used to avoid harming civilians, many Somali women were mixed into Aidid's fighters and thus killed.[100] A reporter covering the September 9 violence wrote the following:

> Americans and Pakistanis clearing roadblocks from the 21st October Road came under attack. A mob of Somali women and children advanced in front of the gunmen and some of the females also carried weapons. The soldiers on the ground called in air support, and within minutes a Cobra arrived, opened up with its 20mm cannon and machine guns, and slaughtered a hundred gunmen, women and children.[101]

Following the killings, international criticism of UNOSOM II military actions in Somalia increased, and dissatisfaction grew among members of Congress. While welcoming home General Loi, the former Italian commander of Italian forces in Somalia, Italy's Defense Minister Fabio Fabbri said he saw a dramatic contradiction between the UN's humanitarian goals and the violent ends being used to achieve them, including "shooting at women and children."[102] The Italian Defense Ministry continued to criticize UNOSOM II's command structure, especially the lack of consultation prior to the undertaking of military operations.[103]

According to Albright, the administration "had fallen into the trap of personalizing the fight with [Aidid], then failing to nab him. US forces had suffered casualties in several incidents and pressure was building to get out."[104] Even Clinton was confused about the direction of US policy in Somalia, ("our position is not well enough formed") despite the fact that US Special Forces had been risking their lives by conducting military raids for the past month.[105]

One week after the Senate's vote, the State Department's coordinator for Somalia, David Shinn, met with UN peacekeeping personnel at UN headquarters in New York to emphasize the negative US press coverage of Somalia and the "sour mood on Capitol Hill."[106] The UN officials seemed surprised when Shinn told them that "if the downward trend line of events in Mogadishu continues, it could be a matter of only weeks before Congress made a serious effort to bring US troops back from Somalia."[107] They replied "how the American public could allow for a failed effort" and "the precedent for international peacekeeping would be terrible."[108] Shinn remarked that "outside the Boston-New York-Washington corridor, most Americans don't care a whit about Somalia unless it involves pictures of thousands of Somalis starving to death."[109]

Feeling under siege and vulnerable, Aidid appealed to international figures, including former US President Jimmy Carter, to help alleviate the conflict between his forces and UNOSOM II by creating an independent commission composed of "internationally known statesmen, scholars and jurists from different countries to investigate the events in Mogadishu since June 5, 1993, and to determine those who are responsible."[110] During a September 12 visit to Washington, DC, for work related to the PLO-Israeli agreement, Carter encouraged Clinton to pursue a new, more peaceful policy direction in Somalia. He told Clinton that there could be no political settlement in Somalia without including Aidid.[111]

In mid-September, recognizing that UNOSOM II was not being supported with the required resources for mission success, US Envoy to Somalia Robert Gosende decided on a different track. Realizing that Montgomery and the US troops in Somalia would not be allowed to do the job, he realized that a change in mission policy was necessary. Gosende thought that UNOSOM II "was being nickel and dimed to death. With death of a few Italians here, a few Nigerians, and once in a while Americans." As a result he sent a memorandum to Washington, DC, recommending a change in US policy, a shift from hunting Aidid to talking with him.[112]

Similarly, National Security Advisor (NSA) Lake informed Clinton that he was "developing options to shift the emphasis more toward a political solution."[113] In the meantime, Secretary of State Christopher was instructing the US Mission at the UN to begin circulating a draft UNSC resolution in response to Boutros-Ghali's latest Somalia report. The draft resolution called for, among other things, greater effort to continue developing a police, judicial, and penal system in Somalia.[114]

Five days later on September 22, the administration initiated a UNSC resolution designed to focus UNOSOM II efforts on developing and pursuing political and economic strategies. According to Albright, "the time had come to modify our approach. . . . In line with our desire to deper-sonalize the conflict, I didn't even mention Aidid in my statement."[115] Five days later on September 27, President Clinton gave a speech at the UN General Assembly that signaled a shift away from "aggressive multilateral-ism" as stated by Albright after UNSC Resolution 814 (March 26, 1993). Clinton instead pushed Boutros-Ghali for a more political solution for Somalia, which he thought was getting too militarily focused.[116]

Unfriendly US-UN discussions and letter exchanges between Christopher and Boutros-Ghali throughout mid-to-late September continued to immo-bilize any US action to inform its troops in Somalia of the diplomatic option and, ironically, stopped them from supporting the requests for more armor and support. Boutros-Ghali continued to resolutely defend continuing military attacks on Aidid and argued that military victory over Aidid was more important for the future of UN peacekeeping than insti-tuting new political initiatives. For example, at a September meeting at UN headquarters, State Department's Somalia Coordinator David Shinn was informed by Iqbal Riza, the assistant secretary-general for peace-keeping that "Boutros-Ghali is still focused on a military solution in south Mogadishu and is not much inclined to resolve the problem politically."[117]

As the administration started to transition from a military policy to a more diplomatic policy, the first casualty was Montgomery's September 14 request for more military resources. Montgomery's request for artillery, Bradley Fighting Vehicles, and tanks was based on his assessment that US and UNOSOM II troops needed greater mobility in and around Mogadishu. General Hoar endorsed the Montgomery request, agreeing that the armor was needed to break through roadblocks.[118] Powell also finally agreed to support Montgomery's request because

> with our commander on the ground pleading for help to pro-tect American soldiers, I had to back him, as I had with the Rangers and Delta Force. With only three days left in my term, I was in Les Aspin's office making one last pitch to him to give Tom Montgomery the armor he wanted.[119]

Aspin informed Powell that he turned down Montgomery's request due to congressional pressure to withdraw from Somalia.[120] In Aspin's view, "The mission for which Montgomery sought the armor—sweeping road-blocks and the like—was an escalation of the 'military' track at just the time that the UN was meant to be looking for political solutions."[121] It would lead to an unacceptable American military escalation, in Aspin's opinion, at a time when the US was trying to disengage from Somalia.[122] Powell felt that he had done what he had to do as "a soldier backing soldiers," whereas "Aspin had done what a civilian policymaker has to do, try to meet the larger objective, in this case, to get us out of Somalia, not further into it."[123]

During Powell's final week as chairman of the Joint Chiefs, he went to Clinton with a recommendation to "approve a parallel American effort to capture Aidid, though he thought we [American military forces] had only a 50 percent chance of catching him, with a 25 percent chance of getting him alive."[124] Since the Pakistani troops that were killed were serving alongside American forces, Powell said, the United States "couldn't behave as if it didn't care that Aidid had murdered UN forces."[125] Clinton agreed to Powell's recommendation.[126]

According to Powell, he presented a different message to Clinton a few hours before his retirement ceremony. Clinton had surprised Powell by calling him to the White House. After Powell was led up to the second-floor residential quarters, he and Clinton sat on the Truman Balcony. Somalia was at the top of Powell's concerns, and he told Clinton, "We could not substitute our version of democracy for hundreds of years of tribablism. We can't make a country out of that place. We've got to find a way to get out, and soon."[127] Clinton responded that he had not thought through the June UNSC resolution to capture Aidid and "that complicated the whole nature of our involvement."[128] What Powell may not have known, however, was that the administration was also attempting to reach a diplomatic settlement with Aidid.

The diplomatic policy already adopted by the administration was not transmitted to the forces in Somalia. Thus the centerpiece of President Clinton's Somalia policy—the effort to transform Somalia into a peaceful democracy—was undermined by lack of policy coordination by American government officials. The administration started backing away from the military option by withholding support for its troops but without giving them the command to stop the attacks or informing them that the diplomatic option had been already adopted. Aspin's decision to turn down Montgomery's request highlighted the impossibility of the two-track policy—continuing military operations without support for the field, and a tentative decision to go diplomatic that was implemented only in Washington, DC.

This momentous failure in communication was to have horrifying consequences for both the forces in the field and the administration, and ultimately for Somalia and future UN efforts to alleviate mass suffering. The breakdown in communication between Washington and forces in the field could have been a result of Somalia's not being a high foreign policy priority: It "never made the 'cut' that separated the big issues from ones considered less deserving of high-level attention in the administration" because Russia and the Middle East were seen by the president as "far more significant than our operations in Somalia."[129] According to David Hackworth, "Powell told Larry Joyce [father of a Ranger killed in action on October 3, 1993] that the president didn't even inform him about the Aidid peace feeler. Because the president never told the military, they could not alter their mission."[130]

Another possible explanation is that Rangers and Delta Force members were sent to Somalia to support a policy toward Aidid that was characterized not by rapprochement but by exile. According to Shinn, "The Special Operations guys were to show Aidid the back door—that that was his only option, and Special Ops would apply the pressure."[131] Lake said "that military track was not wrong just that we were so focused on military track that we were late coming to political track."[132] The US military forces, it was hoped, would reduce Aidid's military capability, creating an opportunity for UNOSOM II to cement coalition unity and proceed in advancing political reconciliation, national reconstruction, humanitarian assistance, and other nation-building functions.[133]

Unfortunately, by the end of September the violence increased beyond even the Somalis' already high expectations and exceeded the worst fears of US administration officials. The US military launched six missions to capture Aidid or his associates. The September 25 mission resulted in the first US Army helicopter to be shot down in Mogadishu.[134] The tactical footprint of these missions would prove deadly for the seventh mission as Aidid's militia had learned from the six previous Ranger and Delta Force helicopter missions; the Somalis were less likely to be caught by surprise.

On October 3 two US Black Hawk helicopters were shot down over Mogadishu while providing air support to Delta and Ranger troops who had captured some of Aidid's lieutenants. Some of the American ground forces reached one helicopter crash site, where they spent the night fighting off hundreds of Somalis. US troops tried to reach the other crash site but gave up because of heavy hostile fire that caused numerous casualties.

It is clear that the American-led forces were taken by surprise by the audacity of the Somali fighters.[135] Unlike the American experiences in other African countries, such as Liberia, the Somalis disregarded the firepower of US soldiers and fought while absorbing high casualties. The Somali fighters could be seen running between the blocks and houses, some of which were converted to defense positions, falling dead as bullets chopped them down or vanishing into some niche or lane. American troops also were not helped by the fact that much of the fighting took place in and around the densely populated and heavily armed Bakaraaha market, which was known as "Guns R Us."

Dawn of October 4 in Mogadishu disclosed that the Rangers and Deltas were indeed under siege and had suffered significant casualties. The fight had killed eighteen Americans and wounded seventy-four, whereas more than 500 Somalis were killed and 700 wounded.[136] By the following morning, most of the US troops had reached their base and the others were rescued by a mix of US and Malaysian forces. One helicopter pilot was taken hostage during the battle (which would later be depicted so well in the book and movie *Black Hawk Down*). According to the Rangers ground forces commander, Lieutenant Colonel Danny McKnight, men from Company A and the AC-130 gunships that had been left out of the force package could have made a difference during the fight.[137] The Rangers had trained at Fort Bragg in early August with three companies, Delta Force, and the gunships, but when they went to Somalia in late August, they were ordered to only bring two companies along with Delta and not the gunships because the United States wanted to keep a low profile.[138]

Also impacting the US military operations was the lack of coordination with UN forces. Especially noteworthy is that even though the US military forces did not form a majority of UNOSOM II as they did UNITAF, its personnel were still under American operational control and tactical command.[139] General Joseph Hoar, Commander in Chief of CENTCOM, insisted that the special operations units, known as Task Force Ranger (TFR) and its commander, General William Garrison, remained under his command. Thus Garrison would report "through Hoar en route to the Pentagon and the White House, with a coordination line to General Montgomery, thus creating two separate US chains of command."[140] Robert Gosende, President Clinton's special envoy to Somalia, opposed the command structure:

> Look at what the Department of Defense did. Montgomery in charge of the Quick Reaction Force and logistics personnel because the US doesn't allow a foreign officer commanding US troops, but he is under Turk Bir [the UNOSOM II Commanding Officer]. It is Crazy. Then Garrison has Delta Force and Rangers. So both major generals are reporting to Hoar at CENTCOM in Tampa. So what you have in Somalia is a stove pop operation going on. . . . with two major generals not talking to each other and having different chains of command.[141]

Besides leaving Montgomery out of the loop, this chain of command also left General Bir and Admiral Howe in the dark regarding Garrison and the operations of the special forces under his command. The result was that UNOSOM II, including Montgomery's 4,000 American military personnel, did not know about Garrison's TFR raid in Mogadishu until after the mission was launched and fighting started. According to one account,

> It was three hours into the raid before the UN forces under-
> stood that it was an ambush of a US unit that was the cause of
> the weapons fire. The probability that TFR might need help
> from the UN forces had not even been considered. Because of
> this, it took the Pakistani and Malaysian armor regiments
> nearly five hours to gather their forces, which were in different
> sectors of Mogadishu, in time to meet at TFR headquarters
> where the second rescue mission was being planned.[142]

The Mogadishu battle news was not broken in the United States until midday. Instead, CNN broadcast live pictures of anti-Yeltsin protesters poised to seize the Russian state television station and storm the Russian Parliament in Moscow. President Clinton's political adviser George Stephanopoulos called national security advisor Tony Lake at the White House situation room to obtain an update before seeing Clinton later that morning after church. Since Lake was not there, the National Security Council (NSC) operator connected Stephanopoulos to Lake's home.

> He [Lake] assumed I was calling about news that hadn't bro-
> ken yet: Several American soldiers had been killed a few hours
> earlier in Somalia. But the first he heard about Moscow was
> from me. "Are you ready for the questions?" I asked. "About
> Somalia?" "No, Russia." He didn't know either. So we decided
> it was best to say nothing now. In Moscow and Mogadishu,
> however, things were deteriorating. Riot police were firing on
> the Russian protesters, and more American soldiers had been
> killed or captured in Somalia. Tony beeped me just before the
> end of church, and I left my pew for "Roadrunner"—the mobile
> communications van in the president's motorcade.[143]

Stephanopoulos, who had already received the news, waited in the limo for the Clintons to emerge from the Sunday morning church service. He gave Clinton the Mogadishu battle news in the limo as it made its way back to the White House. After returning to the Oval Office, Clinton and Stephanopoulos met with Lake to receive more news from Somalia.

> Tony was having a terrible morning, and it showed. He was nor-
> mally restrained in the president's presence, but now he com-
> plained bitterly that he couldn't get straight answers from our

embassy in Moscow, and he suspected that our sources in MOG [Mogadishu] were deliberately keeping information from the situation room. . . . Six US soldiers were already dead in Mogadishu and the firefight was still raging. "We're not inflicting pain on these fuckers," Clinton said softly at first. "When people kill us, they should be killed in greater numbers." Then, with his face reddening, his voice rising, and his fist pounding his thigh, he leaned into Tony as if it were his fault: "I believe in killing people who try to hurt you, and I can't believe we're being pushed around by these two-bit pricks."[144]

So far, the public had supported the American military presence in Somalia, but Clinton believed opinion would turn fast at the sight of body bags. "Americans are basically isolationist," he said. "They understand at a basic gut level Henry Kissinger's vital-interest argument. Right now the average American doesn't see our interest threatened to the point where we should sacrifice one American life."[145]

Clinton turned on CNN, which had begun broadcasting the Mogadishu firefight story, including video of stripped, dead American military personnel being hit with sticks and dragged by ropes through Mogadishu's streets. It also showed images of the battered face of Michael Durant, the captured American Black Hawk helicopter pilot, who was being held hostage along with a Nigerian soldier.

The US deaths in Mogadishu triggered a bitter public backlash against the intervention. After seeing the bodies of American military personnel being dragged through the streets, Americans were bewildered as to why American soldiers were dying on an ostensibly humanitarian mission. Members of Congress started receiving "about 300 calls a day from angry constituents [and then] no one willing to support the UN mission."[146] In attempting to explain their confusion, Thomas Friedman of the New York Times wrote, "Americans were told that their soldiers were being sent to work in a soup kitchen and they were understandably shocked to find them in a house-to-house combat."[147]

In public, Clinton never blamed his national security staff or anyone else in his administration for the Battle of Mogadishu and accepted full responsibility. He kept CNN on his Oval Office television during the afternoon to track the Mogadishu news while still conducting scheduled meetings.[148] During staff meetings, Clinton angrily railed about the Special Forces raid. He asked, "How could they be going after Aidid when we're working on the political end? . . . Why the hell were we chasing after him?"[149] According to Stephanopoulos, who was present for many of the White House meetings after the Mogadishu battle,

On conference calls from the road and behind closed doors at the White House, Clinton complained mercilessly about being blindsided by this national security team, insisting that he had never been fully briefed on how the original mission had evolved at the UN and on the ground. He never forgot Defense Secretary Les Aspin's failure to approve the military's September request for more tanks to protect the troops.[150]

Meanwhile Clinton was continually mystified by the Special Forces operation. "It strikes me as dumb at a minimum to put US troops in helicopters in urban areas where they were subject to ground fire," he angrily complained.[151] Clinton later made the following remarks:

> I did not envision anything like the daytime assault in a crowded, hostile neighborhood. . . . After I left the White House and he was secretary of state, Powell said he would not have approved an operation like that one unless it was conducted at night. But we hadn't discussed that, nor apparently had anyone else imposed any parameters on General Garrison's range of options. Colin Powell had retired three days before the raid and John Shalikashvili had not yet been confirmed as his replacement. The operation was not approved by General Hoar at CentCom or by the Pentagon. As a result, instead of authorizing an aggressive police operation, I had authorized a military assault in hostile territory.[152]

The Battle of Mogadishu was a horrible day for Clinton, who wrote that it "marked one of the darkest days of my presidency. . . . The Battle of Mogadishu haunted me."[153] Albright's reaction was similar to the president's, namely, one of bafflement:

> We had decided on a new strategy, but coordination among officials in New York, Washington and Somalia was not the best. No diplomatic solution was found and there was no letup in Aidid's attacks. The standing orders to the US Ranger force in Mogadishu remained the same—snatch him. . . . I had been a part of the decisions that had led to this. What had we done wrong? It was a nightmare.[154]

The remainder of the week, even while on a scheduled trip to California, Clinton focused on the Somali situation. After returning to his Fairmont Hotel room in San Francisco, Clinton received a conference call from Lake,

Aspin, and two advisers, who informed him that the news out of Mogadishu was getting worse. Mark Gearan, assistant to the president and director of communications and strategic planning, informed Clinton that "at least eleven American soldiers are dead and fifty-eight wounded. Six are missing. There may be hostages. It's Teheran."[155] Clinton asked Aspin, "How did this happen?" Aspin blamed the UN command and control structure in Somalia and its slow response with ill-equipped troops to rescue the American forces.[156]

Lake organized an October 5 meeting for Clinton with congressional leaders in the White House's Roosevelt Room to discuss the Somalia options. According to Lake, "The discussion centered on a withdrawal date."[157] Lake had prepared a ten-page paper outlining four options for Clinton, who was flying back from California aboard Air Force One. At 6:30 PM, Clinton met with advisers and hammered out options. After a few hours of discussion, Clinton left without making a decision, heading to a Democratic fundraiser at the Washington Hilton hotel. At the fundraiser he spoke with Senators Sam Nunn and David Pryor, who told him that Aspin and Christopher's afternoon visit to Capitol Hill to explain the administration's Russia policy did not go well and that Aspin was a "disaster."[158] Except for one question about Russia, Aspin and Christopher addressed numerous questions concerning Somalia. Christopher stood back to let Aspin address most of them. At one point, Aspin asked congressional members what the administration should do in Somalia. As a result of Aspin's "disastrous performance," lawmakers were further convinced "that the administration had no clue as to what policy to pursue."[159]

The following day, Wednesday, October 6, Clinton and his advisers from the previous night reconvened.[160] The meeting was also attended by Robert Oakley, Bush's former envoy to Somalia during the UNITAF operation and former US ambassador to Somalia, who was invited at the request of Lake. Oakley said that the US policy in Somalia had gotten off track by isolating Aidid from the political process and trying to apprehend him.[161] They discussed several other proposals, including General Hoar's proposal to set March 31, 1994, as the withdrawal date for US forces in Somalia.

Based on the meeting's discussions, Clinton agreed to 1) reinforce troops in Somalia with 1,700 additional Army troops, 104 additional armored vehicles and an aircraft carrier, and two amphibious groups with 3,600 combat Marines to be stationed offshore; 2) shift from hunting Aidid to a more political approach by sending Ambassador Oakley; and 3) set a hard deadline for US withdrawal of March 31. Clinton also asked Oakley to negotiate the release of Durant, the American pilot, and the Nigerian soldier using "his own judgment."[162] In his instructions Clinton told Oakley to inform Aidid that "the United States would not retaliate if Durant was released immediately and unconditionally."[163] Accompanying Oakley would be another UNITAF leader, General Zinni, who, while watching the baseball playoffs on television at his home, received a call that he was to report to Andrews Air Force Base the following morning to fly to Somalia "on a special mission."[164]

On October 7 Clinton announced a new Somali policy in an Oval Office address on national television. "Fundamentally," Clinton said, "the solution to Somalia's problems is not a military one. It is political." He also said that the military reinforcements "will be under American command." The implication to the American audience was that the Rangers and Delta forces in the Mogadishu battle were under UN command, when in fact they were under CENTCOM's command. Kofi Annan, UN undersecretary-general for peacekeeping operations, immediately expressed his disappointment and disapproval toward the US withdrawal. He said that the most powerful and well-equipped military in the world had become the weakest link in peacekeeping. "One has to kill a few Americans and the US leaves," he said.[165]

America's and the UN's worst fears of setting a deadline for US troop withdrawal were quickly realized after Clinton's announcement. The UNOSOM II coalition started to crumble. Many of the other twenty-seven governments participating in UNOSOM II rapidly announced the withdrawal of their forces in Somalia. For example, on October 8 Belgium informed Wisner's DOD staff that it "hoped to accelerate its withdrawal schedule, so that troops might begin to depart even as early as November."[166] That same day Shinn met with the German minister for African affairs, who said that all of Germany's troops would soon withdraw because its troops depended on US forces for logistical needs, such as supplies and transportation. Meanwhile, a general from one of UNOSOM II's largest contributors, Pakistan, informed Hoar that "we will leave the day after you do."[167]

Early on the morning of October 8, Oakley and Zinni departed Andrews Air Force Base for Somalia. During the flight they decided that their mission had two absolutes: freeing Durant, the American helicopter pilot hostage, and the Nigerian hostage and negotiating a political resolution with Aidid. According to Oakley, "These prisoners have to be released unconditionally; America does not negotiate for hostages."[168]

After Aidid announced a cease-fire on October 9, the UNOSOM fight with Aidid was over. During the next several days, Oakley and Zinni meet with Aidid's representatives to negotiate for the unconditional release of the American and Nigerian hostages. Clinton's trust in Oakley paid off when Aidid released the hostages on October 14. There was a slight problem in the release because Aidid insisted on releasing them directly to Oakley and Zinni and not to UNOSOM II authorities. Oakley did not think this was the appropriate method because it would cause further problems for UNOSOM II. Therefore, he and Aidid agreed that the Red Cross would take the prisoners and then release them to their national government representatives.[169]

After Durant's release Zinni and Oakley returned to Washington, DC, on October 16 and then visited the White House the following morning to brief Lake, Aspin, Albright, and Christopher. Afterward, they also briefed the new chairman of the Joint Chiefs of Staff, General Shalikashvilli, at a Pentagon meeting. The NSC then announced the creation of an "Executive Committee on Somalia," a structure that imposed top-level accountability on US involvement in Somalia. James Dobbins from the State Department was chosen to head the committee.

As a sign that the UN was ending its presence in Somalia, on November 16 the UNSC passed Resolution 885, which requested that the secretary-general suspend arrest actions against persons not already detained pursuant to UNSC Resolution 837 (June 6), that is, persons who might be implemented in the attacks against UNOSOM II personnel.[170] The resolution was accepted by Aidid's faction and helped ease tensions between the UN and Aidid's forces. During one of their meetings, Aidid informed Zinni that he wished "no more shooting. No more. Too many people will die."[171]

Throughout November and December, the State Department pushed countries to donate to the Somali Trust Fund. The United States proposed a multinational donor conference for the week of November 14 to rehabilitate and train Somali police services. Its purpose was to encourage governments to make financial pledges to the UN for the Somali police program. The United States also encouraged national reconciliation conferences for Somali leaders, but they were not successful. For example, the December 2 National Reconciliation Conference, which occurred over nine days, faced two main obstacles to an agreement. First, Aidid's SNA and many of the other Somali factions opposed each other's involvement. Second, the SNA rejected UNOSOM II involvement. Not surprisingly, the conference bogged down immediately over what role the UN would play in the national reconciliation process.[172]

On December 16 Clinton approved Zinni's US military force withdrawal plan and gave the green light to the operation, which was called "Joint Task Force United Shield" and launched on January 14. It encompassed participation of seven governments and included twenty-three ships and a total of 16,485 soldiers, sailors, airmen, and Marines.[173] On February 7 the United Shield fleet arrived off Mogadishu's coast and started preparations for the final withdrawal of UNOSOM II personnel. For the next three weeks the UN drew down its presence until it controlled only the Mogadishu airport and airfield with the Pakistani and Bangladeshi troops. During the evacuation the UNSC passed Resolution 897, which further reduced UNOSOM II's military effort, and redeployed its remaining military assets to protect remaining UNOSOM II lines of communications and national reconstruction efforts. On February 28 UNOSOM II finished withdrawing from Somalia, which included the Bangladeshi battalion defending the port and airport, which were under siege by Somali mobs eager to loot the UN property that would be left behind. On March 6 UNOSOM II evacuation vessels docked at Mombasa harbor with the mission completed.

On April 21, 1994, Boutros-Ghali admitted defeat and declared that the UN effort in Somalia was effectively over. "I have concluded that the retention of a full-time Special Rep at the undersecretary-general level cannot be justified at the present time in view of the limited possibilities for United Nations political efforts related to Somalia."[174]

The centerpiece of President's Clinton's Somalia policy—the effort to transform Somalia into a peaceful democracy—had been undermined by a two-track policy not working in sync, a determined antagonist in General Aidid, and the broadcast photos of brutality by Somali civilians against dead American soldiers.

Had Montgomery's request for armor been approved and delivered, it might have helped US forces pinned down in Mogadishu's streets, "but the presence of armor would not have prevented the incident nor would it have prevented the casualties that precipitated the need for the reaction force in the first place."[175] Additionally, the armor would have used Mogadishu's main streets, which were "vulnerable to roadblocks and counter-armor ambushes."[176] Also, "the lack of reliable maps and non-standard traffic patterns within the city made it difficult for armored convoys to maneuver."[177] Finally, Somali behavior toward armored vehicles during the February riots in Mogadishu suggests that the armor may have been immobilized by Somalis lying in front of the vehicles.[178]

But debate over the armor-rejection decision is beside the point. It is more important to realize that the US military and Somalia casualties may have been saved if the US armed forces in Somalia had been made aware of the administration's diplomatic track. Since they were never told about the new policy, Delta Force and the Rangers continued with their operations to capture Aidid and his lieutenants.

After the international community departed, Somalia disappeared from most diplomatic and media radars until a few years after the September 11, 2001, terrorist attacks, when Osama bin Laden declared Somalia as the third front, after Afghanistan and Iraq, on the global Islamic war against the United States.

Notes

1. UN Department of Peace Keeping Operations, Lessons-Learned Unit, "Comprehensive Report on Lessons-Learned From United Nations Operation in Somalia: April 1992–March 1995," December 1995, 15.

2. Quoted at July 8, 1993, meeting at the UN. Confidential memorandum, secretary of state to US Mission at UN, "Meeting of Major Somalia Troop Contributors," July 1993.

3. Lieutenant Commander James C. Dixon, "UNOSOM II: UN Unity of Effort and US Unity of Command," Master's Thesis, Army Command and General Staff Coll Fort Leavenworth, Kansas. June 7, 1996, 87.

4. Ibid., 88.

5. Ibid., 110.

6. Confidential memorandum, from secretary of state to US Liaison Office in Mogadishu, "UNOSOM II—Command and Control Problem," June 1993.

7. Confidential memorandum, from secretary of state to American Embassy in Riyadh, "Saudi Participation in UNOSOM II," June 1993.

8. Jonathan Stevenson, *Losing Mogadishu: Testing US Policy in Somalia* (Annapolis, MD: Naval Institute Press, 1995), 138.

9. Commissioner's Report, S/1994/53, 28–29.

10. Ibid., 28–29.

11. Confidential memorandum, "Italy and UNOSOM II Arrangements," secretary of state to USLO Mission in Mogadishu, June 1993; confidential memorandum, secretary of state to US Mission at UN, "Somalia: Italy, UN and US," July 1993.

12. David Bowne Wood, *A Sense of Values: American Marines in an Uncertain World* (Kansas City: Andrews and McMeel, 1994), 201–206.

13. Commissioner's Report, S/1994/53, 29.

14. Quoted at July 8, 1993, meeting at the UN. Confidential memorandum, secretary of state to US Mission at UN, "Meeting of Major Somalia Troop Contributors," July 1993.

15. Confidential memorandum, secretary of state to US Mission at the UN and American Embassy in Rome,"UNOSOM II Operation and Italian Troops," June 1993.

16. Wood, *A Sense of Values*, 207.

17. Ibid., 207.

18. Senators John Warner (R-Va). and Carl Levin, (D-Mich), *Warner-Levin Report,* "Review of the Circumstances Surrounding the

Ranger Raid on October 3–4, 1993 in Mogadishu, Somalia," United States Senate Committee on Armed Services, October 2, 1995, 24.

19. Alberto R. Coll, "The Problems of Doing Good: Somalia as a Case Study in Humanitarian Intervention," Instructor Copy 518, Pew Case Studies in International Affairs, Institute for Study of Diplomacy Publications, School of Foreign Service, Georgetown University, 1997, 9.

20. Warner-Levin, "Review of Circumstances," 25.

21. Madeleine Albright, *Madam Secretary* (New York: Miramax Books, 2003), 143.

22. Ibid.,144.

23. Ibid., 143–144.

24. UN Secretary-General Boutros Boutros-Ghali Report on the Implementation of UN Security Council Resolution 837 (1993). July 1, 1993. S/26022.

25. Admiral Jonathan Howe (deputy assistant to the president for national security affairs 1991–1992; special representative for Somalia to UN Secretary-General Boutros Boutros-Ghali, March 1993–February 1994), interview with author. Jacksonville, FL, December 28, 2005.

26. Ambassador Robert Gosende (President Clinton's special envoy to Somalia, 1993; public affairs officer for President Bush's special envoy to Somalia, Ambassador Robert Oakley, 1993–1994), interview with author, New York, NY, October 22, 2007.

27. Commissioner's Report, S/1994/53, 31.

28. F. M. Lorenz, "Law and Anarchy in Somalia," *Parameters,* vol XXIII, no. 4 (Winter 1993–94): 37.

29. Norman L. Cooling, "Operation Restore Hope in Somalia: A Tactical Action Turned Strategic Defeat," *Marine Corps Gazette*, September 2001, 97.

30. Yossef Bodansky, *Bin Laden: The Man Who Declared War on America* (New York: Forum, 1999), 83.

31. Ibid., 87.

32. Secret memorandum, secretary of state to American Embassy in Rome, "Somalia: Italians Press for Senior Command Slot, Greater Coordination," July 1993.

33. Ibid.

34. Confidential memorandum, secretary of state to American Embassy in Rome, "Italian Ambassador's Meeting with U/S Tarnoff," July 1993.

35. Elizabeth Drew, *On the Edge: The Clinton Presidency* (New York: Simon & Schuster, 1994), 243.

36. *Maanta* means "today" in Somali, and was published six days per week and distributed in twelve cities, including Mogadishu. The UN

also introduced an English-version of *Maanta* for dissemination to international personnel in Somalia, such as those employed by United Nations agencies or NGOs.

37. Commissioner's Report, S/1994/53, 29; Adding credence to the claim that the Italians were working closely with Somali militias and not informing UNOSOM II was a September 5 incident at UN Strongpoint 42 near the Pasta Factory and scene of the July 2 Italian ambush. As Nigerian forces replaced the Italians, they were met by a Somali mob requesting that the Nigerians "negotiate" permission to take over the position. The Nigerian commander objected, whereupon Somali gunmen opened fire on the Nigerians. The Italians did not come to the Nigerians' assistance despite repeated calls because they later said they didn't hear the ambush. William J. Durch, "Introduction to Anarchy: Intervention and "State-Building" in Somalia," in *UN: Peacekeeping, American Policy and the Uncivil Wars of the 1990s*, ed. William J. Durch (New York: St. Martin's Press, 1996), 347.

38. Aidan Hartley, *The Zanzibar Chest* (New York: Atlantic Monthly Press, 2003), 274.

39. Commission Report S/1994/653.

40. CODKA, Issue No. 490, July 19, 1993. USC/SNA Central Committee member, Professor Mohamed Farah Jumale.

41. As quoted in "Somalia: Making Monkeys of the UN," *The Economist*, July 19, 1993, 34.

42. Commission Report S/1994/653.

43. Harry Johnston and Ted Dagne, "Congress and the Somalia Crisis" in *Learning From Somalia: The Lessons of Armed Humanitarian Intervention*, ed. Walter Clarke and Jeffrey Herbst (Boulder, CO: Westview Press, 1997), 197–198.

44. John G. Sommer, *Hope Restored? Humanitarian Aid in Somalia: 1990–1994* (Washington, DC: Refugee Policy Group, 1994), B-4.

45. For example, at an August 4 meeting the US expressed thanks to the Germans for contributing troops to UNOSOM II and also discussed "German aims with respect to a permanent seat on the UN Security Council." Germany agreed to send nearly 1,700 soldiers to Somalia as part of its contribution to the UN's humanitarian assistance operation. It is the first time that Germany had sent military contingents to serve since World War II. Confidential memorandum from US secretary of state to American Embassy in Bonn, "German Political Director Chrobog's meeting with Undersecretary Tarnoff," August 4, 1993.

46. Confidential memorandum from US secretary of state to US Mission at the UN in New York, "Final Report of the Inter-Agency Assessment Team on Somalia," August 1993.

47. Confidential memorandum from US secretary of state to US Mission at the UN in New York, "Somalia: Inter-Agency Assessment Team Briefs UN Secretariat," August 1993.

48. Hartley, *The Zanzibar Chest*, 291.

49. Secretary of Defense Les Aspin's attachment to lengthy analysis and apparent aversion to swift decision-making concerned American senior military officials throughout summer 1993 when many important issues were being placed on hold for consideration of options. Barbara Starr, "Decision time looms for Aspin," *Jane's Defence Weekly* (July 24, 1993): 23.

50. Drew, *On the Edge*, 321.

51. Warner-Levin, "Review of Circumstances," 25.

52. Ibid., 26.

53. Ibid., 26.

54. Ambassador David Shinn (State Department deputy director of the Somali Task Force), interview with author, Washington, DC, April 8, 2004.

55. Warner-Levin, "Review of Circumstances," 25.

56. Confidential memorandum from US secretary of state to US Mission at the UN in New York, "Somalia: Inter-Agency Assessment Team Briefs UN Secretariat," August 1993.

57. Ibid.

58. Shinn, interview.

59. Confidential memorandum from US secretary of state to US Mission at the UN in New York "Somalia: Inter-Agency Assessment Team Briefs UN Secretariat," August 1993.

60. Warner-Levin, "Review of Circumstances," 27.

61. Ibid.

62. Ibid.

63. Ibid.

64. Ibid.

65. Susan Rosegrant, "B 'Seamless' Transition: United States and United Nations Operations in Somalia—1992–1993," Kennedy School of Government Case Program (Cambridge, MA: President and Fellows of Harvard College, 1996), 13. Secretary of State Christopher had previously denied a tank request from the government of Pakistan for its troops in Mogadishu after the June 5 massacre of its soldiers. He wrote that "they are of limited use in dealing with the situation in Mogadishu." Confidential memorandum, secretary of state to American Embassy in Amman, "GOP Requests for Peacekeeping Operations in Somalia," June 1993.

66. Howe, interview.

67. Ambassador Robert Gallucci (assistant secretary of state for Political-Military Affairs, 1992), interview with author, Washington, DC, May 10, 2004.

68. Drew, *On the Edge*, 321.

69. Confidential memorandum from US secretary of state to US Mission at the UN in New York, "Somalia: Inter-Agency Assessment Team Briefs UN Secretariat," August 1993.

70. Patrick J. Sloyan, "The Secret Path to a Bloodbath: How US Policy in Somalia Went from Bad to Worse," *The Washington Post National Weekly Edition*, April 18–24, 1994, 24.

71. Warner-Levin, "Review of Circumstances," 27.

72. Powell, *My American Journey*, 584.

73. Warner-Levin, "Review of Circumstances," 25.

74. Ibid., 25, 26.

75. Confidential memorandum from secretary of state to American Embassy Rome, "Italian Ambassador's Meeting with U/S Tarnoff," July 1993.

76. UN Secretary-General Boutros Boutros-Ghali, "Further Report of the Secretary-General Submitted in Pursuance of Para 18 of Resolution 814 (1993)" S/26317. August 17, 1993.

77. Ibid.

78. Warner-Levin, "Review of Circumstances," 25.

79. Lieutenant Colonel Danny McKnight, presentation at Southwest Missouri State University, Springfield, Missouri, April 26, 2002.

80. UN Secretary General Report on the June 5, 1993 Attack on UN forces in Somalia., S/26351. August 24, 1993. 6–8.

81. Confidential memorandum from secretary of state to US Mission at the United Nations, "Talking Points on the Deployment of Additional US Troops to Somalia," August 1993.

82. Ibid.

83. McKnight, presentation.

84. Warner-Levin, "Review of Circumstances," 5.

85. McKnight, presentation.

86. Ibid.

87. Howe, "Relations Between the United States and United Nations," 169.

88. John Allison, "Force Protection During Urban Operations," in Russell W. Glenn, ed., *Capital Preservation: Preparing for Urban Operations in the Twenty-First Century*, Proceedings of the RAND Arroyo-TRADOC-MCWL-OSD, Urban Operations Conference, March 22–23, "Force Protection-Mogadishu," 178–179.

89. "Remarks Prepared for Delivery by Secretary of Defense Les Aspin at the Center for Strategic and International Studies, Washington, DC, August 27, 1993," news release (Washington, DC: Office of Assistant Secretary of Defense [Public Affairs], 27 August 1993).

90. Madeline Albright, "Yes, There Is a Reason to Be in Somalia," *New York Times*, August 10, 1993, A19.

91. Aspin also listed three conditions that must be met before US.troops could begin to leave Somalia in general and the QRF can be removed from Mogadishu in particular: 1) The security condition in Mogadishu must be complete; 2) Heavy weapons removed from warlords; and 3) Credible Somali police force must be functioning in major population centers. Confidential memorandum from secretary of state to US Mission at UN, "Somalia: Aspin's CSIS Speech on 8/27/93," August 1993.

92. Albright, *Madam Secretary*, 144.

93. Confidential memorandum from US secretary of state to US Mission at the UN in New York, "Final Report of the Inter-Agency Assessment Team on Somalia," August 1993.

94. Albright, "Yes, There Is a Reason to Be in Somalia," A19.

95. Drew, *On the Edge*, 323.

96. Boutros-Ghali statement.

97. Gary Anderson, "UNOSOM II: Not Failure, Not Success," in *Beyond Traditional Peacekeeping*, eds. Donald C. Daniel and Bradd C. Hayes (New York: St. Martins Press, 1995), 271.

98. Johnston and Dagne, "Congress and the Somalia Crisis," 199–200.

99. The House passed the identical amendment on September 28 by a vote of 406–26. Johnston and Dagne, 200.

100. Howe, "Relations Between the United States and United Nations," 175.

101. Hartley, *The Zanzibar Chest*, 292.

102. Confidential memorandum from the US Embassy in Rome to the secretary of state and Secretary of Defense, September 12, 1993.

103. Ibid.

104. Albright, *Madam Secretary*, 144.

105. Richburg, "Aideed Calls for Somalia Cease-fire," *Washington Post*, October 10, 1993, A44.

106. Confidential memo from secretary of state to US Liaison Office in Mogadishu, "Somalia: Meeting with A/SYG for Peacekeeping," September 1993. Shinn met with Iqbal Riza, assistant secretary-general for peacekeeping, Elizabeth Lindenmeyer, desk officer for Somalia, and Lamine Sise, Department of Peacekeeping Operations.

107. Ibid.

108. Ibid.

109. Ibid.

110. Confidential memorandum from secretary of state to the U.S mission at the UN, September 1993.

111. Sloyan, "The Secret Path," 25.

112. Gosende, interview.

113. Brigadier General Ed Wheeler (USA-Ret) and Lieutenant Colonel Craig Roberts (USAR-Ret), *Doorway to Hell: Disaster in Somalia* (Tulsa, OK: Consolidated Press International, 2002), 95.

114. Limited Official Use memorandum from secretary of state to US Mission at United Nations New York, "Draft Security Council Resolution on Secretary General's Report: Somalia," September 1993.

115. Albright, *Madam Secretary*, 144.

116. Gallucci, interview.

117. Confidential memo from secretary of state to US Liaison Office in Mogadishu and various other US embassies, September 1993. The day after the meeting, Kofi Annan, the undersecretary-general for peacekeeping, called Shinn to reinforce the message.

118. Warner-Levin, "Review of Circumstances," 32.

119. Powell, *My American Journey*, 586.

120. Ibid., 586.

121. Warner-Levin, "Review of Circumstances," 5.

122. Drew, *On the Edge*, 331.

123. Powell, *My American Journey*, 586.

124. Bill Clinton, *My Life* (New York: Alfred A. Knopf, 2004), 550.

125. Ibid., 550.

126. Ibid., 550.

127. Powell, *My American Journey*, 588.

128. Ibid., 588.

129. Smith and Devroy, "Inattention Led to US Deaths," WP Oct 17, 1993, A29.

130. Colonel David H. Hackworth (US Army, Ret.) with Tom Mathews, *Hazardous Duty: One of America's Most Decorated Soldiers Reports from the Front with the Truth about the US Military Today* (New York: Avon Boods, 1996), 189.

131. Shinn, interview.

132. Gallucci, interview.

133. Confidential memorandum from secretary of state to US Mission at the United Nations, "Window of Opportunity Opens for UNOSOM," June 1993.

134. Commissioner's Report, S/1994/53, 31.

135. The fearlessness of Somali fighters is legendary. Gerald Hanley, a British officer in Somalia in World War II, wrote that "I never saw a Somali who showed any fear of death, which impressive though it sounds, carries within it the chill of pitilessness and ferocity as well. If you have no fear of death you have none for anybody else's death either, but that fearlessness has always been essential to the Somalis who have had to try and survive against their enemies, their fellow Somalis for pleasure in the blood feud, or the Ethiopians who would like to rule them, or the white men who got in the way for a while." Gerald Hanley, *Warriors: Life and Death among the Somalis* (London: Eland, 1973), 20.

136. The ICRC reported that it counted more than 700 wounded in Mogadishu hospitals with one-third being women and children. "Somalia: ICRC Appeals for Compliance with International Humanitarian Law," ICRC Press Release No. 1759, October 7, 1993.

137. Lieutenant Colonel Danny McKnight, presentation at Southwest Missouri State University, Springfield, Missouri, April 26, 2002.

138. Ibid.

139. Lieutenant Commander James C. Dixon, "UNOSOM II: UN Unity of Effort and US Unity of Command," Master's Thesis, Army Command and General Staff Coll Fort Leavenworth, Kansas, June 7, 1996, 24.

140. Clifford E. Day, "Critical Analysis on the Defeat of Task Force Ranger," research paper presented to the Research Department, Air Command and Staff College, March 1997, 23.

141. Gosende, interview.

142. Day, "Critical Analysis on the Defeat of Task Force Ranger," 23.

143. Stephanopoulos, 213.

144. George Stephanopoulos, *All Too Human: A Political Education* (Boston: Little, Brown and Company, 1999), 213–214.

145. Ibid., 214–215.

146. Johnston and Dagne, "Congress and the Somalia Crisis," 200.

147. Thomas Friedman, "The World: Harm's Way; U.S. Pays Dearly for an Education in Somalia," *New York Times,* October 10, 1993.

148. Drew, *On the Edge,* 317.

149. Ibid., 325 and 326.

150. Stephanopoulos, *All Too Human,* 215.

151. Drew, *On the Edge,* 317.

152. Clinton, *My Life,* 553.

153. Ibid., 550, 552, and 555.

154. Albright, *Madam Secretary,* 145.

155. Drew, *On the Edge,* 317.

156. George J. Church, "Anatomy of a Disaster," *Time*, October 18, 1993, 47.

157. Gallucci, interview.

158. Drew, *On the Edge*, 328.

159. Church, "Anatomy of a Disaster," 48.

160. Meanwhile, at an October 6 Mogadishu airport memorial service for the fallen Ranger and Delta Force members of the October 3 battle, a mortar round hit near the service, killing another American soldier. Remarks by Lieutenant Colonel Danny McKnight at Southwest Missouri State University, Springfield, Missouri, April 26, 2002.

161. Clinton, *My Life*, 551–552.

162. Tom Clancy with General Tony Zinni (Ret.) and Tony Koltz, *Battle Ready*, (New York: G.P. Putnam's Sons, 2004), 270.

163. Clinton, *My Life*, 552.

164. Clancy, Zinni, and Koltz, *Battle Ready*, 272.

165. Annan interview, Sommer, *Hope Restored?* 43.

166. Confidential memorandum from secretary of state to NSC, CIA, DOD, et al. "President's Message for UNOSOM Troop Contributing Countries; conversation with advisor to Belgium PM," October 1993.

167. Confidential memorandum from secretary of state to secretary of defense, JCS and others, "Analysis of Requirements for Additional Pakistani Troops for Somalia," October 1992.

168. Clancy, Zinni, and Koltz, *Battle Ready*, 273–274.

169. Ibid., 280.

170. Commission Report S/1994/653. 7.

171. Clancy, Zinni, and Koltz, *Battle Ready*, 281–283.

172. UN Secretary General report in pursuance of para 4 of Resolution 886 (November 18, 1993), S/1994/12. January 6, 1994.

173. Clancy, Zinni, and Koltz, *Battle Ready*, 293.

174. UN Secretary-General Boutros Boutros-Ghali letter to the UN Security Council, April 21, 1995. 1. S/1995/322.

175. Todd W. Lyons, "Military Intervention in Identity Group Conflicts," thesis, Naval Postgraduate School, Monterey, California, December 2000, 95.

176. Ibid., 95, footnote 120.

177. Major Eric F. Buer, USMC, "United Task Force Somalia (UNITAF) and United Nations Operations Somalia (UNOSOM II): A Comparative Analysis of Offensive Air Support," master thesis, United States Marine Corps, Command and Staff College, AY 2000–2001, 22.

178. Lyons, 77, footnote 103, and 95, footnote 120.

CHAPTER SEVEN

PAST AS PROLOGUE: WITHDRAWAL AND RE-ENGAGEMENT

When President George Herbert Walker Bush entered the White House in 1989, it was hard to imagine that the United States would lead a UN military operation in Somalia four years later, especially in a country that holds little economic and geostrategic value to the United States. Before 1992 the United States had contributed little of its military assets to UN peacekeeping operations even though it encouraged UN multilateral peacekeeping actions as a way to address global security issues in the post-Cold War period and to avoid having these assignments fall to the United States.

Bush arrived near the end of a decade that had witnessed the end of the bipolar world, and his presidency encapsulated a new international political system. In addition to this, Bush himself had decades of international experience—as US ambassador to China, CIA director, and US ambassador to the UN—from which to draw upon in directing his foreign policy goals.

During Bush's four-year term and his successor's first year in office (1993), the UN Security Council, with US support, approved more peacekeeping missions than the UN had attempted in its preceding forty-three years. In 1990 there were fewer than 14,000 UN peacekeepers. In 1993, the number would peak at more than 78,000.[1] Near the end of Bush's term and before the Somalia intervention, the State Department under Secretary of State James Baker opposed further peacekeeping operations because of their ballooning costs and questionable effectiveness.

At the time, Somalia was an unmitigated and unprecedented humanitarian disaster. Hundreds of thousands had died of starvation, and millions more faced famine while being held hostage by feuding warlords whose gangs of teenage boys trolled the cities and countryside confiscating humanitarian relief supplies. It was the first country since the end of the Cold War to implode and exist in a state of chaos without a government.

After the Barre government's fall, the clan elders were pushed aside by warlord-led militias that used their military power to pillage and steal to keep their young soldiers' loyalty. As the country disintegrated, the international humanitarian relief operations became the major source of revenue. The armed gangs stole food, extorted protection money from the NGOs and UN agencies, and charged them for landing and shipping rights. Moreover, they charged outrageous lodging rental rates, which included their own soldiers, who would sometimes rob or kill their clients.

On August 13, 1992, Bush ordered Operation Provide Relief to airlift a UN guard force and humanitarian supplies into Somalia. As the crisis continued to spiral out of control, Bush decided in November to send tens of thousands of American troops to Somalia to lead an unprecedented humanitarian aid mission titled by the UN the United Task Force (UNITAF)—or Operation Restore Hope by American officials. American national security was not a primary issue for UNITAF's launch in December 1992, when expectations for the humanitarian mission were high and coupled with predictions that it boded well for a new era in international cooperation. Created by UN Security Council (UNSC) Resolution 794, UNITAF was authorized as a Chapter VII mission to use force to support humanitarian operations in Somalia. In passing the resolution, the UNSC deviated from its custom of inserting UN military forces only with the consent of disputing parties. In Somalia, there was not a national government to approve the UN mission, and the warlord-controlled militias were too preoccupied with looting humanitarian relief shipments, fighting among themselves, and jockeying for national leadership roles to give their consent to the UN mission.

Bush acted on his belief that the United States could exert worldwide leadership in managing humanitarian crises by utilizing the US military to intervene in Somalia when others were unable or unwilling to take the lead. The international community and the American public also supported Bush's philosophy as evidenced by remarkably broad support for intervening in Somalia: endorsements of his decision extended from UN Secretary-General Boutros Boutros-Ghali to bipartisan support on Capitol Hill, to a diverse collection of humanitarian relief groups, and to national and international media.

According to its leading enthusiast—President Bush—the US military intervention to support UN and other NGO humanitarian operations in Somalia was morally correct and the right thing to do to save thousands of lives. Utilizing the US military in humanitarian aid operations was not new to Bush as he had used it two times before the Somalia intervention—in post–Gulf War northern Iraq to provide relief to Kurds and in Bangladesh immediately after a natural disaster. His doctrine on the US military's role in alleviating global suffering was formed in the cauldron of the UN headquarters hallways as US ambassador to the UN and from memories of visiting a famine zone in Sudan in the early 1980s.

In purely military terms the UNITAF mission was a huge success, with scarcely any casualties to US and UN military forces. After arriving in Somalia they quickly secured relief routes and significantly shut down banditry, which allowed humanitarian aid to flow to needy populations. After the starvation ended, the international community made considerable progress in restoring Somalia to the community of nations. But the prospects for long-term peace in Somalia seemed dubious as long as the warlords continued to jockey for power, block reconstruction efforts, and hold more than a million refugees and internally displaced people hostage to their ambitions. The warlords had plunged Somalis into war with themselves.

Further compromising the UN's success in Somalia was the fact that the UN secretary-general's office did not have previous experience in running a Chapter VII mission, especially with a large number of troops with a use-of-force mandate.[2] There was, therefore, little by way of precedent to guide the nonconsensual intervention by the UN in Somalia. The scale of physical devastation, famine, and inability to deliver humanitarian assistance, compounded by the absence of a government, provided the justification for entering the virgin territory of forceful international intervention.

UNITAF was replaced by the UN Operation in Somalia II (UNOSOM II), which was authorized by the UNSC to try to develop civil society groups and nation-build focusing on judicial, police, and political development and rehabilitation. Warlord Mohamed Farah Aidid and his followers proved too cunning and powerful to be marginalized and thus reacted violently. Aidid believed that he was the rightful president of Somalia and that the UNOSOM II-imposed peace and settlement plans would cost him too much. Before UNOSOM II could facilitate its nation-building objectives, the June 5 fight between Aidid's supporters and Pakistani troops thrust it into a bloody conflict. The following day the UN accused Aidid of being responsible for the killing of twenty-four Pakistani troops.[3] UNSC Resolution 837 instructed UNOSOM II forces to capture those responsible, which strained its undermanned and under-resourced mission.

You can find a number of excuses to explain the international nation-building failure in Somalia—a brutal warlord, ineffective UN-US cooperation, a nation undermined by clan loyalties—but there are a few fundamental reasons why it failed. First, the United States' chronic inability to get the UN to take over the UNITAF mission more quickly, second, the lack of resources given to UNOSOM II, and third, a muddy assignment of US and UN roles and responsibilities in Somalia. Secretary-General Boutros-Ghali's insistence on UNITAF forces implementing a nationwide disarmament program was not supported by the United States and was violently opposed by many Somalis, including key warlords, such as Aidid.

Boutros-Ghali stalled the UNITAF transition to UNOSOM II, hoping that US forces would stay in Somalia in order to help achieve one of his key objectives, which he had stated from the operation's beginning—to disarm all Somalis throughout the country.[4] In order to get Boutros-Ghali and the UN to accept the necessary follow-on mission, however, the United States agreed to retain in Somalia a small military component in order get most US troops out of Somalia as rapidly as possible.

It would be quite wrong, however, to imagine that the United States handed the Somalia mission over to the United Nations with the creation of UNOSOM II. One of the mission's key military leaders was US Army Maj. Gen. Thomas M. Montgomery, who was the first US general ever to wear the blue beret of the UN, whereas the UN Secretary-General (UNSG) special representative was retired US Admiral Jonathan Howe, who had chaired the November 1992 National Security Council (NSC) Deputies Committee meetings that presented the military force intervention option in Somalia to President Bush.

In the horror and tragedy of the October 3 Battle of Mogadishu, President Bill Clinton and members of Congress declared that US troops would never again serve under UN command. However, the simple fact is that most of the American troops, including those fighting and dying in the October 3 fighting were directed by Americans participating in an US planned mission, which operated exclusively under American command in Somalia. All the political sides in American politics—Clinton, Congress, Republicans, and Democrats—were using the UN as political cover for losing focus on the Somali mission and blaming it for the American military casualties. The UN as a legitimate functioning institution was permanently damaged in the minds of many Americans. Most notably, the United States supported the withdrawal of UN forces from Rwanda during the genocide there.

In addition to being hurt by the slow UN transition into Somalia, UNOSOM II was also crippled by the failure to provide the promised staff and assets. The UNSG Special Representative, Admiral Howe, desperately tried to get the required resources to achieve his mission, even resorting to communicating directly with the US NSC's international organization director, Richard Clarke, for assistance and support.[5] Howe believed that the transition delay was damaging to the mission's goal of stabilizing

Somalia and that as a Chapter VII peacekeeping operation, UNOSOM II must be "given the resources with which to solve problems in a timely manner [and] when it comes to resources, timing is everything and resources are critical in the early stages."[6]

Another explanation for the mission's failure was the result of the 1992 US presidential elections, which brought a wintry blast of political action toward Somalia. President Bush's election loss prompted him to act in Somalia, but the White House transition to Clinton cast a sudden shadow over the transition from UNITAF to UNSOM II. The new Clinton administration sent contradictory signals on the US position in Somalia by trying to get its military forces out while at the same time helping the UN succeed in the follow-on mission, which was more ambitious and broader in scope than UNITAF. The Clinton administration's political goals in Somalia did not match its commitment to military forces and their requirements to achieve the mission.

President Bush's November 1992 decision to quickly turn Somalia into a security zone where food aid delivery would be unencumbered by bandits—and the belief that US troops could do this and return by his successor's inauguration—was as absurd a political fantasy as the Clinton administration's decision in March 1993 that the United Nations would magically turn Somalia into a peaceful and stable state with a functioning government. According to the State Department's point person on Somalia, Ambassador David Shinn, Somalia was a "good mission" but

> where they got it backwards was not to get into something at the end of your term if not continuing with Presidency and or if there is a change of parties. We know from past experience that at transition of new administration, they are focused on finding where the toilets are and finding people for different positions.[7]

After the October 3, 1993, US firefight with Aidid's supporters in Mogadishu that resulted in eighteen American deaths, President Clinton's abrupt broadcast announcing the withdrawal of US troops from Somalia sent a message around the world that harming US troops would result in their quick exit. In the wake of America's withdrawal from Somalia, US forces, once perceived as invincible, were diminished in the eyes of many Somalis. When the Americans arrived, the Somalis viewed them as the powerful victors over Saddam Hussein's large army.[8]

The American casualties in Somalia shocked US policymakers and the Pentagon into opposing any future humanitarian actions. United States opposition to reinforcing the UN mission in Rwanda was directly tied to its experience in Somalia. In her 2002 Pulitzer Prize–winning book, *A Problem From Hell: America and the Age of Genocide,* Samantha Power writes that the "lesson of Somalia" was that the Pentagon now feared that "a small engagement by foreign troops would end up as a large and costly one by Americans."[9]

On April 7, 1994, Lieutenant General Romeo Dallaire, force commander of the UN assistance mission to Rwanda during the genocide there, requested permission from the UN to use force. According to Dallaire, the Rwandan extremists knew that "when confronted with casualties, as the United States was in Somalia or the Belgians in Rwanda, they will run, regardless of the consequences to the abandoned population."[10] At the UN, US Ambassador Madeleine Albright wrote that "fearing another Somalia," UN headquarters "didn't want to be viewed as taking sides, so it turned the request down."[11] She believed that "the only solution would have been a large and heavily armed coalition led by a major power, but because of Somalia, the US military wasn't going to undertake that."[12]

Asked directly if he believed the UN would have sent forces to Rwanda to help prevent genocide if the US intervention in Somalia had never happened, Dallaire replied, "The way Clinton reacted scared a lot of people about going into another mess. It certainly played a large factor in the lack of international response to Rwanda."[13] Confirming Dallaire's observation, Clinton wrote that Somalia played a large part in the lack of US action to stop the Rwanda genocide—"with the memory of Somalia just six months old, and not vital to our national security interests that neither I nor anyone on my foreign policy team adequately focused on sending troops to stop the slaughter."[14]

The first casualty of crossing the "Mogadishu Line," a term coined after the Mogadishu battle and meaning the point at which peacekeeping becomes war, was Haiti. About one week after the Battle for Mogadishu, on October 11, 1993, the USS Harlan County was scheduled to dock at the harbor in Haiti's capital, Port-au-Prince, and unload 250 American and 25 Canadian troops to help restore the democratically elected government that was overthrown by a military junta. The ship was turned away from docking by stone-throwing youths, who followed the armed junta's orders to oppose the American landing. Among the anti-American signs held by protesters was "Remember Mogadishu," an overt warning that Haiti would be turned into another Somalia for American forces. The USS Harlan County left the harbor without unloading any of its troops and supplies because US officials feared the loss of American lives less than two weeks after the Mogadishu battle.

Another repercussion of the US experience in Somalia is seen in how the United States has conducted the war on terrorism. Before the

September 11, 2001, terrorist attacks, Clinton tried to target al-Qaeda leaders, including Osama bin Laden, and operatives in Afghanistan, but US military leaders balked out of fear of the bloody Somalia experience. According to President Clinton, "I had asked General Shelton [General Henry Hugh Shelton was chairman of the Joint Chiefs of Staff at the time] and Dick Clarke [referred to in other places in this book as Richard Clarke] to develop some options for dropping commando forces into Afghanistan. I thought that if we took out a couple of al-Qaeda's training operations it would show them how serious we were, even if we didn't get bin Laden or his top lieutenants. It was clear to me that senior military didn't want to do this, perhaps because of Somalia."[15]

A direct legacy of the Mogadishu fighting in particular and the Somali experience in general for Americans is the lack of respect they command from al-Qaeda and bin Laden, who said that Somalia highlights the fact that American soldiers are unprepared to fight extended wars and will "run in less than twenty-four hours."[16] He also wrote that al-Qaeda's

> battle against America is much simpler than the war against the Soviet Union, because some of our mujahideen who fought here in Afghanistan also participated in operations against the Americans in Somalia—and they were surprised at the collapse of American morale. This convinced us that the Americans are a paper tiger.[17]

Recriminations of the early 1990s US and UN intervention in Somalia have lingered, even though the US has recently realized re-engaging Somalia is warranted. Nearly two decades after the international intervention in Somalia, the country today remains a political and security vacuum in terms of not having a functioning and controlling national authority. Mogadishu's streets still swarm with armed militias and bandits demanding money from travelers and shaking down merchants. Although street crime or even battles among militias are not a major international concern, Somalia's lawlessness in the post September 11, 2001, era provides an abundant area for al-Qaeda and other terrorists to operate. For example, Somali-based al-Qaeda operatives planned the 1998 bombings of the US embassies in Tanzania and Nairobi.

In the post–September 11, 2001, era and after nearly a decade of absence, the US is again playing a role in Somalia. However, rather than humanitarian principles for justifying intervention, the US has intervened for security reasons in light of September 11, 2001, and the war on terrorism. Within months of the September 11, 2001, attacks, the US deployed troops in neighboring countries and created strategic partnerships with particular Somali leaders, including warlords, and regional neighbors, such as Djibouti, Ethiopia, and Kenya, in an effort to maintain military pressure on those Somalis thinking of harming US interests.

Al-Qaeda and terrorism concerns led the US to deploy nearly 2,000 troops in Djibouti in 2003 and to support a string of Ethiopian armed invasions in Somalia, including major incursions in December 2006 and January 2007, in order to destroy Islamist forces attempting to create an Islamic republic and providing sanctuary to foreign al-Qaeda forces. US military support for Ethiopia included providing intelligence to its military forces. The United States also launched air assaults in Somalia, including a January 8 AC-130 gunship strike on reported al-Qaeda sites in southern Somalia that killed five to ten people suspected to be linked with the terrorist group. The following month, President George W. Bush's press secretary, Tony Snow, used the American experience in Somalia to defend keeping US forces in Iraq:

> Have the United States leave before the job's done in Iraq, and invite al-Qaeda—give al-Qaeda the biggest recruiting tool of all, which is to say we made the Americans leave. Osama bin Laden cited the American departure from Somalia as the way to recruit and train people for September 11th.[18]

The challenges and problems experienced by the United States and UN in Somalia provide significant lessons for future UN Chapter VII missions and dealing with countries that no longer have effective and functioning governments. Drawing on these lessons will better enable the UN and its members, especially the United States, to ensure that future missions are properly coordinated and resourced, and most important, that goals and objectives are reasonable and commensurate with local populations and their leaders.

A major lesson from the UN experience in Somalia is that the UN should be careful about conducting peace enforcement missions within states experiencing internal strife and without a national agreement. If the UN should undertake a peace enforcement mission in such a context, then it should be a narrow mission confined to clear goals, and force should be rarely utilized.

In addition, the UN and international forces should work with local authorities in building up national institutions. As UN peacekeeping missions operating without the consent of local and warring parties, both UNITAF and UNOSOM II had little guidance from previous UN missions, but the UNSC decided that the humanitarian devastation in Somalia validated a forceful UN intervention. These missions were experiments in whether the UN could carry out a Chapter VII peacekeeping operation against adversaries who did not want the mission to succeed.

Another major lesson of the international experience in Somalia is that forced disarmament in internal conflict and without a national agreement may be unachievable, especially without exposing international forces to hostility. In many societies, such as in Somalia, the cultural importance of guns, coupled with the practical need for self-protection, makes it all but impossible for foreign forces to disarm militias or homeowners. Therefore, enforced disarmament of societies under Chapter VII and without the consent of the warring parties should be reconsidered.

A fourth major lesson that can be applied to the future challenge of the post–Cold War era is that the US military must develop unity-of-effort procedures with the armed forces of other nations. Other national forces may have different operational procedures and philosophies, a challenge that exhibited itself in Somalia and caused tremendous coordination and command problems for UNOSOM II leaders. For example, during the Somalia operation, the Italian ambassador to the UN stated that Italy's forces "do not like being told what to do without being consulted as part of the decision-making process."[19]

In the wake of the US and UN departure from Somalia in 1994, the country quickly reverted to an anarchic condition similar to the chaos that provided the UNSC justification for authorizing UNITAF. For example, in 1993 Aidid was powerful enough to force the US and UN to quit Somalia. He also had the blood of tens of thousand of Somali's on his hands in his unsuccessful effort to become president. He declared himself president in June 1995, but his claim went unrecognized by most Somali factions and the international community.[20] His self-declared reign ended about one year later when he died in an inter-clan firefight, which seemed appropriate considering that he attempted to take the Somali presidency by the barrel of a gun and use it against foreign or domestic foes alike.[21]

UNOSOM II's nation-building failure led to major reassessments in Washington and New York of the value of such operations. Both US and UN officials downgraded the desirability and likelihood of such missions being carried out in the future. As a result of Somalia, Clinton ordered a review of US participation in UN peacekeeping forces that resulted in the May 1994 Presidential Decision Directive 25 on "Key Elements of the Clinton Administration's Policy on Reforming Multilateral Peace Operations." It was a strong reversal from the administration's initial supportive policy for assertive multilateralism. It stated that US support for peacekeeping operations must be contingent on a conflict's threat to international peace and security, or on a determination that the operations "serve US interests."

Bush's 1992 decision to lead the Somalia intervention was one of the last foreign policy decisions he made. It changed the face of international interventions and the US role in attempting to alleviate humanitarian crises and restore government to imploded states. Although the intervention saved hundreds of thousands of Somali lives and helped nearly save a country, many blame the Somalia experience for preventing the use of US troops to alleviate or prevent subsequent humanitarian emergencies, including the Rwanda genocide, and for operationally and psychologically handcuffing US policy in the war on terror.

If one considers that before the intervention in 1992, tens of thousands of Somalis were dying, and that after UN troops left in 1994, the situation did not revert back to widespread famine, the international mission in Somalia was a success despite the enormous financial and human cost to the international community, especially the United States. Politically, the Somalia mission's success is debatable.

Notes

1. There were fifteen peacekeeping operations mounted from 1948 to 1998 and twenty-six peacekeeping operations launched between 1989 and 1996. Boutros Boutros-Ghali, "Introduction," in *The Blue Helmets: A Review of United Nations Peacekeeping* (New York: United Nations Department of Public Information, 1996), 3.

2. The 1960 Congo peacekeeping mission could be compared to Somalia, except that Chapter VII authority was not given by the Security Council. It began as typical peacekeeping mission but turned into a peace-enforcement mission without UNSC authorization as the violence increased in the Congo.

3. Aidid subsequently claimed that UNITAF and UNOSOM II forces killed more than 13,000 Somalis and wounded more than 39,000, Commission Report, S/1994/653, 55.

4. Another of Boutros-Ghali's key demands that created tension with US officials and didn't help the transition process was his insistence that UNITAF military forces deploy throughout Somalia, including to northern Somalia, an area that had not experienced the dramatic humanitarian suffering that occurred in the south.

5. Richard A. Clarke (National Security Council, director, Office of International Programs, 1992; Department of State, assistant secretary of state for politico-military affairs, 1989–1992; and deputy assistant secretary of state for intelligence, 1985–1988), telephone interview with author, July 16, 2004.

6. Jonathan T. Howe, "Relations Between the United States and United Nations in Dealing with Somalia," in *Learning From Somalia: The Lessons of Armed Humanitarian Intervention*, eds. Walter Clarke and Jeffrey Herbst (Boulder, CO: Westview Press, 1997), 182–183.

7. Ambassador David Shinn (State Department deputy director of the Somali Task Force), interview with author, Washington, DC, April 8, 2004.

8. Some of the perceived power of American forces influenced forces in nearby countries, such as Sudan, where "the expected Sudanese government offensive against southern rebel forces in early 1993 did not occur, some diplomats believe, because the northern government feared that it would be the next object of US humanitarian interventionism." Herman J. Cohen, *Intervening in Africa: Superpower Peacemaking in a Troubled Continent* (New York: Macmillan Press Ltd, 2000), 110.

9. Samantha Power, *A Problem From Hell: America and the Age of Genocide* (New York: Perennial, 2002), 366.

10. Romeo Dallaire with Brent Beardsley, *Shake Hands With the Devil: The Failure of Humanity in Rwanda* (New York: Carroll & Graf Publishers, 2003), 240.

11. Madeleine Albright, *Madam Secretary* (New York: Miramax Books, 2003), 149.

12. Ibid., 152.

13. Lieutenant General Romeo Dallaire, force commander of the UN assistance mission to Rwanda, 1993–1994, discussion with author, Berkley, California, March 14, 2007.

14. Bill Clinton, *My Life* (New York: Alfred A. Knopf, 2004), 593.

15. Ibid., 804. Clinton promoted Clarke to be the National Security Council's chief counterterrorism adviser.

16. Bin Laden interview, ABC News, May 28, 1998, as quoted in "Remembering Mogadishu: Five Years after the Firefight in Somalia, Some Say US Forces Abroad Still Are Reeling from It," G. E. Willis, "Remembering Mogadishu," *Army Times*, October 12, 1998, 16.

17. Yossef Bodansky, *Bin Laden: The Man Who Declared War on America* (New York: Forum, 1999), 83.

18. Tony Snow (White House press secretary for President George W. Bush, April 2006–September 2007). Interview on *Meet the Press*, February 18, 2007.

19. Quoted at July 8, 1993, meeting at the UN. Confidential memorandum, secretary of state to US Mission at UN, "Meeting of Major Somalia Troop Contributors," July 1993.

20. William J. Durch, "Introduction to Anarchy: Intervention and 'State-Building' in Somalia," in *UN: Peacekeeping, American Policy and the Uncivil Wars of the 1990s*, ed. William J. Durch (New York: St. Martin's Press, 1996), 365.

21. Aidid died on August 1, 1996, from injuries sustained in a fight with rivals on July 24. Aidid's son, Hussein Aidid, succeeded leadership of the Habar Gidir sub-clan and SNA. He was a Corporal in the United States Marine Corps and served in Somalia as an interpreter-translator for the American forces commander from December 18, 1992, until January 5, 1993.

POSTSCRIPT

> Since the withdrawal of UNOSOM II, the security situation in Somalia has been characterized by political instability, inter-clan conflict, banditry and general lawlessness; however, conditions vary greatly from region to region.
>
> *Boutros Boutros-Ghali, UN Secretary General, January 16, 1996*
> *UNSG report on the situation in Somalia*

The UN and US military intervention in Somalia occurred at a multilateral moment at the end of George H. W. Bush's presidency. Saving Somalia with a humanitarian relief operation and then attempting to build a functioning and stable Somalia was an enormous mission. It was a cooperative effort that involved militaries from more than thirty countries and a range of NGOs, UN agencies, and the International Committee of the Red Cross (ICRC). Because the UN was unwilling to act with a robust military mission, President Bush offered US military forces to lead the humanitarian mission under a UN mandate that was largely organized, sustained, and financed by the United States. The Somalia mission was a kind of laboratory for the testing of this multilateral position.

Bush's decision to intervene in Somalia was very much part of a particular historical moment for US Foreign Policy, a moment of intense multilateralism spawned largely by the end of the Cold War and the President's experience as a diplomat at the UN. Bush's successor, President Bill Clinton, soon learned that multilateralism interventions were more limited and difficult than imagined. For example, even though he promised that US military forces would be deployed for a short time in Bosnia in the mid-1990s, they are still there, whereas the 1999 Kosovo mission was conducted under NATO rather than UN auspices due to lack of UN Security Council consensus.

Clinton's heir, President George W. Bush, continued to turn US Foreign Policy away from multilateralism toward unilateralism, which reached its apex with the US invasion of Iraq in 2003 that most states opposed. Ironically, the invasion has revived discussion in the United States on the worth of multilateralism. For example, in Afghanistan the US currently finds itself leading NATO's first extended bloody engagement that also includes support from several UN agencies operating under a UN mandate. Despite the fact that the Afghanistan mission is characterized by a serious lack of member contributions to military forces, the US is in better military shape there than in Iraq where it does not have either NATO or UN support.

There is abundant evidence that the demands of the ongoing US military missions in Afghanistan and Iraq, coupled with its continuing alliance and defense obligations around the globe, are close to exhausting its armed forces—that is, "overuse" on its way to a "broken force."[1] As a result, Secretary of State Condoleezza Rice labeled current US military interventions in the greater Middle East region as a "generational commitment" that can only be solved by "increasing the size of the force available to our civilian leadership."[2]

Besides increasing the size of the US military as considered by Rice, another option is for the United States to return to a revised version of the multilateralism of the early 1990s. As the United States experienced in Somalia and is learning in Afghanistan and Iraq, the key goal in nation-building is to induce peace and stability in volatile and violent regions, which entails extended military missions. At the forefront of any peacekeeping operation is security, followed by humanitarian relief, economic support, and political reconstruction.

Ironically, the US is currently doing this to combat the Jihadist front for al-Qaeda in Somalia. As detailed in the last chapter, in January 2007 the US launched military aerial strikes on al-Qaeda suspects in southern Somalia. It was also reported by the UN that 7,620 Islamic militants from Somali went to Lebanon to fight alongside Hezbollah forces against Israeli forces in the summer of 2006 in exchange for Iranian and Syrian financial and military assistance.[3] The US military strike laid the groundwork for an American-backed Ethiopian military invasion of Somalia in order to eliminate Islamic fundamentalist military and political forces controlling Mogadishu and large parts of southern Somalia. The US-Ethiopian alliance formed as part of the Bush Administration's war on terror is calculated to eradicate Islamic fundamentalism in the region.

Concurrently with the formation of the US-Ethiopian alliance, President George W. Bush's administration is encouraging and committing support for an all-African peacekeeping force under the auspices of the African Union to assist Ethiopian forces supporting Somalia's transnational government. The arms-length approach to Somalia is different from the US intervention in 1992–1994, a result of lessons learned from enmeshing ground troops in the chaotic country.

One of the challenges that is overcome by this arms-length relationship is the interoperability questions that the US military forces experienced working with other national forces that were encumbered with operating caveats and restrictions that prevented other military forces from participating fully in joint robust military operations. As described in this book, the unilateral restrictions placed on Italian forces in Somalia by its own political forces and contrary to the wishes of the UN command highlights the difficulty that US military forces faced operating with other national forces under a UN mandate. Unilaterally supporting national military forces, such as Ethiopia, or mandates by regional organizations, such as the African Unit, as surrogates without placing US troops on the ground is a possible solution to currently overextended US military forces. Although not the early 1990s multilateral exhilaration surrounding the Somalia intervention, it is also not the unilateral emphasis of current US military operations in the greater Middle East.

Notes

1. Lieutenant General James Helmly, chief of the Army Reserve, as quoted in a letter from the Project for the New American Century to Congress on increasing US Ground Forces, January 28, 2005.

2. Quoted in a letter from the Project for the New American Century to Congress on increasing US Ground Forces, January 28, 2005.

3. Report of the Monitoring Group on Somalia pursuant to Security Council resolution 1676, November 2006, 24.

BIBLIOGRAPHY

Books

Albright, Madeline. *Madam Secretary: A Memoir*. With Bill Woodward. New York: Miramax Books, 2003.

Bodansky, Yossef. *Bin Laden: The Man Who Declared War on America*. New York: Forum, 1999.

Boutros-Ghali, Boutros. *Unvanquished: A U.S.-U.N. Saga*. New York: Random House, 1999.

Clancy, Tom. *Battle Ready*. With Tony Zinni and Tony Koltz. New York: G. P. Putnam's Son, 2004.

Clarke, Walter, and Jeffrey Herbst, eds. *Learning From Somalia: The Lessons of Armed Humanitarian Intervention*. Boulder, CO: Westview Press, 1997.

Clinton, Bill. *My Life*. New York: Alfred A. Knopf, 2004.

Cohen, Herman J. *Intervening in Africa: Superpower Peacemaking in a Troubled Continent*. New York: St. Martin's Press, 2000.

Dallaire, Romeo. *Shake Hands With The Devil: The Failure of Humanity in Rwanda*. With Major Brent Beardsley. New York: Carroll & Graf Publishers, 2003.

Drew, Elizabeth. *On The Edge: The Clinton Presidency*. New York: Simon & Schuster, 1994.

Drysdale, John. *Whatever Happened to Somalia*. London: HAAN, 1994.

Fogarassy, Helen. *Mission Improbable: The World Community on a UN Compound in Somalia*. Lanham, MD: Lexington Books, 1999.

Hackworth, David H. *Hazardous Duty: One of America's Most Decorated Soldiers Reports from the Front with the Truth about the U.S. Military Today*. With Tom Mathews. New York: Avon Books, 1996.

Hanley, Gerald. *Warriors: Life and Death among the Somalis*. London: Eland, 1993.

Hartley, Aidan. *The Zanzibar Chest*. New York: Atlantic Monthly Press, 2003.

Hempstone, Smith. *Rogue Ambassador: An African Memoir*. Sewanee, TN: University of the South Press, 1997.

Hirsh, John L., and Robert B. Oakley. *Somalia and Operation Restore Hope: Reflections on Peacekeeping and Peacekeeping*. Washington, DC: United States Institute of Peace, 1995.

Hubbard, Mark. *The Skull Beneath the Skin: Africa After the Cold War*. Boulder, CO: Westview Press, 2001.

Johnston, Philip. *Somalia Diary: The President of CARE Tells One Country's Story of Hope*. Atlanta: Longstreet Press, 1994.

Lewis, I. M. *A Modern History of the Somali*. Athens, OH: Ohio University Press, 2002.

Little, Peter D. *Somalia: Economy without State*. Bloomington: Indiana University Press, 2003.

Lyons, Terrence, and Ahmed I. Samatar. *Somalia: State Collapse, Multilateral Intervention, and Strategies for Political Reconstruction*. Washington, DC: Brookings Institution, 1995.

Makinda, Samuel M. *Seeking Peace From Chaos: Humanitarian Intervention in Somalia*. Boulder, CO: Lynne Rienner Publishers, 1993.

Maren, Michael. *The Road to Hell: The Ravaging Effects of Foreign Aid and International Charity*. New York: The Free Press, 1997.

Natsios, Andrew S. *US Foreign Policy and the Four Horsemen of the Apocalypse: Humanitarian Relief in Complex Emergencies*. Westport, CT: Praeger Publishers, 1997.

Powell, Colin. *My American Journey*. With Joseph E. Persico. New York: Random House, 1995.

Power, Samantha. *A Problem from Hell: America and the Age of Genocide*. New York, Perennial, 2002.

Roberts, Craig, and Ed Wheeler. *Doorway to Hell: Disaster in Somalia*. Tulsa, OK: Consolidated Press International, 2002.

Robinson, Piers. *The CNN Effect: The Myth of News, Foreign Policy and Intervention*. New York: Routledge, 2002.

Romeo, Dallaire. *Shake Hands with the Devil: The Failure of Humanity in Rwanda*. New York: Carroll & Graf Publishers, 2003.

Sahnoun, Mohamed. *Somalia: The Missed Opportunities.* Washington, DC: U.S. Institute of Peace Press, 1994.

Schraeder, Peter J. *African Politics and Society: A Mosaic in Transformation.* Boston, Bedford/St. Martin's, 2000.

Sommer, John G. *Hope Restored? Humanitarian Aid in Somalia: 1990–1994.* Washington, DC: Refugee Policy Group, 1994.

Stephanopoulos, George. *All Too Human: A Political Education.* Boston: Little, Brown and Company, 1999.

Stevenson, Jonathan. *Losing Mogadishu: Testing U.S. Policy in Somalia.* Annapolis, MD: Naval Institute Press, 1995.

Strobel, Warren P. *Late-Breaking Foreign Policy: The News Media's Influence on Peace Operations.* Washington, DC: US Institute of Peace Press, 1994.

Wood, David Bowne. *A Sense of Values: American Marines in an Uncertain World.* Kansas City: Andrews and McMeel, 1994.

Chapters

Allison, John. "Force Protection During Urban Operations." In *Capital Preservation: Preparing for Urban Operations in the Twenty-First Century,* edited by Russell W. Glenn, 165–194. Santa Monica, CA: RAND, 2000.

Anderson, Gary. "UNOSOM II: Not Failure, Not Success." In Beyond Traditional Peacekeeping, edited by Donald C. Daniel and Bradd C. Hayes, 267–281. New York: St. Martin's Press, 1995.

Boutros-Ghali, Boutros. "Introduction." In *The Blue Helmets: A Review of United Nations Peace-keeping,* edited by United Nations Department of Public Information, 3–9. New York: United Nations Department of Public Information, 1996.

Cohen, Herman. "Intervention in Somalia." In *The Diplomatic Record: 1992–1993,* edited by Allan Goodman, 51–80. Boulder, CO: Westview Press, 1995.

Durch, William J. "Introduction to Anarchy: Humanitarian Intervention and State-Building in Somalia." In *UN: Peacekeeping, American Policy and the Uncivil Wars of the 1990s,* edited by William J. Durch, 311–365. New York: St. Martin's Press, 1996.

Howe, Jonathan T. "Relations Between the United States and United Nations in Dealing with Somalia." In *Learning From Somalia: The*

Lessons of Armed Humanitarian Intervention, edited by Walter Clarke and Jeffrey Herbst, 173–190. Boulder, CO: Westview Press, 1997.

Johnston, Harry, and Ted Dagne, "Congress and the Somalia Crisis." In *Learning From Somalia: The Lessons of Armed Humanitarian Intervention*, edited by Walter Clarke and Jeffrey Herbst, 191–204. Boulder, CO: Westview Press, 1997.

Kanstiner, Walther H. "U.S. Policy in Africa in the 1990s," In *U.S. and Russian Policymaking With Respect to the Use of Force*, edited by Jeremy R. Azrael and Emil A. Payin, 105–116. Santa Monica, CA: RAND, 1996.

Oakley, Robert B. "The Urban Area During Support Missions: Case Study: Mogadishu: The Strategic Level." *In Capital Preservation: Preparing for Urban Operations in the Twenty-First Century*, edited by Russell W. Glenn, 309–354. Santa Monica, CA: RAND, 2000.

Woods, James L. "U.S. Government Decision Making Processes During Humanitarian Operations in Somalia." In *Learning From Somalia: The Lessons of Armed Humanitarian Intervention*, edited by Walter Clarke and Jeffrey Herbst, 151–172. Boulder, CO: Westview Press, 1997.

Articles

Annan, Kofi. "UN Peacekeeping Operations and Cooperation with NATO." *NATO Review* 478, no. 5 (October 1993): 3–7.

Bolton, John R. "Wrong Turn in Somalia." *Foreign Affairs* 73, no. 1 (January/February 1994): 56–66.

Clark, Jeffery. "Debacle in Somalia." *Foreign Affairs* 72, no. 1 (1993/1994): 109–123.

Clarke, Walter, and Jeffrey Herbst. "Somalia and the Future of Humanitarian Intervention." *Foreign Affairs* 75, no. 2 (March/April 1996): 70–85.

Croker, Chester A. "The Lessons of Somalia." *Foreign Affairs* 74, no. 3 (May/June 1995): 2–8.

Dworken, Jonathan T. "Restore Hope: Coordinating Relief Operations." *Joint Forces Quarterly* (Summer 1995): 14–20.

Huntington, Samuel. "New Contingencies, Old Roles." *Joint Forces Quarterly* (Autumn 1993): 38–3.

Lorenz, F. M. "Law and Anarchy in Somalia." *Parameter* XXIII, no. 4 (Winter 1993–94): 27–41.

Menkhaus, Ken. "Somalia: Political Order in a Stateless Society." *Current History* (May 1998) 220–228.

Schraeder, Peter J. "The Horn of Africa: U.S. Foreign Policy in an Altered Cold War Environment." *Middle East Journal* 46, no. 4 (Autumn 1992): 570–593.

Sloyan, Patrick J. "The Secret Path to a Bloodbath: How U.S. Policy in Somalia Went from Bad to Worse." *The Washington Post National Weekly Edition* (April 18–24, 1994): 24–25.

Stevenson, Jonathan. "Hope Restores in Somalia?" *Foreign Policy,* no. 91 (summer 1993): 138–154.

Waal, Alex De, and Rakiya Omaar. "Doing Harm by Doing Good? The International Relief Effort in Somalia." *Current History* (May 1993): 198–202.

Weston, Jon. "Sources of Humanitarian Intervention: Beliefs, Information, and Advocacy in the U.S. Decisions on Somalia and Bosnia." *International Security* 26, no. 4 (Spring 2002) 112–142.

Unpublished Material

Baggott, Christopher L., "A Leap Into the Dark: Crisis Action Planning for Operation Restore Hope." Monograph, Army Command and General Staff College, School of Advanced Military Studies, Fort Leavenworth, KS, December 20, 1996.

Buer, Eric F. "United Task Force Somalia (UNITAF) and United Nations Operations Somalia (UNOSOM II): A Comparative Analysis of Offensive Air Support." Master's thesis, United States Marine Corps, Command and Staff College, AY 2000–2001.

Curry, Michael J. "21st Century Combat and the Operational Logistics Link." Monograph, School of Advanced Military Studies, United States Army Command and General Staff College, Fort Leavenworth, KS, AY 98–99.

Day, Clifford E. "Critical Analysis on the Defeat of Task Force Ranger." Paper presented at the Research Department, Air Command and Staff College, Maxwell Air Force Base, Alabama, March 1997.

Dixon, James C. "UNOSOM II: UN Unity of Effort and U.S. Unity of Command." Master's thesis, Army Command and General Staff College Fort Leavenworth, KS, June 7, 1996.

Jones, Dorian F. "The Viability of Large Scale Amphibious Operations on the Eve of The Twenty-First Century in Light of Military Operations Other Than War (MOOTW), High and Low Technology Weapons, and Weapons of Mass Destruction." Master's thesis, U.S. Army Command and General Staff College, 1997.

Lyons, Todd, W. "Military Intervention in Identity Group Conflicts." Master's thesis, Naval Postgraduate School, 2000.

Reports

Amnesty International Annual Report, 1992.

Clarke, Walter S. "Somalia: Background Information for Operation Restore Hope 1992–1993." Strategic Studies Institute Special Report, Department of National Security and Strategy, US Army War College, Carlisle Barracks, PA, 1992, 37.

Dagne, Theodore S. "Recent Political Developments in Ethiopia and Somali," Congressional Research Service Report for Congress, May 31, 1991. Washington, DC: Congressional Research Service, May 31, 1991.

Gallagher, Robert. "Support for the Mission." UN Technical Team Report on Somalia to the UN Secretary-General [not dated].

Hansch, Steven, Scott Lillibridge, Grace Egeland, Charles Teller, and Michael Toole. "Lives Lost, Lives Saved: Excess Mortality and the Impact of Health Interventions in the Somalia Emergency." Report, *Refugee Policy Group,* November 1994.

ICRC Somalia Report, July 9, 1992.

Office of U.S. Foreign Disaster Assistance (OFDA). Somalia Situation Report No. 10, "Somalia—Civil Strife." June 23, 1992.

———. Somalia Situation Report No. 11, "Somalia: Civil Strife." August 14, 1992.

Prendergast, John. "The Gun Talks Louder Than the Voice: Somalia's Continuing Cycles of Violence." Discussion paper, *Center of Concern,* July 1994.

UN Commission of Inquiry Report, Established Pursuant to Security Council Resolution 885. January 6, 1994. S/1994/653.

UN Branch Office Somalia Unit in Nairobi. "Framework for Possible Resumption of UNHCR's Activities in Somalia." Report, February 27, 1991.

UN Department of Peace-Keeping Operations, Lessons Learned Unit. Report of the seminar (June 19–20, 1995, New York) "Lessons Learned from the United Nations Operation in Somalia at the Strategic and Operational Levels," August 1995.

———. "Comprehensive Report on Lessons-Learned From United Nations Operation in Somalia: April 1992–March 1995." December 1995.

UN Secretary-General Boutros Boutros-Ghali. Report submitted in pursuance of paragraph 4 of Resolution 886 (1993). January 6, 1994. S/1994/12.

———. "The Situation in Somalia." Report, August 24, 1992. S/24480.

———. "The Situation in Somalia." Report, March 11, 1992. S/23693.

———. Consolidated inter-agency 90-day Plan of Action for Emergency Humanitarian Assistance to Somalia." Report, addendum. April 21, 1992. S/23829 Add.2.

———. Further report, submitted in pursuance of paragraph 18 and 19 of Resolution 794 (1992). March 3, 1993. S/25354.

———. Report on the implementation of UN Security Council Resolution 837 (1993). July 1, 1993. S/26022.

———. Report on situation in Somalia. August 24, 1992. S/24480.

———. Report on the June 5, 1993 attack on UN forces in Somalia. 5. August 24, 1993. S/26351.

———. Report on the Situation in Somalia. December 19, 1992. S/24992.

———. Report on the situation in Somalia. January 19, 1996. S/1996/42.

UN High Commissioner for Refugees (UNHCR). Situation report for Northwest Somalia, Somalia Unit-Djibouti, September 20, 1991.

———. Regional Bureau for Africa report, "UNHCR's Plan of Action for Somalia," June 14, 1991.

———. Situation report for Northwest Somalia, Somalia Unit-Djibouti, October 18, 1991.

———. Situation report for Northwest Somalia, Somalia Unit-Djibouti, October 31, 1991.

———. Situation report for Northwest Somalia, Somalia Unit-Djibouti, December 12, 1991.

UNICEF Somalia Situation Report. June 1992.

UN Under Secretary General James O. C. Jonah. "Exploratory Mission to Somalia." Report, January 3–6, 1992.

Clarke, Walter S. "Somalia: Background Information for Operation Restore Hope 1992–1993. Strategic Studies Institute Special Report, Department of National Security and Strategy, U.S. Army War College, Carlisle Barracks, PA, 1992.

Westcott, Jan. "The Somalia Saga: A Personal Account 1990–1992," *Refugee Policy Group,* November 1994.

Magazines and Newspapers

Africa Confidential. "Somalia: Time to take Stock." 33, no. 8 (April 17, 1992): 4.

Albright, Madeline. "Yes, There Is a Reason to Be in Somalia." *New York Times,* August 10, 1993, A19.

Caputo, Robert. "Tragedy Stalks the Horn of Africa." *National Geographic* 184, no. 2 (August 1993): 88–121.

Church, George J. "Anatomy of a Disaster." *Time* (October 18, 1993): 40–49.

Cooling, Norman L. "Operation Restore Hope in Somalia: A Tactical Action Turned Strategic Defeat." *Marine Corps Gazette* (September 2001): 92–106.

The Economist. "Armed Relief." 323, no. 7758 (May 9, 1992): 48.

———. "Making Monkeys Out of the U.N." 328, no. 7819 (July 10, 1992): 34.

———. "Somalia: Death by Looting." 324, no. 7768 (July 18, 1992): 41.

Oberdorfer, Don. "US Took Slow Approach to Somali Crisis: Delay in Action Attributed to Civil War." *The Washington Post,* August 24, 1992. A13.

Oberdorfer, Dan. "The Path to Intervention." *The Washington Post,* December 6, 1992, A1, A35–A36.

Perlez, Jane. "Somali Fighting Keeps Aid From a Suffering City." *New York Times,* December 11, 1991, A7.

Richburg, Keith B. "U.S. Envoy to Somalia Urged Policy Shift Before 18 GIs Died." *The Washington Post,* November 11, 1993, first section, A39.

Sloyan, Patrick J. "The Secret Path to a Bloodbath: How U.S. Policy in Somalia Went from Bad to Worse." *The Washington Post National Weekly Edition,* April 18–24, 1994.

Willis, G. E. "Remembering Mogadishu." *Army Times* (October 12, 1998): 16–20.

Other Publications

Coll, Alberto R. "The Problems of Doing Good: Somalia as a Case Study in Humanitarian Intervention." Instructor Copy 518, Pew Case Studies in International Affairs, Institute for Study of Diplomacy Publications, School of Foreign Service, Georgetown University, 1997.

Farrell, Theo. "United States Marine Corps Operations in Somalia: A Model for the Future." Amphibious Operations: A Collection of Papers, The Occasional, Number 31, Geoffrey Till, Mark J. Grove, and Theo Farrell, The Strategic and Combat Studies Institute, October 1997.

Menkhaus, Ken, with Louis Ortmayer, "Key Decisions in the Somalia Intervention." Case #464, Pew Case Studies in International Affairs, Institute for the Study of Diplomacy, School of Foreign Service, Georgetown University, 1995.

Rosegrant, Susan. *Seamless Transition: United States and United Nations Operations in Somalia—1992–1993*. Kennedy School of Government Case Program. Cambridge, MA: President and Fellows of Harvard College, 1996.

———. *Seamless Transition: United States and United Nations Operations in Somalia—1992–1993*. Kennedy School of Government Case Program. Cambridge, MA: President and Fellows of Harvard College, 1996.

Warner, John, and Carl Levin. *Warner-Levin Report,* "Review of the Circumstances Surrounding the Ranger Raid on October 3–4, 1993 in Mogadishu, Somalia." United States Senate Committee on Armed Services, October 2, 1995.

INDEX

public announcement of US
military intervention, 81
reaction to Kunder's report, 45
reaction to newspaper articles July
1992, 43
Senate asked, to deploy armed
personnel to Somalia, 54
sent team to brief President-elect
Clinton, 79
supported proposal for UN
standing army, 55
visit to southern Somalia,
103
Byrd, Senator Robert
amendment to cut off funding for
Somali mission, 154
objections to keeping US forces in
Somalia, 147

Carter, President Jimmy, 156
Casualties, lack of communication
cause of, 167
Cease fire agreement, 104
CENTCOM, 74
Central government in Somalia, lack
of, 30
Civil war in Somalia
launched in protest to
Ethiopia–Somalia nonaggression
pact, 5–6
US weapons used in, 9
Clan militias, against Darods and
Marehans, 11
Clans
Darod, 3
external threats as unifying factor,
2
fighting between, 108
Hawiye, 7–8, 52
Issaq, 5–6
government of, 1, 2
Marehan, 5
Mijerteen, 5
rivalry between, 1, 3
Clarke, Richard, pressured by NGOs
to bring in military, 67

Clinton administration
Carter encouraged to pursue
peaceful policy, 156
compared to Bush administration,
107
contradictory policy about Aidid,
153
contradictory signals on US
position in Somalia, 181
early foreign policy decisions, 110
goals of, for Somalia, 121
lack of communication with forces
in Somalia, 158
supported multilateral nation-
building, 109
UNSC resolution on developing
politics economics 156–158
Clinton, President Bill
accepted full responsibility for
Battle of Mogadishu, 162
announced new Somali policy, 165
approved sending Special Forces,
150
confused about direction of US
policy in Somalia, 155
Jeremiah sent to brief on Somalia
plans, 79
ordered US military withdrawal, 136
as presidential candidate, 66
as president-elect, met with Bush,
to discuss Somalia, 73
reaction to Battle of Mogadishu,
162–163
security team, leaderless, 105–106
Cohen, Herman, 7, 16, 54
declared Somalia in midst of civil
strife, 14
saw Aidid as primary villain, 56
spearheaded Policy Coordinating
Committee meetings, 39–40
Colonial legacy
clan schisms, and, 3
Somalia land divided by, 2
Communication
Clinton not informed of battle for
hours, 161

About the Author

Kenneth R. Rutherford, PhD, MBA, lost both his legs to a landmine in Somalia. Dr. Rutherford has testified before Congress and published articles in numerous academic and policy journals, including *World Politics*. He has also coedited two books, *Reframing the Agenda: The Impact of NGO and Middle Power Cooperation in International Security Policy* (Greenwood Press) and *Landmines and Human Security: The International Movement to Ban Landmines* (State University of New York Press). He has traveled worldwide to promote the economic and social rights of those disabled by cluster munitions and landmines. He is co-founder of Survivor Corps, formerly known as Landmine Survivor Network (LSN), which played a leadership role in the Nobel Peace Prize–winning coalition that spearheaded the 1997 Mine Ban Treaty. In 2005 Dr. Rutherford served as a Fulbright Scholar in Jordan, where he was appointed to the faculty at the University of Jordan. He is an Associate Professor of Political Science at Missouri State University. Dr. Rutherford lives in Springfield, Missouri with his wife Kim and their four children: Hayden, Campbell, Duncan and Lucie.

Also from Kumarian Press . . .

Human Rights and Humanitarianism:

Humanitarian Alert: NGO Information and Its Impact on US Foreign Policy
Abby Stoddard

Nation-Building Unraveled? Aid, Peace and Justice in Afghanistan
Edited by Antonio Donini, Norah Niland and Karin Wermester

Humanitarian Crises and International Intervention: Reassessing the Impact of Mass Media
Walter Soderlund and E. Donald Briggs

New and Forthcoming:

The World Bank and the Gods of Lending
Steve Berkman

Surrogates of the State: NGOs, Development and Ujamaa in Tanzania
Michael Jennings

World Disasters Report 2007: Focus on Discrimination
Edited by Yvonne Klynman, Nicholas Kouppari and Mohammed Mukhier

Peace through Health: How Health Professionals Can Work for a Less Violent World
Edited by Neil Arya and Joanna Santa Barbara

g green press
INITIATIVE

Kumarian Press is committed to preserving ancient forests and natural resources. We elected to print this title on 30% post consumer recycled paper, processed chlorine free. As a result, for this printing, we have saved:

6 Trees (40' tall and 6-8" diameter)
2,097 Gallons of Wastewater
4 million BTU's of Total Energy
269 Pounds of Solid Waste
505 Pounds of Greenhouse Gases

Kumarian Press made this paper choice because our printer, Thomson-Shore, Inc., is a member of Green Press Initiative, a nonprofit program dedicated to supporting authors, publishers, and suppliers in their efforts to reduce their use of fiber obtained from endangered forests.

For more information, visit www.greenpressinitiative.org

Environmental impact estimates were made using the Environmental Defense Paper Calculator. For more information visit: www.papercalculator.org.

Kumarian Press, located in Sterling, Virginia, is a forward-looking, scholarly press that promotes active international engagement and an awareness of global connectedness.

Humanitarian
        Mission Versus

              war

Political Support / issues

issues at home?